MW00809724

VulnerABLE

VulnerABLE

How to notice the power
of vulnerability through
lettuce, laundry, and love

JULIA RUGGIERO

New Degree Press

VulnerABLE

How to notice the power of vulnerability through lettuce, laundry, and love

ISBN   978-1-64137-224-4 *Paperback*

978-1-64137-225-1 *Ebook*

To my mom, for helping me find the passion
and emotion in my voice: Lettuce.

To my dad, for teaching me to not let criticism
define my whole being: Laundry.

To Michael, my best friend, for showing me unconditional
love and acceptance, teaching me how I can listen
to and work together with others: Love.

Thank you to Doan Winkel, for always supporting
me along my creative journeys and inspiring me
to embrace my voice with confidence.

Contents

How to Use This Book

—

If you are having trouble communicating with others, or even with yourself, there are some great tools in this book to notice the power that our words can have on ourselves and others, and how we can use our voices to empower one another. Books that share people's experiences have helped me grow in more ways than I would have ever imagined, but I know the danger of them. My perspective is *not* the only perspective, but I want to offer you the permission to feel okay standing alone. I hope this book helps you realize that you do not have to listen to 100,000 different opinions and try to mold and fit each and every viewpoint out there. This book is a collection of experiences from myself and others, mixed in with tips and reminders that you can use to take action and embrace *your* unique being and voice, as well as find that empathy for others. When you are vulnerable, you are able to create a deeper connection with yourself and others, which first starts by becoming comfortable with who you are. This is one of the hardest parts of the process, but it helps us rise in more ways than we may have ever thought possible. Since this book is a collection of ideas, here is a little guide for how to use this book:

First, finish the entire dish of lettuce.

Just like the common phrase "don't waste your food; finish everything on your plate," I would first suggest reading the book from beginning to end, in order. Each chapter title is a quote, some of which you may have heard or even said to others or yourself before. Withhold any judgment while reading, because you may just find a nugget of wisdom even if this is not your cup of tea.

Second, fold the pieces of laundry one by one as needed.

After reading the book in order of the parts and chapters, refer back to the specific chapters based on how you are feeling. Read what you think would help you most at that time. Use this book as a guide. If you ever have a thought pop up in your head, like, "I'm crazy" or "I'm the only one," take a look at that chapter. If you're on the go, for a quick summary of points, head down to the bottom of the chapters to summarize actions you can take in that moment to bring your mind back to peace.

Third, continue to study the love.

Treat this book like a friend and have a conversation with it. Feel free to carry it around with you in the car or in your bag to pull out when a thought gets in your head that you can't escape. We can read a book so closely but still lose touch with some of the messages that resonate with us most. Keep studying the love. Use this book as a darn canvas if you want—highlight the heck out of it! Use a notecard as a bookmark and jot down some mental health reminders. Anything that helps you process the material in a way that will stick with you. I then invite you to not only think of what you experience, but also who else may benefit from the words in this book.

My hope is that, in reading this book, you will discover the meaning behind vulnerability in a relatable and unique manner, and notice vulnerability in even the smallest of situations. I hope to instill the same sort of passion and excitement that I have for your voice in you. Ultimately, I want you to see this book as a tool to help you to embrace the imperfect and encourage others to love themselves and one another.

Introduction

———

Vulnerability.

Define that.

What do you first think of when you hear the words "vulnerability" or "vulnerable?"

You may think vulnerability means weakness, strength, confidence, fear, or *insert any word here.*

My initial impression of vulnerability was not anywhere near pleasant when I was a child.

When I used to hear this "dirty" word, I would quickly think of when I would hear the word most: in the news. I thought of vulnerability the same way I did the worst news story possible when a news anchor, journalist, or passerby described a person in a state of attack or harm.

If you asked me as a child, I probably would have defined vulnerable as "worthless and powerless."

I would briefly imagine people who were criticized, weak, less than, or smaller than those who kept their emotions inside.

I saw fear and extreme weakness.

As for myself, I feared vulnerability at a young age due to judgment and past experiences when my voice was pushed to the side. I looked for my worth in the opinions of others but had a hard time locating my voice there. I did not even know what the word vulnerability meant for a long time: I thought it was synonymous with "complaining."

However, when we really listen to our inner voice, what do we hear?

When you sit back, breathe, and think of the word vulnerability, what do you truly think of?

**

I'll do this exercise too. I am closing my eyes right now...

Never mind. Closing my eyes is making me want to fall asleep.

Anyways, after a little dive into new perspectives and some serious reflection, I started to watch vulnerability bloom like a flower in front of me over time.

It all started with my admiration for other people's personalities.

I was continually awe-inspired by people who felt comfortable around others, letting loose and owning their true selves.

As a child, I would cling to those who promoted confidence in their everyday lives through their actions. My cousins, the popular girls and guys in middle school—they seemed to have it all together.

I always wanted to grow up like that person who came into the room dancing around, not letting the fear of coming across as "different" control their being, so that they could inspire others to be themselves and break out of their shell. I had so many role models.

What I didn't realize then was that those people were embracing their vulnerability, unapologetically.

Now, when I think of vulnerability, there are a lot of thoughts that pop into my mind, not only negative. I close my eyes and clearly see multiple people who inspire me by using their voices to speak their purpose.

I see the connection between me and my friends, sharing how we feel and what we identify with.

I see ultimate strength.

I see love in relationships.

I see acceptance.

And I see the word "able."

I knew I wanted to explore and share how I was realizing the importance of vulnerability in my own life at a young age. I wanted to overcome the fear of uncertainty in my life and help others who struggle with the same fear. Most of what I saw in the mainstream media and in my everyday social life left me feeling afraid to be myself, as well as compassionate for the other people who were criticized for being themselves.

Why is now such a critical time to explore the power and importance of vulnerability?

Because so many of us are uncertain in our lives.

Where do I start?

I sure as heck don't want to start here, but I have to: I am starting with my deepest, darkest fears.

Fear

What exactly *is* fear, I had to ask myself? If we do a search on trusty ol' Google, we see a particularly scary definition: "an unpleasant emotion caused by the belief that someone or something is dangerous, likely to cause pain, or a threat."[1]

Why do we have fears?

Let's use spiders as an example.

Is anyone else afraid of spiders?

Okay, so let's say you see a spider on the door handle and you're late for a meeting.

HECK NO, you think. *I am not touching that spider. Nope, I'll wait until it passes.*

You hold to your word and wait. You attempt to shoo it away with a piece of paper, standing far away from the spider, and extend your hand to try to knock it down. You decline

---

1   "Definition Of FEAR". 2019. *Merriam-Webster.Com.* https://www. merriam-webster.com/dictionary/fear.

to look it in the eye, refusing to pick it up in a cup and take it outside to live among you and not trap you.

Finally, the spider passes and you leave for a while, but you come back home to it at night, not sure when it will come back out to inconvenience you again.

Well, for starters, we quickly jump to conclusions, making assumptions about our fear. We may think that spider is going to bite us, or even think to the extremes, that it'll eat us for dinner. We have uncertainty about what the spider will do to us, and we realize that the situation is many times out of our control because no, we cannot talk sense into a spider to keep it from biting us. And—shocker—oftentimes we cannot easily talk sense into another human.

We try and shoo away what we fear most, avoiding everything we can to invite the fears into our lives up close. No, we don't have to make a decision right away to kill the innocent spider, but if we just worked through the fear, maybe we can tolerate it.

So, how about human examples, shall we?

Have you ever wondered if you were going down the right path in life?

Are you a student? Have you ever refrained from asking a question in class in fear that everyone would think you look dumb?

Have you ever withheld your voice in your friend group because you assumed your ideas or thoughts held no worth?

Have you ever chosen not to disclose what you were thinking in front of family members, afraid that they will treat you differently for the rest of your life?

Situations like this happen to all of us, whether we feel like we do not have a voice in our family, friend group, job, classroom ... *insert any other situation here that applies to you.*

I feared vulnerability because I felt that when I spoke up, I was immediately judged. I would come to this conclusion by overanalyzing the looks of people around me after I spoke, or even after I walked into a room. I would assume that after I spoke and someone laughed or whispered, that I was hated by someone, somewhere. I would walk away from a situation, whether in class answering a question or talking to a group of friends, and replay what I said over and over again, asking myself if that sounded okay and if others misinterpreted my messages.

Billions of people are afraid.

Not of spiders or scary monsters.

Of themselves.

And, for me, something as simple as publicly sharing a story about lettuce (I'll get to that in just a minute) helped me realize I didn't need to be afraid of others. And I most definitely didn't need to be afraid of myself.

I became vulnerABLE.

What does it mean to be VulnerABLE?

Now that we have a handle on the word fear, let's get into the good stuff: vulnerABILITY.

Maybe you've felt pushed to the side, or not worthy of sharing your voice throughout the course of your life just like me.

Maybe you've felt that your story is not good enough, inspiring enough, interesting enough, or unique enough.

Noticing the word "able" in vulnerable reminds me to refuse to let fear, especially the fear of being judged, to control my worth. This simple but powerful tweak of the word vulnerable was coined when I was trying to come up with a name for a mental health awareness movement that I hosted on my wellness social media account, called Campus Oils. I reached out to six individuals who were willing to take over my Instagram story to share a summary of their journey with mental health and ways they cope when times are tough. I remember sitting on the floor, trying to figure out a clever name for the movement that would engage others to think more about the concept of vulnerability.

One day, while my boyfriend was playing video games on the other side of the room, he casually said to me, "Why don't you just capitalize the word 'ABLE' in vulnerable?"

"GENIUS!" I screamed. "That's exactly the message I want people to take away from this campaign! We are ABLE to be vulnerable! We are vulnerABLE!"

People express how shocked they are that I—someone who struggles with vulnerability—am so comfortable writing and speaking about personal aspects of my life. I thought about it for a moment and realized that I truly admired the power of vulnerability but only practiced it in safe settings, whether on a retreat, in certain classes at school, or with friends.

Becoming vulnerable is not as easy as it may seem. It was a process for me. Being myself was not as easy as I thought. I carried my anxiety and vulnerability piggyback every single day (no wonder my back and shoulders are so sore all the time).

For me, much of that centered on the fear of being the only one, of being alone and of being judged.

A series of small, simple, and purposeful actions led me to combat my fear.

I became ABLE to be vulnerable.

As author Brené Brown points out, vulnerability is indeed, "uncertainty, risk, and emotional exposure."[2]

Vulnerability is not one thing, one act, or one decision. It's exposure: the consistent embrace of uncertainty and risk. Vulnerability isn't canon-ball jumping into an icy lake; it's slowly creeping into the water one inch at a time. Exposure

---

2   Brown, Brené. 2013. Daring greatly: how the courage to be vulnerable transforms the way we live, love, parent and lead.

suddenly makes you realize that—in the words of Elsa from *Frozen*—the cold doesn't bother me anyway.[3]

✳✳

Anything I write in this book, people can take and use how they please. Someone may call me inexperienced, saying my voice isn't worth sharing. But what gives me empowerment is knowing one of my stories may be useful to you. Me giving away much of my life story is me "emotionally exposing" myself, creating uncertainty for what could happen.

Then, what's the positive of exposing ourselves emotionally, you may be asking?

Brené also defines vulnerability as "the birthplace of love, belonging, joy, courage, empathy, and creativity."[4]

In other words, vulnerability is the source of connection.

That definition tastes a little sweeter and looks more appealing, yes?

We want to belong. We want to work past shame. We want people to truly understand us with empathy, not just sympathy. The only way to do that is by sharing our vulnerability.

In her first Ted Talk, Brené defines shame as a "fear of disconnection, something about me that makes me unworthy

---

3 Walt Disney Animation Studios ; directed by Chris Buck, Jennifer Lee ; produced by Peter Del Vecho ; screenplay by Jennifer Lee ; story by Chris Buck, Jennifer Lee, Shane Morris. Frozen. Burbank, Calif. :Walt Disney Pictures, 2013.

4 Brown, Brené. 2013. Daring greatly: how the courage to be vulnerable transforms the way we live, love, parent and lead.

of connection." She adds, "The less you talk about [shame], the more you have it."[5]

One of the most important points Brené discusses is that "people who have a strong sense of love and belonging believe they are worthy of love and belonging." She teaches us to embrace vulnerability and understand that whatever it was that makes you vulnerable makes you beautiful. I've had the pleasure of hitting some of those realizations about my own life, and I am here to share what I've learned about myself and others with you.

Sometimes vulnerability, the truth, is not only hard for us to say but also hard to hear. When someone is mad at us, sad, sick, scared—when we hear others' true feelings—it may not always be easy. But let's not push these moments of feeling away. We tend to think so much that we forget to feel what is actually happening rather than what we are trying to force ourselves to feel.

The 'Negatives' of Vulnerability

My hope is that you read this book and think, *HECK YES, vulnerability is the source of connection! I CAN embrace my vulnerability!*

But later you may come across a Google search or article using the word vulnerability in a negative way, triggering past fears and thoughts. You may see synonyms of the words and

---

5   "The Power Of Vulnerability | Brené Brown." 2019. *Youtube.* https://www.youtube.com/watch?v=iCvmsMzlF7o.

associations; you may see other people experience criticism for their true, authentic word.

Understanding the whole scope of vulnerability is important and tough. We want to make sure to not lose sight of the positives of vulnerability. Let's get this out of the way now and learn about the uncomfortable: the negative side.

Exploring the word "vulnerable" on Merriam-Webster dredges up some interesting facts about the core root of vulnerability, dated years back:

> *Vulnerable* is ultimately derived from the Latin noun *vulnus* ('wound'). 'Vulnus' led to the Latin verb *vulnerare,* meaning "to wound," and then to the Late Latin adjective *vulnerabilis,* which became 'vulnerable' in English in the early 1600s. 'Vulnerable' originally meant 'capable of being physically wounded" or "having the power to wound' (the latter is now obsolete), but since the late 1600s, it has also been used figuratively to suggest a defenselessness against nonphysical attacks. In other words, someone (or something) can be vulnerable to criticism or failure as well as to literal wounding.[6]

Yes, vulnerability is the source of connection, truth, and openness, but it is also where temptation, susceptibility to emotional harm, and exposure lie.

---

6   "Definition Of VULNERABLE". 2019. Merriam-Webster.Com. https://www.merriam-webster.com/dictionary/vulnerable.

When people are labeled as in a vulnerable state, maybe they just went through a breakup, or a family member is sick, or just found out they're sick. We will repeat that we are not immune to new experiences. At any point in time, any one of us can be labeled as being in a "vulnerable" state.

Some synonyms of the words are:

Weakness.

Defenselessness.

Destructibility.

Yikes.

In reality, we could receive backlash when expressing our true authentic self. We may speak up about our truth just to be shut down or made fun of by others. We can be taken advantage of.

And when we speak up, we may think the worst is inevitable. *Someone will laugh at me when I present*, you may think. *What if I mess up and look like an idiot in front of everyone?*

What if he/she spreads my secret when I tell them what has been bothering me?

What if no one cares what I have to say?

Think about a situation that tried to knock you down to your lowest point. A breakup? A mental health flare-up? An illness or death in the family? A fight with friends? When someone else was making fun of another?

How did you handle it, and what did you learn from the experience? How did you use your voice? Where was vulnerability present?

There are tons of situations where we may be susceptible to harsh words thrown at us. We may "suffer" an embarrassing moment one time or another. But the benefits of vulnerability outweigh the costs, and we are just getting started in our small journey through what it means to be vulnerABLE.

**

I'll get it out there right away—we all may be overthinking it.

The prospect of being vulnerable may seem absolutely terrifying, no matter the situation. Sometimes we don't want to speak up, worried that we may ruin our reputation, a job offer, maybe even a friendship. We may not want to speak up about our passion or choices because we are afraid of being shut down. For example, you may have a huge crush on someone, but do not want to tell them how you really feel. Why? Maybe because you don't want your current relationship with them to change. You may not want to take that risk, because playing it safe is the easy option.

The reality of vulnerability right now is to hold in your feelings: it's the appropriate thing to do. Hold in your feelings, and you're crazy and unstable if you need to go to therapy and learn how to appropriately handle them. Hold in your feelings, because it is not appropriate to show emotion. Hold in your feelings, until they burst and you feel like a deer in headlights.

Vulnerability is not the norm.

What are the reasons we don't we feel comfortable sharing our reality with others? Why is it so difficult for us to share our actual thoughts and feelings? No, not just admitting that we are feeling sad, but admitting why—the actual reasons—we feel hurt and sadness within ourselves. There are a lot of factors holding us back from being vulnerable: not wanting to face the unknown, not wanting exposure, not being in control, not wanting to change a situation from what it is.

This is personally a struggle that I challenge myself to work every single day: to practice what I preach. To notice not only my worth and talents, but others'. I and many others need to realize that everyone goes through their own experiences and we don't always need to beat ourselves up trying to find the one answer that will change our lives. We just need to find new experiences. We need to settle on the idea that answers are gray instead of black and white.

**

But wait, before we get started, who is Julia Ruggiero? Who exactly is the brownish-blonde-haired girl who spends a lot of her time watching *National Geographic* videos about animals and still rides her childhood Razor scooter (which is getting way too small for her 5′6″ height)?

Sounds credible, right?

I, Julia Ruggiero, am here to share with you the future of vulnerability: realizing our own worth, others' worth, and how we can work together. I hope to help others figure out that we are in this life together, even when our experiences are different.

Well, not to brag, but—I'm sort of a professional in feeling anxious. I worry like any other human being on this planet, I don't enjoy doing laundry or washing dishes, I often forget to wear my retainers at night or take out my trash, I cry while watching almost every movie (even most comedies), and I sucked my thumb until I was seventeen years old.

Do you trust me yet?

Surprisingly, there is a lot more to my life. And I am really hoping that my thumb-sucking does not define me.

Well, who is Julia Ruggiero when she is not complaining about doing her laundry? That's a loaded question, as it is for anyone.

I am currently a friend, cousin, speaker, and writer.

I am also an advocate for mental health awareness.

I grapple with debilitating anxiety.

I struggle with body image and binge-eating. I've had my bouts of depression, obsessions, and compulsions, as well as living daily with a phobia of vomiting.

I have experience in being rejected, criticized, and misunderstood. I have experience seeing others in my life rejected, criticized, and misunderstood. I make mistakes all the time.

But, most of all, I am human. I feel guilt, shame, and extreme sensitivity at times. I have trouble speaking up. I can be judgmental and am guilty of not listening to others. I am learning every single day from imperfection and experience, and challenging myself to improve.

Through countless interviews; years of self-reflection, listening, and speaking with others; my unique experiences; jobs in customer service and sales; and extensive research in communications during my time in college and beyond, I've learned a good amount about the importance of vulnerability.

Okay, cool, but what insight do I have regarding vulnerability?

Why should we discuss vulnerability?

Rumor has it there are a ton of people out in the world who would rather swim with sharks than admit they still suck their thumb.

Rumor has it that there are a ton of people who are terrified of speaking on stage, or even in front of their family members.

But why? Maybe you are reading this and still suck your thumb, or you are thirty-five years old and still don't know how to do a load of laundry. And you live your life ashamed of these things because of the ever-present fear of judgment. You may feel ashamed because you think you're abnormal, a bad person, lazy, stupid, *insert any other harmful word that may pop up in your thoughts.* You may think you're the only one.

Psst. Hey, you! There are billions of people on this planet. Yes, someone else doesn't know how to use a dishwasher.

Someone else suffers from extreme depression. Someone else feels like they are alone. And *all* of your stories are important, because all humans are stories in themselves if we really listen to one another.

Why join in on this whole concept of vulnerABILITY? Being vulnerable is cathartic. Having the opportunity to be honest is a step in the right direction to allow yourself to heal. Yes, I've been writing stories about my life in this book and waking up the next day in a panic, thanking God that what I wrote has not been published yet. Vulnerability is not always easy, and you may ask yourself often things like, *Why the heck did I write in a published book that I sucked my thumb until I was seventeen?* But then you'll realize you don't have to be ashamed of that anymore, because there are people out there who will accept you and who will be able to relate to you because, in the words of the great Dr. Seuss, "Those who matter don't mind." Vulnerability inspires vulnerability.

In the coming pages, you'll learn about the presence of vulnerability in the lives of many.

This book will explore experiences that not only I but also many other individuals have behind closed doors that have shaped a huge part of our lives. It opens up the possibility of listening and learning about others, as well as learning more about ourselves in the process. My plan is to create awareness through the stories in this book. If we can state our opinion, what makes another person's opinion less worthy?

Questions that I challenge you to ask yourself while reading this:

- Although I cannot control the thoughts that pop into my head, am I judging others through my actions?
- Do I feel like I am being attacked?
- And do I make others feel unsafe?
- Do I feel that gossiping is the only way to connect with certain people?
- Who do you allow to have control over you? Do your fears take the wheel?

For example, I'll admit some of my struggles here: I've gossiped many times. I've spread rumors. I would stoop to a lower level just to be accepted by a group. I've judged others who have had anxiety before I understood it myself. I've been frustrated with others.

Wait, whaaat?

Yes, as a matter of fact, I have hurt someone else's feelings before. I am impatient. People have been mad at me. And it sucks to admit that, as it probably does not feel great for anyone to admit that about themselves.

I've been upset with others.

I felt like people were quick to ignore me before they could even engage in dialogue.

And I am not a squeaky clean perfect human either.

I also started to gossip about myself over time. Self-depreciation is unhealthy, and it was a part of my daily routine.

We get stuck in a cycle of blaming others, blaming ourselves, and feeling unsafe to engage with others because we are either too scared or just worried we are right and the other person is wrong.

The world has a lot of healing to do, and even as I am writing this, I have trouble wrapping my mind around the concept of vulnerability and acceptance at times.

So, I am talking about it in the way I know how to: by asking both myself and other people how we feel—not only about how they found peace within themselves, but how they felt along the way.

That's what I'm curious about.

Now I am moving to positively expose things about myself in hopes of helping others, spreading my own secrets such as my thumb-sucking because it's part of who I was and who I am today, and I am learning to embrace the parts of my life I was once so ashamed about due to comparison and trying to maintain an image.

You'll also hear a collection of stories about me—and my own personal journey to help my understanding of vulnerability come full circle through my experiences, including:

- Depression
- Bullying
- Jealousy
- Romantic relationships
- Family
- Friendships

I now believe the smartest people in the world are those who actively work to understand other voices and opinions before promoting their own. I learn more from the people who discuss the positives and negatives of both sides of a story, walk me through how they formed their opinion, and then open their ears to hear mine, too.

**

I offer my experience of life to help guide your own journey. Here's a brief snippet of what I've learned in my journey learning about vulnerability: sometimes we feel stuck inside our own mind, keeping in so many details of our lives that we think will tear our relationships apart. People have very similar thoughts and experiences that they may go their whole life never admitting. We feel bad for being a certain way. We feel wrong for being ourselves.

I felt compelled to write this book because everyone has a unique message to share with the world. In this book you will hear from many voices explaining why they did or did not speak up in various walks of life. I want to highlight the human reality and let you know that you do not need to be considered "special" to have a voice in this world.

More people are letting down their guard and becoming vulnerable, but more people are finding ways to criticize these people. I hope to help you accept yourself and others through learning about three words that hold such strong importance: lettuce, laundry, and love. You'll find out how to recognize that everyone has something special they were meant to share with the world.

I want to help others refuse to give up. I want to share the tools I've developed over time for anyone who chooses to read this. To keep the tools relatable to them in their memory bank and use for later when needed.

With vulnerability comes criticism. And I am not just talking about people who stand up on a stage and speak to an audience of 30,000+ people, sharing their life story.

I am also talking about when you are standing in your pajamas trying to tell your parents that you do not want to go to your family Thanksgiving gathering because you are feeling anxious and upset for a reason that is not too clear to you yet.

Remember, there are billions of other people just like you (I'm one of them) who are struggling with something in our lives. And for many of us the steps towards fulfillment begin with being vulnerable.

Simply admitting you *don't* have things figured out to yourself and to others—well, that's called being vulnerable.

See? That wasn't that hard, right?

I hope this book helps you realize that someone else out there is making a ton of mistakes and learning from them. I hope this helps you feel supported and like you are not alone. Because you, reading this book, have gone through a lot. I know you have, even if you can honestly say that you feel 100 percent happy at this very moment. Life is a collection of feelings that come and go. You've handled a lot to get to the point in life that you are at now. We just have to figure out what has become of us. How are we making ourselves feel? How are we making others feel?

**

You do not need to stand up on stage and broadcast how long you may have sucked your thumb or your most embarrassing moments to be vulnerable. You don't have to be vulnerable by going on YouTube and posting a video about your biggest fear. This is also about microlevel connection, pure human connection with one another.

This is about understanding ourselves and one another, developing compassion for the beautiful voice that lives inside of us. You don't have to be rich or poor to have a voice; you don't have to be a woman to be vulnerable—you just have to be you.

Even if you do not read this book word for word, even if you read one page or one line in a chapter and it resonates with you, you may be able to find that voice within yourself that is waiting to emerge, despite the shame and fear. I hope to spark a conversation between me and you. I hope that you can find worth in your unique voice.

We are all ABLE.

Welcome to the vulnerABLE movement.

PART 1

'I CAN'T CUT MY OWN LETTUCE'

"Sometimes when we dare to walk into the arena the greatest critic we face is ourselves."

—BRENE BROWN[7]

7 Brown, Brené. 2013. Daring greatly: how the courage to be vulnerable transforms the way we live, love, parent and lead.

I can't cut my lettuce.

Yup, you read that correctly. It sounds like a pun or a meme or something, but it's just reality.

Nice to meet you; my name is Julia Ruggiero, and I can't cut my lettuce.

Why? Well, I had trouble cutting a huge wedge of lettuce for one reason:

I am a massive germaphobe.

How do wedges of lettuce and germaphobia correlate in the slightest? And how does this relate to vulnerability?

I had just gotten off the second flight in my journey from Pittsburgh to Utah. I was traveling with one of my closest friends and her family; it was still morning when we landed. We were all exhausted and hungry by the time we settled into our hotel room. Although we could have used a little nap, we wanted to make the most out of the day and did not hesitate to jump into the car to head to Park City for lunch.

My excitement suddenly turned to fear and shame in a matter of hours because of the food I chose to eat.

As tired as I felt, the scenery in Utah was beautiful and I wanted to take in every moment. Stomachs rumbling, we walked up to a quaint brewery for lunch. The walls were lined with Mason jars, the sunlight shining on every individual jar. We all took our seats, and when I picked up the menu, all I knew was that I wanted something refreshing and to chug as much water as possible. The salads sounded incredible, so I quickly chose one and was ready to *dig in.*

As I handed my menu to the waiter and moved my cup of water forward, I accidentally hit my unwrapped knife, which touched the table. I did not think much of it and continued to talk with everyone about our plans for the rest of the week. I knew the minute my salad hit the table I was going to eat it in less than two minutes.

I finally saw the waiter heading toward us, and when his tray got to my eye level, my shoulders instantly fell. The waiter plopped a wedge of lettuce down right in front of me that felt like the size of the Statue of Liberty.

Why did my shoulders fall?

I realized that I would have to use my knife to cut the lettuce.

My thoughts were going in circles:

I'm going to need to use my knife, won't I?

The same knife that touched the table ... the dirty, germ-infested table?

I don't want to risk sickness when I'm traveling!

I can't catch the stomach virus and throw up, I just can't.

I just want to enjoy the week and not have any problems.

No way!

I looked around and saw everyone's unused knives sitting at the table. I started to weigh my options.

Okay Julia, all you have to do is ask someone, "Do any of you mind if this knife touched the table? Just to lay it out there, I am a germaphobe and I do not want to eat with my knife that fell on the table. If you aren't using yours, can I switch with

you?" I could even ask the waiter for a new knife. Or I could
suck it up and use the knife, working through my fear...

But then people would look at me funny.

I am making this a big deal.

There are bigger problems in the world; why am I fixated
on my knife?

What if everyone has questions about my fear of germs?

What if someone makes fun of me?

The slightest act of asking for someone to pass me a knife
or grab me a new one felt like the biggest bother. You would
have thought that I was asking someone to jump out of
a plane with me. I wished the concept of my knife touching
the table were not this bizarre and complicated.

Instead, I kept my mouth shut and started to tear at the
lettuce with my fork. I was very hungry, and each piece that
I was able to break off was miniscule. But I continued to eat,
hoping that no one would notice.

Not long after all of the people seated at the table started
to eat, everyone saw that I had not yet cut my wedge of lettuce.

"Are you going to cut that?" one asked.

Another joked, "You know, if you use your knife, you
can eat your meal!"

They giggled, thinking I was just messing around with
them.

I started to make excuses, explaining that everything
was fine and that I did not want or need to cut the wedge.
A couple of minutes passed by, and little pieces of lettuce

were falling off the plate. I kept dropping whatever my fork picked up.

I let every single person at the table make a comment, and I still kept my mouth shut.

Eventually, a voice said, "Here, I'll do it." My friend cut up the lettuce with her unused knife in less than five seconds.

I was absolutely mortified.

I'm a grown-up, I thought to myself, *and I can't even work up the courage to speak!*

While she was sliding the lettuce back to me, I buried my head into my lap. Every single person at the table I felt comfortable around, but for some reason I still did not want to admit I was afraid of a knife.

My eyes were welling up with tears from embarrassment. *Julia, there is no excuse for this*, I thought. *Seriously, grow up. You're being dramatic.* I thought if I said these criticisms to myself first, it wouldn't hurt as much if someone else said those words to me.

I fought to hold back my tears, not because I was angry at the people around me, but because I was so afraid of how crazy I would look when I said my knife brushed the table for a millisecond and I assumed the table was covered in germs that could possibly give me the stomach flu. All right, how am I going to say that out loud on the first day of a trip to a ton of people?

No one will want to travel with me ever again! I thought.

**

Everyone at the table did not understand my fear.

I couldn't blame them for that, because I did not even give them a chance to listen to me. I always assumed no one in the world would give me the chance to explain. I let that assumption hold me back from experiencing the possibilities using my voice could bring.

I was afraid that I would still look crazy if I explained my fear of germs.

People could not read my mind. It was my responsibility to speak up and own my decision, whether I told the whole story or not. I was mad at myself for being ashamed of my decisions.

If I believed that I was allowed to be vulnerable and embrace my voice, cutting lettuce may not have been as difficult. I would have embraced my truth, and helped the people around me understand how I was feeling.

What was holding me back from admitting why I did not want to use my knife?

I started to recall the things I'd heard through the years when my anxiety flares up.

"Julia, you are acting childish."

"It's not that big of a deal."

"You worry too much!"

"There is no possible way in the world you can get sick from that."

I used to blame everyone for their criticisms toward me. I looked at each comment as an attack. A threat.

In reality, most comments were actually said to try and help me get over the fear that popped up in my life every single day. I was blaming everyone else when I was taking each comment to heart, fueling the negative side of the comments and beating myself up in my own mind.

Many people do not understand what I am feeling, I kept needing to tell myself. *And people everywhere are going to feel like they are mistreated unless voices come together and speak up. Vulnerability and understanding may just be the big secret to changing our lives, one voice at a time.*

I started to think about how small of a situation this was, but how getting used to not speaking up could stick with me as bigger situations in my life arose.

A scary thought crossed my mind when pondering how upset this seemingly small situation made me feel.

If other people feel stuck, insecure, embarrassed, and deflated in their own lives over and over again, how do they keep the drive to continue moving forward? How will they handle facing the issues when times are tough?

I wanted to know how others felt in times of embarrassment, confusion, and fear. Why do people give up on tasks they once wanted to grow at? Do they think no one will take the time to understand them? Do people give up hope instead of facing their insecurities head on?

**

We are all broken.

Every single one of us.

We crave fulfillment and connection. We tend to judge people and suppress our own mistakes. We make ourselves the protagonist in almost every story. And when we are broken down again and again, we may feel disconnected, misjudged, and alone.

This is a story of my own journey to find fulfillment and connection.

To do that, I'd have to learn to be vulnerable.

This part of the book details my quest to embrace my own voice, my own opinions, my own thoughts, my own ideals, my own quirks, and all the things that make me ... me.

And for a woman afraid to share why she needed a new knife, it required me to re-examine everything.

Think of the lettuce story. Think of the way I was talking to myself, the assumptions I made, and the harsh thoughts that I fueled in my mind.

Now think about this: Have you thought to yourself that you have no worth? If this ever happens to you, take a moment to reflect on how you view yourself. When your voice is judged or affected, you may turn against yourself, believing criticisms and losing confidence in yourself. When you assume someone will judge your voice, you may filter what you say.

Through these coming chapters, I will re-introduce you to a voice you may be all-too-familiar with: the voice within us holding us back from cutting our lettuce. The voice of self-criticism. Self-depreciation.

Lettuce symbolizes insurmountable mounds, or challenges, that arise in our own lives that we are responsible for growing from and working past as time progresses.

Part 1 will help you to learn about the whole scope of vulnerability, and how to stay mindful of your own thoughts and responses. You will learn some winks of wisdom to foster positive thoughts. You may notice more about how you talk to yourself.

Whether influenced by our shame, anxieties, or our fears, we will explore how our thoughts are just merely thoughts, why we do not give ourselves permission to be vulnerable.

Although we cannot always control what happens to us and what thoughts pop into our minds, we can control how we act and use our voice. We will learn that it's possible to move from self-doubt to accepting ourselves and accepting our true voices.

Each chapter title in Part 1 will begin with a quote. These quotes are common phrases that we say to ourselves in times of disappointment and disapproval, phrases that we start to believe—phrases that hold us back from reaching our true potential and recognizing our worth.

Being vulnerable with someone else is one story, but you also have to be vulnerable with yourself.

Maybe you would have easily been able to tell the people eating at the table that you couldn't cut your lettuce. Maybe you would have just cut and eaten your lettuce, despite the possibility of a dirty, table-touching knife. Through these chapters, my curiosity allowed me to explore why people may feel like they can and can't cut their hypothetical wedge of lettuce.

Chances are there is someone else in the world who feels like they can't cut their own lettuce, either.

Is it you?

P.S. How wild is it that I'm writing this story publicly for you—my reader—when just a few months earlier I couldn't even tell the closest people in my life. Maybe there's something to this whole being-vulnerable thing. Into the deep end of the pool we go!

CHAPTER 1

'I'm the Only One'

———

Stories that incorporate real-life examples usually start with a childhood experience, right?

Well, I hated a six – or seven-year-old girl for over ten years.

Yup, hated and judged this little girl.

I was ashamed of her, felt embarrassed to even think of her, and never wanted to talk about her.

That little girl's name is Julia. And yes, you guessed it— *my* name is also Julia. That's not a coincidence.

Yup, hi, it's me.

There is no other six – or seven-year-old on this planet that I hate, but looking back to when I was little is the worst feeling for me to relive, and the strangest thing is:

I don't even fully remember over 90 percent of what I am going to write about.

**

Self-hatred.

Self-loathing.

What do these words mean and why do they prey on our thoughts?

I recently stumbled across PsychAlive, a nonprofit resource that contains interesting information in regards to psychology. To be honest, I always wanted to pursue a career in psychology, but after taking an AP Psych class in high school, learning at a rapid pace anything and everything we could about the variety of research on mental health, I started to self-diagnose myself to an unhealthy degree (instead of just learning without overthinking to get an actual degree).

I was caught up reading posts by Jo Barrington on Psych Alive, who writes about multiple different topics, including self-loathing. She includes research to come to the conclusion that starting from childhood, "we have all been subjected to situations and times in which we were made to feel like we were somehow bad, inadequate, or desperately needing to prove otherwise." She further describes self-loathing as the "critical internal voice or internal coach … as though it might just be your conscience." We think these critical thoughts we possess in our heads are what our conscience is saying to us. We can often find ourselves caught up in thinking that we are awful human beings, driving ourselves to insanity, bringing us close to the brink of giving up all hope for a happier life.

Barrington goes on to explain:

[The self-loathing process] is diametrically opposed to your self-interest. Whereas your conscience will tell you not to have that one drink too many, this process first lures you into taking that drink and then attacks you viciously for having taken it. Your conscience may nag at you to revisit a conversation in which you may have not been kind for instance, and from there you can think about it and decide what you would like to do. The internal enemy either justifies your having been rude by attacking the other person, *He deserved it, he is such a jerk!* or berates you furiously for your part, *You are always so touchy and mean. No wonder no one likes you!*[8]

Her words opened my eyes to the fact that I do treat myself like the examples she mentioned above. I do not always accept myself when wrestling with feelings and thoughts about my own worth and potential. And, reading Barrington's words, knowing her article was not just directed toward me, helped me realize that many other people are struggling with the same form of self-hatred.

**

8   Barrington, Jo. "Self-Loathing: Where Self-Loathing Comes From And How To Stop It". 2017. *Psychalive*. https://www.psychalive.org/self-loathing/.

As much as I hated that little girl—myself, as a child—I also don't really remember why I hated her or even the actions that led me to this feeling.

It's one of the challenges of self-loathing behaviors: we fixate on the symptoms, not the root cause.

What I do remember: I loved attention as a child. I do not have any siblings and my parents both worked hard. They were stressed and busy a majority of my life. My mom was a caregiver for multiple family members for as long as I can remember, and my dad busted his butt to work two jobs just to make sure we brought in an average income.

I remember bits and pieces of small stories from my childhood, such as the annual Kris Kringle event in elementary school.

In second grade, my class and I headed over to the school cafeteria, where the air smelled of smiley fries and chicken nuggets, the white walls lined with blue trim. Kris Kringle was our school's Christmas event where we could shop a variety of little gifts for our friends and family.

My friends and I ran, giggled, and split up to pick out the items that first caught our eyes. Our little hands were full of picture frames that said "I love Dad" or "I love Grandpa," as well as tennis bracelets and stuffed animals.

Those darn stuffed animals.

So, what happened at that Kris Kringle sale?

I looked over at one of my friends to meet up with her, and as I was scanning the room to find her, I saw the fluffy, brown, stuffed animal bear with a super cool, intricate design laying across the room. My friend saw the bear too, and happily picked it up and went to go check out her items.

I want that bear! It's so cool! Why can't I have it?! Why didn't I get to it first? I thought to myself.

I do not remember the conversations in between the school day and the time I returned home, until I called my friend up on her home phone who bought the bear and took it home.

Here is my attempt to interpret the call between my friend and me.

Hey! I said.

Hi Julia! she said from the other line.

Can I have that bear you got today at Kris Kringle? I asked abruptly.

No, I'm sorry! she said nicely, sounding a bit confused.

I don't care. I want it. So bring it tomorrow, I said, quickly hanging up the phone.

To this day, I replay this scenario, trying to remember my tone and every little word I said to my friend. It eats me alive to know I can't go back and change how I used my voice.

I have always been a pack-rat—you can see it in almost all the home videos from when I was a child. Flash back to three-year-old me on Christmas, I would take my presents and lay them out in a line so I could see all of them. Even at eight years old, I would lay out all of my toys and games just to see everything at once. When I was a teenager, I would lay out my shoes and jewelry just to see how much I had. Collecting more and more became a stress reliever for me from a young age, and as I got older, I was more ashamed of this habit. My friends from college would come to visit during holiday breaks, cleaning out my closet, surprised with how much junk I had stored behind the doors. Friends would comment on my collecting habit constantly, calling my room the "eye-spy room." Although I agreed with them, I was so self-conscious about it.

I always wanted more stuff. I wanted to prove I was my own individual with my own interests. I felt fulfilled when I would purchase a new shirt or stuffed animal. But when I bought one thing, it always led to the habit of buying more ... and more ... and more.

Even though I was a child, I remember that I hurt my friend's feelings with my selfishness. And this was not the only story I have in my memory bank. When I think back, I let these stories define me. I let that fixation on material items define me. I make myself out to be an absolute monster.

I would tell my friends that I was the star of a new show on Disney Channel named *Lizzie From Mississippi*, and yup, I was Lizzie (if you were wondering, this was around the same time Hannah Montana was already released as a show on Disney Channel. Very original, Julia). I also told a guy in my class—whom I had a *huge* crush on—that I rode to school in a limo every day and got extra Jolly Ranchers every day at home. Totally not true. Jolly Ranchers were all the hype back then (still kinda are).

Oh, and I used to tell people that I had a hundred sisters—and apparently told one of my friends to eat a tissue in second grade if she still wanted to be my friend.

Wow, I am freaking out knowing I just published all of that. Yup, that's who I was, but not all that I am.

I always hear quotes saying, "People never change." Hearing this heightened my feelings of shame, and I defined myself as the person I once was—as a child!

We grow! Life changes! We have the capacity to improve and learn. But I lost complete sight of that as I entered adulthood.

As a child, I was insecure and jealous of others; I wanted to be the best at everything and anything. I constantly needed to prove to the world I was worthy.

I used my voice constantly as a child—to interrupt others.

I was a kid. I learned from it. By fourth grade, I was already feeling ashamed of the way I treated others.

I started to become a pushover in early grade school, going from constantly using my voice to letting other people define it. I was bullied in the coming years and felt that I deserved it.

I went from being the one who wanted all of the attention to someone who lost their own voice. I lost confidence in my own voice and ideas.

When I talked about this in therapy, my therapist would ask me, "Would you be mad at a seven-year-old right now for acting like that?"

"No," I replied.

"Okay, why are you mad at yourself?" she would ask.

"Because I should have known better. I was probably old enough to know right from wrong."

"Okay, but what about if you were talking about this with a current seven-year-old? How would you handle it?"

"Well, they are so young yet, and we just have to continue setting a good example, disciplining when needed, making sure they know to not only care for themselves, but also care for others," I said, immediately seeing what my therapist trapped me into.

I was so harsh on myself, but so understanding toward and willing to help others.

I did not want to grow up. I wanted to start over. I wanted to live a childhood that brought me no shame of the way I treated others. And, because I do not remember my past clearly, I created stories in my head, making me more and more anxious. I wanted things to be perfect.

Now, I have this fear of seeing others get hurt or lose someone or something close to them. Even though in this example it was a small stuffed animal bear, I still hate knowing how I made my friend feel. I want to take part in something that someone can celebrate, not that makes them feel deflated and alone.

Realizing 'I Am Not Alone'

I was talking to some friends when I started writing this section of the book, going back and forth on whether I wanted to include this "embarrassing" section.

My friends started to reminisce about their childhood, sharing stories with me when they wished they weren't so "annoying" or "loud" or "childish" as a kid.

But the part that shocked me most was when they were done telling me the story and would say, "Don't repeat that to anyone, though. I was so stupid; it's embarrassing."

Someone else feels ashamed of the way they acted as a child, I thought.

And wanna know what I immediately thought? *Oh my goodness, we all have shame. DUH.*

We all go through disappointment, even more similar that we ever thought. Many times people started their childhood stories by saying, "I never thought I would tell this story out loud…"

That takes *guts*. It really does.

It took me a long time to realize, but when I shared my voice and someone else shared their voice with me, I felt comfort and connection, realizing for once that I was not alone, and that change is possible.

**

Embarrassment can also be defined as discomfort. Discomfort arises when we think we are going against a social norm. A journal by Kiersten Weir, published by the American

Psychological Association, touches on the topic of embarrassment. Weir includes comments from Christine Harris, Ph.D., a psychologist at the University of California, San Diego, who said that "embarrassment serves the function of immediately and strongly displaying, 'Oops, I didn't mean to do that.'"[9] We want to justify what we did wrong, but when we feel guilt for justifying what we are doing, we hobble into thinking we are awful human beings. I am personally embarrassed to say that the Kris Kringle story is just one of the many times I acted as a controlling bully.

That unpleasant feeling of embarrassment pops upon us *quickly*. If we are sitting in a classroom, we can do one thing, such as burp or accidentally trip when walking to get water, and immediately want to hide in a ditch and never show our faces again from a fear of judgment.

In Wier's writing, she mentions that "embarrassment may repair social relationships and even advertise positive character traits, but at the same time, that sheepishness could lead you to make less-than-stellar decisions."

Researchers found that we tend to feel more embarrassment in front of people we know rather than strangers. Embarrassment can be absolutely crippling, threatening our decisions, wellness, and performance in many situations. An example Weir uses driven by her research is buying condoms.

---

9   Wier, Kristen. "Oh No You Didn't!". 2019. *Https://Www.Apa.Org.* https://www.apa.org/monitor/2012/11/embarrassment.

Many humans would rather be anywhere else than in a convenience store in their local town buying condoms, or even consulting a doctor, thinking they sound "stupid" or like they are "overthinking."

Covering up embarrassment can lead to lies, excuses, and blame.

Weir ends the article with one of my new favorite life mantras: "The good news, though, is that others may not judge us as severely as we judge ourselves. ... So, the next time you trip on the sidewalk, forget an acquaintance's name or realize your fly has been down all day, take a deep breath and try to shake it off. Your ruby-red cheeks and nervous smile may be broadcasting your best traits."

Guilt and Shame

Why does it take guts to speak about what we are withholding from the world? Why is it hard to talk about the past or even the future? Why are we afraid of experiencing embarrassing moments?

Because we are working against our guilt and shame, facing head-on how we feel inside.

Confronting ourselves.

Accepting ourselves and sitting with those uncomfortable feelings. It's not easy, nor is it always fun to pay attention to our shameful feelings.

This process can feel heartbreaking. It can be a long and tedious process of growth and healing, and you may feel like you've been thrown in the dark. But even when you are in a dark place, there is light surrounding you—you just may not be able to see it yet. What are our eyes and ears focusing on?

Are we focusing on outside approval? Resisting vulnerability to guarantee acceptance from the people around us?

Protecting ourselves from the unknown?

Are we afraid our voices will be shut down? Or abandoned?

Have we been abandoned or abandoned others because of a disagreement?

We need to be vulnerable with ourselves first and foremost, facing these shameful situations head onto forgive our former selves.

Guilt

Let's first discuss the looming question: what exactly is guilt?

Guilt is different from shame, but our minds can have a difficult time differentiating between the two. Brené Brown powerfully states that where shame is when we feel like we are wrong for being who we are, guilt is that we did wrong.

Simply put, guilt is "a feeling of deserving blame for offenses."[10] Let's think back to my childhood example. I acted foolishly, and knowing that I was in early grade school, I felt like I had to be old enough to know right from wrong. I am

---

10   Brown, Brené. 2019. "Listening To Shame". *Ted.Com*. https://www.ted.com/talks/brene_brown_listening_to_shame.

guilty of being a bully. Even though it was a while ago, I feel guilty that my behavior caused people to feel upset or frustrated with me.

Maybe someone came to you upset and conflicted after they were caught cheating on their romantic partner. They believe their act of cheating went against not only their own values but also the boundaries and values their partner held onto within the commitment of the relationship.

How does guilt differ from shame?

Shame

Shame is the humiliation we feel because of a foolish action. Brené also adds that it's a painful experience "of believing that we are flawed and unworthy of love and belonging." She describes shame as feeling that "we are wrong."

There are many ways shame can present itself in our daily lives in both small and large situations. Maybe your face heats up and your eyes well up in tears because you burped in that important meeting in front of all of your colleagues or in a room full of your classmates.

When I was approaching my teenage years, my little cousin and I were in the family room with my mom and dad, who were watching television. I was laying down playing on my iPod when my cousin quickly climbed on my back, standing on his two feet. I was startled and ticklish, and the minute he stood on my back, I flinched. He slipped off onto the ground, crashing onto the hardwood floor. After a moment, he started to scream and cry, while I stood there in horror, shocked, hoping he wasn't severely hurt.

For years after, I was worried that his headaches were somehow from the time he fell. I felt irresponsible for playing on my iPod while my cousin wanted to goof around. I felt a lack of confidence to take care of my cousin in the coming years, afraid that I would screw up again. I defined myself from that situation, thinking I could never have children. Wowza, that escalated quickly.

Although this example may seem small to many, these feelings of shame arise in all kinds of situations.

How the Dynamic Duo of Guilt and Shame Prey on Our Vulnerability

I lived with the guilt of knowing that I hurt people's feelings and that I had to somehow turn back time and change what I did to ever have a chance to improve my attitude in the future. I fixated on my guilt and was ashamed of myself.

When we are guilty, we let these feelings of regret spiral into shame. We then feel humiliated, unworthy, and worn out from trying to fix what we believe we messed up. We start to become okay with the guilt, believing we really are bad people with no chance to improve. This mindset does not give us an opportunity to change or to ask for help when needed. We feel like we lose control of ourselves, and deserve nothing more. We start to let that affect the way we view ourselves, and feel afraid to speak up, thinking we already ruined our chances to make a positive impact on the world.

It's important to remember that it takes time to grow and to not to lose grasp of this message. You cannot go from ten years old to twenty years old in one day. Growth takes time, learning takes time, and it's an absolutely beautiful and rewarding process to experience. It's a privilege to wake up in the morning, given another chance to grow.

Focusing on the past and on our downfalls throws us into an unhealthy spiral of shame in the way we view ourselves. We take even the smallest of situations and beat ourselves up, letting our past performance define our future.

In college, I would go to spiritual direction sessions to learn more about the Bible and my relationship with God. I remember my spiritual director and I were in a deep conversation discussing the meaning of a specific Bible verse, when she paused and asked me if I loved myself.

"Yeah, I think so," I quickly replied. "When I am sitting alone in my room, I know that I am smart and willing to learn. I appreciate my anxiety at times, looking at it as a friend who thinks they have my best interests at heart. I make mistakes, but know that I have the capability to rise."

I thought for a couple of moments and continued, "Although, when I am out in the open, I realize my confidence does not always follow me outside of the confines of my room. While I know that I am capable, I let others make me feel like I am not. I let others remind me that I am imperfect and because of this, that I may not have what it takes to work past my struggles."

She paused for a moment, nodded her head once, and smiled. "God's voice isn't your regret and guilt. God's voice isn't your fear. God made you perfect in his image. You're perfect as you are, Julia. Try and remember that, through God's lens, you are where you're supposed to be."

What are we fixating on?

No matter your religion or connection to faith and a higher power, this is such an important message to remember in times of panic and sadness. In times of guilt and shame:

Someone out there recognizes that you are where you are supposed to be right now, at this moment.

Someone out there will not try to change you for who you are.

Someone out there knows that you have more to you than the mistakes you've made in your life.

Someone out there truly grasps the concept that we are not perfect, is okay with that, and embraces the imperfect parts of their own lives to lead as an example.

Are you that someone to yourself?

**

Temporary guilt is said to help with moral development and understanding our decisions and what other decisions they lead to. Guilt helps us analyze how we are treating others and how we can improve. Where shame hops into the picture, photobombing, saying, "You look awful and always will! There is no need to try because you are a *failure*." Surprisingly, shame is way harsher than that, too.

According to Dr. Joseph Burgo, guilt arises from a feeling of awareness. In other words, a responsibility to know the actions we took in a situation. He describes this notion further by saying:

Shame may result from the awareness of guilt but apparently is not the same thing as guilt. It's a painful feeling about how we appear to others (and to ourselves) and doesn't necessarily depend on our having done anything. … I once said something hurtful at a dinner party, and on some level, I intended it to be hurtful. Afterward, I felt *guilty* because I could see that I had hurt my friend. More painfully, I also felt *ashamed* that I was the sort of person who would behave that way. Guilt arose as a result of inflicting pain on somebody else; I felt shame in relation to myself.[11]

I learned from Alexis de Los Santos, a wonderful therapist from Awaken Into Love, a platform that helps bring awareness to relationship obsessive compulsive disorder (ROCD), that guilt and shame can work together to create disconnection from ourselves and one another. She describes how thoughts hijack our viewpoint on welcoming love into

11   Burgo, Joseph. "The Difference Between Guilt And Shame". 2019.
     Psychology Today. https://www.psychologytoday.com/us/blog/
     shame/201305/the-difference-between-guilt-and-shame.

our lives, telling ourselves things such as, *I shouldn't feel a certain way. I am a bad person for feeling this way. If I feel guilty enough, then I will mend my mistakes.* These thoughts are typically accompanied by words like "should" and "shouldn't."

We don't even need to do anything wrong—we may just *assume* we are wrong, *assume* we've done wrong, and give up on whatever we aspire to be in life.

**

All people, no matter who comes to mind, experience guilt and the pain of shame. There are two types of people I want us to focus on right now: those who choose to own up to their feelings and those who give up without even trying.

I was watching Marie Kondo's show, *The Magic of Tidying Up*, based off her bestselling book about decluttering and finding peace and comfort in the space you live in. Kondo, who has written multiple bestselling books, rose to success after people noticed her KonMari method: her plan for organizing your belongings and parting from clutter that does not "spark joy" in your life. When I think of her book, I also think of decluttering the mind by taking action and going through the hard part of getting rid of the items that no longer serve us.

When we are cluttered and engulfed in sadness, we start to form a habit of looking at our *whole* life as baggage. A small but powerful quote that stuck with me from *The*

Magic of Tidying Up is when expert organizer Marie Kondo herself admitted: "Even my house gets cluttered."[12]

There is so much power in that quote. What does it mean?

Even the people we may think have everything together in their life, even the people who declutter their space and become an expert in their field, still have moments of imperfection.

We all make mistakes. We may try as hard as possible to make ourselves look perfect, but in reality we all have parts of ourselves that are a work in progress.

We are afraid that we are the only one going through bouts of guilt and shame, and then we let those painful feelings of shame eat us alive.

I still find it hard to talk about my emotions, especially in front of certain people.

But when we speak up, we realize that others feel sadness, shame, and guilt, and that we are all in this together, more than we may ever realize.

Speaking Up and Connecting with Others

In an article from the *Wall Street Journal*, interestingly enough, research from the Virginia Tech Carilion Research Institute describes how we are actually less intelligent than usual in certain smaller group settings. The article explains, "If we think others in a group are smarter, we may become

---

12   "Tidying Up With Marie Kondo." 2019. *Netflix*.

dumber, temporarily losing both our problem-solving ability and what the researchers call our 'expression of IQ.'"[13] We do not want to say something others may think is dumb or stupid, so we resort to nervous talking, not saying anything at all, or judging others when that's exactly what we do not want to happen to ourselves. As a result, we may sound exactly how we do not want to since we fixate so much on our performance rather than the actual happenings around us. Panic, fear, and fixation on our emotions emerge from nervousness in small group situations. We tend to drive ourselves crazy to find answers, to find ways we can prove ourselves to be smart, when we learned earlier that embarrassment can be positive.

Look at everything getting in the way of us connecting with one another! When we are too afraid that we are the only one feeling, looking, or acting a certain way, we waste time figuring out how we are actually very similar to the person next to us.

'The Perfect Timing'

What happens when we take the plunge and speak up? Do we have to wait until "the perfect time" to use our voices? Or will that time come when we least expect it?

In my high school creative writing class, my teacher explained that we would have twenty minutes to write about

---

13 Bernstein, Elizabeth. 2019. "Speaking Up Is Hard To Do: Researchers Explain Why ". *WSJ*. https://www.wsj.com/articles/SB10001424052 9702041364045772070202525853492.

anything we wanted. She set the timer, sat down, and told us to go.

The minute her finger hit the start button on her timer, I knew what I had to write. I felt no hesitation as each minute passed by. My eyes stared intently at the computer screen, and my fingers started to type as fast as they could. I do not remember how the words flowed so smoothly from my fingers to the keyboard, but I kept going.

When the timer stopped, I pulled my hands back and took a big deep breath in and out.

"Okay, now we are going to read our words to the class," my teacher said as she stood back up from her chair.

Wait, what? We have to read this? Seriously? Darn it, I thought. *I have no clue what I just wrote.*

I did not have time to read my whole essay back and make any changes. My heart started to beat faster and faster when it came closer and closer to my turn to speak.

"Julia, it's your turn!" Her voice snapped me out of my thoughts. I swallowed hard and started to read:

I wish I had known to study more for this test, I thought to myself. The pounding in my chest reaches my throat and I gasp for air while the tears stream out of my eyes. As I sit in the bathroom stall at school when I should be in history class, I feel the anxiety overpowering my mind. On top of everything that is bothering me at this present moment, I started to develop a fear that if I do not go back to history right now, my teacher will give me detention for "taking my good old time." That worry makes my attack ten times worse. But if I go try to get help and confront someone, telling them that I am having an actual anxiety attack, it will look like I just want attention or want to get out of my next period's anatomy test.

Perfect. I feel like there is no one who understands why I am upset almost every night of the week and I have resorted to my hiding place in an inclosed cube with a toilet to comfort me. The best part is that I don't even know one reason as to why I am so upset. Maybe it's because I am going to fail the anatomy test. Maybe it is because someone laughed at me in class. Maybe it is because of a small argument I was in with a girl in my class last year that no one probably even remembers now. This is the day in the life of a seventeen-year-old teenager with an obvious anxiety disorder. But this has become normal for me. I wish I had one person to talk to all the time when I feel like this. But I've already made that mistake. I would vent constantly to one person and they started to talk about how annoying I was and would constantly make fun of me though I told them some of my biggest problems. As a result, I feel alone, not able to really say how I am feeling and not always able to trust people.

As I wipe my tears as best as I can and calm my breathing, my heartbeat still keeps its rapid pace. After a few more moments, I walk out of the stall pretending to yawn because hey, it has become obvious to me that my watery eyes can pass as a yawn any day.

I stopped reading, took another big deep breath in, and looked up.

Okay, I did it. All done. I just admitted how I suppress my anxious feelings. I just shared with my peers how I hide when things get tough. Was that just one big stupid complaint? Was that even considered "creative"?

I thought about how many times I had gone through this process, hiding in the bathroom and crying as quickly as possible in the middle of class. When I looked up I felt afraid that I would be seen as weak.

But what happened next shocked me the most.

Multiple students in my class approached me, explaining that they were able to relate to what I wrote. A couple of students thanked me for reading my story, and explained how they felt the same way on a regular basis. I had no idea that the straight-A student next to me was afraid of failure. I had no idea the girl sitting in front of me was afraid to speak up.

I did not know how yet, but in this moment, I wanted to help others somehow, in some way, feel like the bathroom did not have to be the only place they felt safe.

But the problem was I still didn't know where that safe space was in my life, either.

Reading that essay was a defining moment in my life, as it helped me notice that others break down in silence and that I was not the only one.

"I'm the only one." ----------> "I'm NOT the only one. We are in this together."

Let's pause and check in with ourselves.

What were times in your life when you felt that you were the only one? Think about a time you experienced the wave of immense shame. Think of a time you felt guilty and were motivated to change your actions. Has anyone else approached you, afraid they were the only one? Think about the uniqueness you can offer to the world, and how being "the only one" can carry a strong impact to deliver to others. Breathe and express thanks for you being allowed to be you. Know that being the only one is better than not being here at all.

What to expect:

- Expect to be "the only one" for a while in some situations. And that it is okay. One day, I was scrolling around on Facebook and saw my cousin had typed at the end of one of his posts, "everything seems the same all the time now." Change is possible. Your voice has the possibility to spark something new, fresh, and beautiful. Expect to come across as different when you channel your inner authenticity, but when you start to speak up, even if it takes a while, you'll find someone who has felt a similar way the whole time, with their own distinct experience to follow. It starts with someone speaking up. Let it be you. Different is not synonymous with alone. Difference is not negative. It's empowering, and a beginning step to spark immense change.

- You are not the only one who passed gas in an important place. You are not the only one who smelled funky after a workout at the gym. You are not the only one who peed your pants as an adult. Contrary to certain "norms," these examples are *normal*.
- We sometimes feel like we are on the headlines of every magazine, scrap of paper, and even on some strips of grass out deep in the wilderness. There are tons of people in the world, with unique experiences that happen to be relatable and similar to our own, if not the exact same. Even if you are in the headlines all the time, there is someone out there who sees *you* before they see the headline.
- From your experiences, you may see things that other people cannot yet see. When trying to tell others that I was feeling more anxious than usual, or people not believing how much my stomach hurt. There will be people, even some of those closest to you, who will look at you funny at times. One of my biggest pet peeves is when other people flash judgmental stares to one another, trying to deflate the presence of someone just simply being their authentic self. I am saying this because unfortunately we probably do this to other people as well, and awareness is the first step in creating massive change.

What you can do:

- Think of ways you can work with others. Notice others' talents and share a giggle at both of your embarrassing moments and how you continue to grow each and every day.

- Notice how you talk to yourself. Are you relying on the internal self – depreciation to get you through the day?
- Close your eyes and imagine how amazing it can be to be "the only one" in a situation. Imagine yourself in your room, dancing around to your favorite song. Imagine yourself driving down the empty road with all of the windows down. I truly used to be embarrassed of dancing around in my room. If I caught sight of myself in the mirror, I would judge myself for a reason I could not figure out. But it feels so freaking great to stop judging myself and sing so loud and smile until my mouth aches. We are in this together. Yes, that also means you making peace with self-criticism. Stand up to that shame and say, "I hear you, but I'd rather not take your advice."

CHAPTER 2

'I'm Fine'

———

Thanksgiving 2018 felt different.

I remember waking up later than usual, my parents and I quietly shuffling around downstairs preparing for the day. Everything was quiet, and my dad took a quick nap on the couch before the day's festivities began.

Later on, while finishing our Thanksgiving meals at my cousins house, I stood behind the couch scanning the room. My eyes passed my parents, and I did a double take when looking at my dad. Recently, he had been in and out of doctor appointments, checked for unexplained weight loss and a few other health barriers. Multiple appointments and tests later, they still had no clue what was wrong.

I remember when my eyes passed my dad who was sitting across the room, I immediately thought that his skin looked pale, with a slight yellow tint. But I was always told that I tend to overthink, so after looking once more, I tried to stop overthinking and enjoy the rest of the holiday with my whole family.

Two days later, I lazily crawled out of my bed to head downstairs to grab some tea after hours of laying and reading. I was hit with a burst of cold air and quickly put on socks, slippers, and a blanket wrapped around myself. I tiptoed downstairs and into the kitchen, thinking that my mom was taking a nap.

With no prior warning, I heard my mom say from the living room, "Julia, Dad is sick." My hands were buried in the sink, fishing out the mugs lying beneath the plates, when I paused, hands still soaking in the water. I pulled my hands away, splattering water all over the floor as I walked to the doorway from the kitchen to the living room. "What?" I asked, trying to think back to the way my dad's skin looked on Thanksgiving.

"He is jaundice and keeps losing weight—we are not sure what's wrong, but people are noticing."

I tried not to overthink. One of the biggest worries that kept me up at night is something happening to my parents. I was continually thankful for how healthy they both were the majority of my life; I could not even begin to grasp something serious being wrong.

Because of all the times I have been criticized for my anxiety and overthinking, I tried to quickly calm down and imagine this all blowing over in the next week. Despite my attempt to forget about everything happening, my anxieties grew as the days passed. My dad also tried not to overthink. Although he was jaundice, he did not see the yellow discoloration of his skin himself, constantly reminding us that he would wait for his doctors' appointments in the coming weeks to get checked.

My mom and I begged him over and over again to go to the emergency room to get checked right away, just in case. He kept denying that anything was wrong. "I feel so great, Julia. I am not sick! I'll be fine until my next appointment!"

**

The Sunday morning after Thanksgiving, my dad was planning to drive me back to school. I woke up to my parents talking loudly and blasting the television.

"Hey, Mom and Dad! Can you please talk a little lower?" I yelped sleepily, still trying to get my last thirty minutes of rest in for the morning.

"Sorry Jul," my dad said from the bottom of the steps. I could hear him pacing back and forth from the creaky sound of the wood floors. "You may need to find a ride back to school later; I am going to go to the emergency room."

My eyes quickly opened wide as I hopped to my feet and started asking thousands of questions.

"What made you want to so suddenly?" I kept repeating worriedly.

He started to describe a couple of noticeable red flags that he experienced minutes prior. Immediately, when my mom left for work, I packed a quick bag and drove with my dad to the emergency room.

After waiting hours in the hospital, enduring multiple scans, and learning his room assignment for the next couple of days, we waited to find out if the jaundice—yellow skin—was because of his liver, pancreas, or an infection.

I did not go back to school for an extra day, playing mind games with my dad from a $5.99 puzzle book we found at the hospital book store.

Since he was sitting through multiple appointments and various days of doctor visits, I got a ride back to school the next day to try and stay distracted. "Stop overthinking," I would say out loud before bed. "It'll be fine."

**

On November 29, 2018, I was sitting in my "Persuasion" class at school when I felt my phone buzzing uncontrollably on my foot that was propped up against my backpack. I was mortified, knowing my teacher might hear my phone buzzing as I forgot to silence my phone yet again. Hurriedly reaching down to stop the buzz, I saw multiple calls from my dad and mom. After the fourth call, I grabbed my phone, left class, and walked through the hallway to call my parents and check if everything was okay.

The moment I raised the phone to my ear and heard my dad say, "Hey Jul," I could feel the tone in his voice fall.

"Hey, uh, I don't mean to worry you," he started. "And I am so sorry I have to say this."

I stood in the dead center of the hallway while people passed me on each side. I drowned out the sound around me when I heard my dad say: "It's cancer, Julia. I'm sorry, Julia. It's not good; I'm sorry."

**

He explained to me that he was officially diagnosed with stage-three, inoperable pancreatic cancer. My heart sank as I heard my worst nightmare unfold as I stood miles and miles away from home. I ran to a space away from all the chaos and paused. I took a big deep breath in and out, opening my eyes to what felt like tunnel vision as I tried to fixate on the ground, propping myself up against the wall to make sure I would not lose my balance.

As we both cried over the phone, he told me to stay strong and keep up the good work in school. He understood my shock, confusion, and frustration, having found out when he was around my exact age that his own father had lung cancer.

"I want to fight though, Jul. I told the doctors to let me fight. I'm not leaving you anytime soon. You and your mom are my whole world," he said as his voice cracked. He was stuttering and apologizing, trying to make sure I hung up the call in a good headspace.

**

In times of a tragic event, humans tend to assess what they could have done to make the situation better, less tragic. This brings me back to the concept of guilt, specifically survivor's guilt—a term used especially for those who have witnessed or been involved somehow in losing a loved one in the wake of a tragedy. In 2018, students from Marjory Stoneman Douglas High School in Parkland, Florida, experienced one of the deadliest mass shootings in U.S. history. In early 2019, the concept of survivor's guilt gained heightened attention in the media when some of the survivors of the Florida tragedy took their lives. Experts working in the mental health field immediately started raising awareness about survivor's guilt and the grief that accompanies it.[14]

The common feeling that someone with survivor's guilt has, as with guilt in general, is that the situation, no matter what it may be, could have been prevented. One may tend to throw the entire blame on themselves.

Although not exactly survivor's guilt, when I found out that my dad was diagnosed with cancer, I initially thought: *Why him? He does not deserve this, it should have been me. Was it something I did? Maybe I could have prevented this diagnosis at some point in my life.*

I tried finding every reason that made even the slightest bit of sense to place the blame on myself, and in turn try to find a way to fix the diagnosis when there wasn't anything I could do to completely get rid of the diagnosis right then and there other than staying positive and lifting my dad up.

---

14 Chuck, Elizabeth. "Spate Of Suicides Puts Spotlight On Survivor's Guilt". 2019. *NBC News*. https://www.nbcnews.com/news/us-news/parkland-newtown-apparent-suicides-put-spotlight-survivor-s-guilt-n987011.

I let guilt and fear take over my whole body but tried my best to shut down the feelings, trying to keep a strong face for my friends and family surrounding me.

When Life Happens

Right before my dad was in and out of the hospital, my mom started a new job working at a cafeteria to make some extra money, in addition to caregiving for families in the surrounding area. My parents sold our house and moved into the former home of my grandmother, who had passed away in January 2018. I was returning to college for the last weeks of the first semester of senior year, preparing for finals, and had started a new antidepressant medication weeks prior to my dad's diagnosis.

That sure is a mouthful. I asked myself, *How do I handle all of this? How do I rise? How can I help my parents when I am in a bad place?*

"I'm an inconvenience."

I had such a hard time processing everything happening all at once. It made me even more upset to think about the stress on my parents and the emotional exhaustion they were experiencing. I especially did not want to inconvenience my parents with my own struggles. I did not want to make everything about me when my dad needed the highest care, especially at this time.

"Don't make it all about you," I constantly warned myself.

When I would come close to speaking up about how I was feeling, I would remind myself again to not be selfish. "Julia, you're healthy and blessed. Nothing should be wrong," I would tell myself time and time again.

My parents were unaware of the severe bouts of depression I was experiencing after my relapse in 2018 of breakdowns and shutting myself away from everyone. I tried to keep my feelings in behind closed doors and work on my struggles all by myself. I would go to a therapist and picked up my newly prescribed medication behind their backs. When my dad called to tell me the news of his diagnosis, I became even more strategic in hiding my depression, frantically trying to find ways to improve emotionally so that I could support my parents through this time. I would have rather attempted to run forty miles without stopping than open up to my family about how I was feeling. I felt embarrassed, not even knowing how to look anyone in the eye without feeling like I was worthless.

Depression is unlike any other feeling I've had before. When I felt sad growing up, I always asked myself, "Is this depression?" That is a common question we all may ask ourselves when we are going through a tough time in our lives, confused as to whether certain feelings of sadness and deflation are actually signs of depression.

My mind would make me feel drained and afraid, and when I felt the most depressed, I could hardly pinpoint what was wrong. I had trouble keeping my eyes open most of the day every day, sleeping in for hours and taking multiple naps instead of talking about the pain I felt inside.

When my depression would strike hard, even though I tried to keep a smile on my face and channel my inner pep when I was around others, there were still nonverbal signs of depression that I tried so hard to cover up.

All my self-care was thrown out the window as I woke up later and later each day, napping, shopping, or eating any time my anxious thoughts started to act up. I snoozed my alarm for hours. Yup, that's right—hours upon hours, because I was too tired to get up to even change the alarm time so I wouldn't have to hit the snooze button every five minutes.

When I fully woke up, I threw my damaged hair up in a messy bun, unkempt at the top of my head.

"Julia, you've been sleeping so much," one of my friends said to me time and time again, looking me in the eyes until I double – then triple-promised that everything was okay.

I would go months without combing my long hair, showering over the knots as they built into tangled dreads. When I tried combing my hair, I ripped and forced the knots to come out, desperate to untangle them so I wouldn't have to cut my hair short. Almost every single day, I would feel too drained to take care of myself, falling asleep on the knotty hair as the tangles continued to build up among my thick curls.

The knots in my hair spoke volumes. The bags under my eyes spoke volumes. The slowness in my movement spoke volumes. My inability to use my voice spoke volumes. Days, weeks, months would pass as my self-care declined further and further.

I started to move back into obsessive habits that started when I was younger, such as binge-eating and compulsively shopping to fill the void I felt inside of me.

My weight fluctuated often. Sometimes I would eat nothing but bread, cookies, and fried foods to "calm" my nerves. One day, I would feel so anxious that my body would reject food, losing a ton of weight in a short amount of time. Not long after going days without eating meals, I would break down and experience random sparks when I would binge-eat an absurd amount at a time and think about food almost every second of every day. People would call me out for "always wanting to eat," and that they "never knew anyone else who thought of food more than me." Some would even cheer when I would get up and go to the gym, sharing smiles around the room that I was "finally going to work out."

I avoided my phone, had a hard time focusing on school work, dreaded going into my shifts for work, and stopped creating content for my hobbies and projects.

The only escape for me was writing the words in this book. As I started to pour my feelings down on paper and expressed my passion for wanting to give others the chance to be vulnerable, I was struggling myself. Using my voice on this piece of paper that you are reading right now helped me process and organize my thoughts. These words helped me embrace my passion for vulnerability. And the more I wrote, the more I wanted to speak up unapologetically every day instead of hiding behind a mask.

Although I was expressing my feelings while writing, I kept hiding them when out in public. I would walk outside of my dorm, put on the best happy face I could, mixed with a heightened peppy attitude, and went about my day. Friends noticed that I was hiding out in my dorm room and leaving events early. The constant, "Julia, wow, thanks for replying to my text for once!" Or the infamous, "Wow, you actually came back into my life!" Each time I heard those words, especially on the days I felt my lowest, I held back tears, and held back using my voice so I would not come off as defensive. "Haha, yeah, I am a piece of s***—I know!" I would joke back, making sure I walked away the bad guy.

My mind was constantly running as I battled my outward emotions to stay as calm as possible so people wouldn't look at me differently. What was really on my mind? I constantly thought about how hard it must have been for my dad to hear the news of his diagnosis. I constantly thought of how hard it would be to be vulnerable with others, sharing the news of his diagnosis and upcoming, rapid life changes. I constantly thought of how I could please others and still try to find a free hour in my day to relax and do something I wanted to do.

My dad inspired me by showing his emotion and sharing his vulnerable side with me during such a hard time in his life. You could tell by the tone in his voice and the shakiness on the other side of the phone that vulnerability is not always easy, especially when you're being vulnerable in front of someone you love. We may tend to think vulnerability, exposing ourselves emotionally, is easier in front of certain friends, family members, and even to a romantic partner.

Around the same time my dad was diagnosed with cancer, my mentor and boyfriend's mom, Jennifer Antkowiak, was diagnosed with renal cancer. Jennifer, a former news anchor and current top-tier wellness advocate for DoTERRA essential oils, is like a second mother to me. She sparked my motivation to explore the possibilities of entrepreneurship, as well as gain the courage to speak publicly to large audiences. When she first spoke out about her cancer on a public platform weeks and weeks after the diagnosis and successful removal surgery, she acknowledged the difficulty of being vulnerable with the ones we love most:

> There is something about looking your kids in the eyes and being vulnerable with them. We try to put on this front that everything is okay all the time. I felt like I was put on earth to help everyone stay calm, but at this point in my life, I feel very weak and vulnerable. Other people see that differently. My kids always tell me how much of a hard worker I am, but in my head right now I feel afraid. Sometimes the perception we have of ourselves is not accurate. Although

what I am going through is not easy, I realize now the difficulty and strength of vulnerability.

Life will always throw us a new set of challenges that switch up the way we view vulnerability. Maybe you've lived your whole life thinking there's no need to share how you feel with others, but there are downfalls to holding in our emotions.

There are experiences that try to knock us down so far, so many times, that we feel bruised and disoriented with every step, not knowing how we can move through life any further. Whether this is loss, sickness, rapid change, or any barrier that pops up in our face faster than a jump-scare in a movie, we have a choice: will we see how long we can last without using our voice, taking action to face the unknown that vulnerability carries? Or will we release our emotions and thoughts unapologetically, walking next to the unknown?

Some may argue that vulnerability is just like oversharing. We may even think that ourselves.

When I think my feelings don't matter, I assume I can't speak up. I say to myself:

Stop complaining.
Depression isn't real.
You're too dramatic.
You're childish.
Get over it.

Those are just some of the societal norms that hold me back from speaking up to the people in my life. I started to believe the meaning of the quotes above myself, thinking the ideal world is a place where we all act perfect. Because, hey, we are in the habit of looking and displaying the perfect parts of our lives, right?

I was afraid that if I spoke up about my depression, people would expect my feelings to quickly blow over.

What if I am still depressed one year later? With minimal improvement? People will start to get annoyed with me. So I have to withhold my voice until it's time.

Woah, wait—did you catch that?

"So I have to withhold my voice until it's time."

"...withhold my voice until it's time."

"...until it's time."

Ahh, the good ol' "whenever I'm ready" fixation. Remember when we talked earlier in the book about the perfect time to speak up?

Yes, there are many moments in life when we are not yet ready. Say we are being forced to go on a rollercoaster but just ate two corn dogs and chili and feel nervous on top of that. Say someone is peer-pressuring you into drinking a large amount of alcohol when you're not ready to completely forget the night ahead. Maybe you'll never be ready for that. The list of examples could go on forever.

But when it comes to speaking up, helping others, taking care of ourselves, taking a step in the direction we dream to move into, we do not want to use the same tactics of avoidance that we do when deciding if we want to jump over a pool of sharks on a motorcycle. We try to put a "perfect time" on everything. We may even do too much to try to fit our lives in this notion of "in time." Or we wait, wait, wait until that magical, "ready" moment pops up in our lives.

What are our values? Are we actually waiting for something because we believe we should and value our time ahead? Or are we avoiding because of fear?

Through my time working through obsessive-compulsive disorder (OCD) and other anxious tendencies, I learned a lot about how we place so many expectations on future situations in our lives. It's common to believe that if we don't feel or act a certain way in a specific situation, it's "not right for us." For example, think about something as innocent as a first kiss. I remember I thought that my first kiss would be at night under the lights at an amusement park, with "Best Love Song" by T-Pain playing in the background. My first kiss was the farthest thing from that. I was standing in my middle school cafeteria at the farewell dance for the eighth-graders and quickly pecked my boyfriend at the time. We even texted before and planned the whole thing. Scandalous.

At the time I was overjoyed, but days after felt unsatisfied, wishing I could have made the moment more special for the both of us. Although I am no longer dating the same person I had my first kiss with, and given that I was only thirteen years old, I still think the moment went how it should have, even though that's not the expectation I once had.

Kiyomi LaFleur, owner of Awaken Into Love, an online platform building awareness of relationship obsessions, frequently talks about how we "are always 'shoulding' on ourselves."

Have you ever said to yourself *I should feel this way*? *My relationship should be like this* or *my education experience should be like that* or *my job should be like this*?

People all over the world online and in person also try to tell us how we "should" feel. We then have that opening to spiral into doubt and get into the habit of placing high expectations on ourselves and others.

Let's connect this all back to vulnerability: what if we think we shouldn't say how we truly feel or admit that we are hurting because of *blah blah blah*?

One of my boyfriend's favorite quotes in the world is from the movie *Dazed and Confused*, which helps describe "the perfect timing":

> **Cynthia**: God, don't you ever feel like everything we do and everything we've been taught is just to service the future?
>
> **Tony**: Yeah, I know, like it's all preparation.
>
> **Cynthia**: Right. But what are we preparing ourselves for?
>
> **Mike**: Death.
>
> **Tony**: Life of the party.
>
> **Mike**: It's true.

Cynthia: You know, but that's valid, because if we are all gonna die anyway, shouldn't we be enjoying ourselves now? You know, I'd like to quit thinking of the present, like right now, as some minor insignificant preamble to something else.[15]

Why are we always preparing for something when it comes to using our voice and taking the leap? Yes, it's effective and helpful to project a plan and adhere to our values. But how does the student graduate? How does the entrepreneur grow their business? They learn along the way. It's a process. Life is a process. Development is a process. Improvement is a process. But the student had to finally decide to start school, yes? The entrepreneur had to face the difficulties of building a business to grow, yes? We put many projects, tasks, and even our emotions off for later. Then we get into a habit of "doing everything later."

If we waited until someone was not going through as much as we were, we would be waiting for our whole lives.

The perfect moment to share our voices is now. We keep withholding our true feelings and trying to find obstacles and covering our emotions up so far until it we drown.

We may think we inconvenience others by expressing our feelings.

But we don't wanna fall so hard that we are the ones who can't get up anymore. Because if we are able to find our

15 Linklater, Richard, Jason London, Rory Cochrane, and Milla Jovovich. 1998. Dazed and confused. [U.S.A.]: Universal Studios.

way and get up off the ground, we can be a guiding hand to another one who has fallen. Offer your voice so you can help and influence yourself and others to embrace ourselves.

I write these words to you so I can hopefully hold your hand along your journey, feeling like the words in this book can be a place of calmness and understanding of yourself and others. Over time, I learned that speaking up, whether to a therapist, to someone in your life, through creative writing, or even to a crowd of thousands, can make life easier to process in the long run. We can own our feelings instead of putting on a face that we cannot live up to. We tend to put on a mask that we think has more worth over our own, true, authentic self.

Sometimes we have to be brave—that's the only option. We have to learn to step into the uncomfortable, the unknown. We have to stop avoiding everything when something gets tough. We have to take care of ourselves even when it's hard.

Nothing is guaranteed in life. Jennifer and my dad taught me that if there is a life you want to create, you have to make it happen. Even when we feel like giving up. Right now in this moment is an opportunity even if we get shut down. So why do we have to shut ourselves down first? To protect ourselves from others doing it first?

The more I cover up my depression, the more I wait for a time I expect to be the perfect time.

The more I hold myself back from embracing my voice.

The more I hold myself back from stepping into bravery.

The more I put off taking care of myself.

The more I cannot take care of others.

The more others are guessing and assuming my voice instead of me owning it.

I learn every single day more and more that my feelings are not insignificant.

We all need to care for others, but we can't forget about caring for ourselves.

Just because my dad is going through a hard time does not mean I should quiet my own emotions. We can walk hand in hand together, supporting one another along the way. People may seem perfect at first but we all have flaws. People may seem like they are going through a worse situation, but we all matter The power comes when you can show your concern for others, while showing that same unconditional love and care for yourself.

We try to put on this front that everything is okay. We spend more time figuring out how to cover up how we feel then we do trying to fix it. We start to believe everything is okay. We get overwhelmed and exhausted and, soon after, risk a breakdown.

The Process of Realizing

Another example of overlooking our self-care and happiness is found in Tesa Drew's powerful story of the path to recovery from anorexia nervosa. My friend Tesa, from @recoveryisarollercoaster on Instagram, uses her voice to inspire others through teaching them about her experience with anorexia and anxiousness. Before she was using her voice to help others on social media, she experienced a prior time when she did not think she even had to use her voice.

She describes her time with anorexia by saying, "You are visibly wasting away. People can often see that you are sick. Scarily, other eating disorders may not be as visible, such as bulimia and binge-eating. It can be harder to see, so we have to encourage people to use their voices if they are going through a difficult time."

Tesa experienced a variety of other health complications with her eating disorder, through purging, skipping meals, and constant exercise. She was frequently nauseated and developed severe anemia, needing a blood transfusion. Tesa passed out at a cheer competition, and in grade 11, her weight was at one of its lowest points. She did not go through a process of recovery until two years later. "If I would have spoken up when I felt at my worst, it could have been a lot easier," she admitted.

I was curious to learn about the motivation behind deciding to speak up.

She shared with me how speaking up was a process, saying, "Figuring out who I actually was as a person was hard. For example, my own voice and the voice of my eating disorder was hard to differentiate between. I used to think that these voices were one and the same. Going through treatment, you learn to differentiate the two voices."

It is true that illness voices, voices and intentions of stress and anxiety, are hard to differentiate from intentions of our own. When Tesa was in the deep depth of her illness, she described herself telling lots of lies, deceiving herself and others. She used lies and excuses for her behavior, such as saying, "it's just one time I am skipping this meal" and "oh you're not that bad, not that sick, not that small."

"There was a time when I hit an endpoint, there was no lower than where I was," Tesa recalled.

Tesa described how change sparks when you are authentic with yourself and reach out for that help. "The biggest jump forward in my recovery process is honesty. Being honest and saying that I can't go out today if I could not go out but not taking it personally myself when others did the same was crucial. Lying is what can keep you sick in your illness."

"I thought that I would sound crazy because of the conflicting voices in result of my illness. My thoughts would work like an angel and devil on my shoulders. The devil would say, 'Don't eat dinner' when the angel would tell me to eat," Tesa explained. "There are so many times looking back where I could have spoken up, but it was not normal to speak up about what others may view as 'problems.' I honestly thought I did not have a problem. I wanted to think I was a smart girl and would have noticed if I was anorexic. I never once thought, *wow this is my low point*. I thought, *this is what it is and what I have to do right now*."

When she started to realize the severity of the disorder and the toll it was taking on her physical and mental health, she noticed the triggers that arose when she felt at her worst. "When people told me, 'You're so skinny and tiny,' those words act as motivators to keep fueling the eating disorder."

She is continually inspired by others' vulnerability and wants to pay it forward in her own life, speaking out to help others. She described that "seeing how much other people's stories inspired me made me decide that I was going to use this for the good and help people who may not be reaching out for help yet. I never want anyone to feel the way I did, to be sacred to admit or feel guilty or ashamed of what they are going through. I want to help others realize that these aspects of their lives are not their fault."

Tesa offered her advice to channeling our most authentic selves: "You spend so much time beating yourself up and feeling isolated. Continue connecting with people who struggle with eating disorders themselves. We have to either speak up, or someone else does to find that connection. Either welcome vulnerability by listening, or create a space for vulnerability by speaking out. It makes the journey feel much easier."

The Guessing Game

Sometimes we may choose to not use our voices to speak up but hope others realize that we are not okay when we say we are fine. Do you ever feel like proving a point to someone, or waiting for someone to figure out if and why you're upset or feeling a certain way?

We may play this game more often than we think—it could be giving someone a pouty face when you don't get the reaction you want, or giving a teacher backtalk in class due to your anger from a bad grade on a paper.

When we are in a state of pain, anger, or any other strong emotional state, our actions and thoughts are affected in the present moment, even though emotions change and fluctuate over time. When we are in a vulnerable state, overcome by emotions from experience, it's hard, but we choose how we react.

My boyfriend is here to tell the tale of how much he hates playing the guessing game with me.

Let's set the scene: he and I are sitting down trying to decide where to eat. I want to go to get a burrito bowl, but he wants pizza. We always get burrito bowls when we are together, so he states his opinion, "I would rather have pizza today. Is that okay?"

"Yeah," I reply, my voice flat.

"Are you sure?" he asks, looking straight into my eyes to try and read my untold emotions.

"Yup," I say dryly.

"What's wrong?" he asks.

"Nothing," I say with a pouty face, trying to get my way without saying it so I don't look like the bad guy if he doesn't get what he wants.

Now this is just a silly (but relevant) example of hiding my real feelings, still trying to get what I want while trying to get my boyfriend to figure it out and make the decision himself.

At times, I am super stubborn and sport an attitude when I do not get my way, as do many of us. But I do not want to come across as annoying and admit my harsh feelings, thinking I will inconvenience or upset someone. I want people to figure it out. I want people to notice my emotions. But sometimes I am more passive-aggressive than effective.

Even though I do not say anything, my emotions show that there is something wrong.

Think about if you're mad at your friend for canceling plans. Do you choose to ignore them?

Remember the lettuce example from the beginning of the book? I did not speak up and was upset when I was teased for not cutting my lettuce.

Are we making people guess how we feel by pouting, ignoring, or using subliminal messages?

Speaker and psychotherapist Mel Schwartz discusses the notion of always needing to be right. A point that I found extremely interesting was when he explains that "our educational system is rooted in the construct of right and wrong. We are rewarded for what are deemed to be correct answers and the ensuing higher grades, which generally lead to more successful lives. Being right affirms and inflates our sense of self-worth."[16]

Let's put this commonly learned behavior in everyday situations. If we are wrong or do not get our way, we may feel a lack of worth. He goes on to say that the feeling of being right, or "winning" a situation, heightens our pulse. This feeling of being right is addicting and tries to control our whole being.

People can't always assume what is going on in our lives. It's our responsibility to be vulnerable. Some people will ignore or shut down our vulnerability, but many simply do not know the extent to what we are feeling.

What does this all mean? Let's end with an example from Cardin McKinny.

Emerging From the Geek Glasses

Cardin, whom I knew as @theoilgeek on Instagram, was one of the very first Instagram accounts I found to learn how to use natural products in super fun and exciting ways. She always posted my favorite beauty tips and essential oil diffuser blend recommendations. Little did I know, Cardin was hiding behind the glasses of the oil geek.

---

16   Schwartz, Mel. "Why Is It So Important To Be Right? | Psychology Today". 2019. *Psychology Today*. https://www.psychologytoday.com/ intl/blog/shift-mind/201103/why-is-it-so-important-be-right?amp.

One day when I was scrolling through Instagram, I noticed that Cardin changed her branding from the infamous "Oil Geek" to "Cardin Healing."

My branding mindset was curious why she changed the well-known name of her brand. Just seeing the same Cardin Healing echoed to me that her branding change was personal and powerful. I was intrigued and excited to hear the details of the change. Late one night, I saw a notification saying that Cardin hopped on a live video, and although I tuned in a couple of minutes late, her eyes were filled with tears as she thanked the community of her page with open arms for the acceptance of her brand change. As I continued to listen, I learned that Cardin was healing in her own life with self-respect and her recent divorce. When I had the chance to talk with her personally, I asked her about the transition from her old brand to the new. "I am coming out from behind the geek glasses," she said with a smile. She was starting to realize that we are all working through a process of healing and growing into new experiences, and she broke out of that space of holding back her voice to a space where she could talk with others about the real: the authentic part of herself and others.

"For years, I tried to stay quiet, drowning in the self-doubt and sadness. There were challenges in my life that felt absolutely insurmountable." She explained that back in high school, her home was vandalized. Terrible words exchanged from bullies at her school, and she felt wrong for being who she was and having the feelings she felt.

"I am inspired knowing there are so many hearts that need to be heard. If I have this ability to share my voice to help others feel heard, I'll do it. Silence leads to illness. Social media is a place of perfection. I like the contrast." So she shared with the world her vulnerability. "It's safe to be who I am," she said with a smile.

"There have been so many times others vulnerability inspired me. When I first met my now-friend Tiff Peterson, I was so at home with her presence. She would say to me, 'You can shine; you don't need to be afraid to shine.' She extended her friendship and allowed me to show some of my wounds. My group of friends tell me that when I am my most authentic self that they love this version of me most of all. 'Please be that,' they say to me. 'I feel so connected and inspired by you.'"

With Cardin Healing, Cardin could embrace her emotions, admitting she is not always okay, but continually growing. She is always healing and inviting others to embrace that reality in their own lives, too.

"I was finally okay at where I was in my life without anyone else's permission. I was giving my permission to their permission."

"I'm Fine" ----------> "I Am Healing."

Do you notice that you say, "I'm fine" when you are really feeling immense hurt and sadness? Is your story left untold? Do you feel like you have trouble explaining how you are feeling and think it's an easier escape to tell others that you are fine when you really are not feeling at peace?

What to expect:

- There may be times when we try to tell ourselves that we are fine. There may be times when we truly do not believe anything is wrong. There may be times when we feel like we cannot overpower someone else's voice by admitting we are not okay. The same rules apply to the variety of different times that may appear in our lives: "You are able to be vulnerable."

- When we try to control everything that happens, situations can spiral. When we let go a little bit and accept how we are feeling, healing has the opportunity to enter into our lives. When we admit we are upset and not just "fine," we are exposing ourselves to those emotions. It's terrifying at times and may be uncomfortable. We all have certain situations when we feel obsessed and anxious more than others may feel. Maybe it's because your crush did not text you back, or the best friend you're fighting with won't reply. Maybe it's because you have an important test that's a week away, or you are having a kid and afraid of the life changes ahead. Even if it is something that seems so minuscule to you, you also have something that makes you anxious or nervous. We may let our past define us. We may allow our anxiety to protect us so much that we try not to expose ourselves to work on healing. We have to fight this urge to hold our feelings inside all the time and letting these feelings bottle up, instead of honestly talking about how we feel in a calm.

What you can do:

- If you're feeling a certain way, think of your feelings in a way that other people can relate to at the present moment in their lives. What's something that you feel inside that no one believes? Are you feeling depressed? Worried? Overwhelmed? When you feel these feelings, compare the way you feel to the pain you get when you stub your toe. That cramp you feel in your stomach. Just because others cannot see how you feel does not mean it's not there. Embrace what you are feeling with a quick and simple, "I'm okay with you being you. I'll be me." Describe how you feel in relatable ways and listen to what others are asking and saying. Describe it in a way others will understand it, and then give them a rundown of what is happening to you. Because, in all honesty, even though it is so important to help people understand what we are going through and the truth behind what we feel, we most likely would not wish our unpleasant feelings on even our worst enemies. We want others to understand how we feel, but do not want to give others that feeling and run away.

- Allow others to take care of you. Be happy that others are taking care of you, even if you think it's out of pity. We may not want to ask someone for help, afraid we will come across as needy or incapable. But think about it this way: why do we have teachers? Why do we have role models? Why do we have advisors? Why do we have training sessions? Why do companies have customer service options? Because they help support us in our learning and growth journey.

- Check in with yourself throughout the day. Make a chart, whether through a bullet journal, in your agenda, on a piece of paper on your bedroom wall, or even an application on your cell phone to track how you are feeling throughout the day. Just because something bad happened in the beginning or middle of the day does not mean the rest of the day is doomed for you.

CHAPTER 3

'I Can't Do It'

—

It was a chilly Friday morning in November and people were filing into a local coffee shop to grab their warm coffee, tea, or choice of snacks. Although I was surrounded by loud chatter and the *clickidy-clack* of fingers typing, I was captivated as I learned about passion and purpose. Brianne, a boutique owner from Pittsburgh, wrapped her hands around her cup of coffee and looked me in the eyes, saying, "My dad always said to me, 'It takes just two seconds of courage to get to where you want to go.'"

Woah, I thought as I lost focus for a second, reflecting on that comment over and over again. *That's a game changer for vulnerability!*

Brianne Conley (Bri) is the owner of a trendy and unique boutique, Number 14 (No. 14), in Lawrenceville, Pennsylvania. Bri named her boutique No. 14 for a *number* of reasons, literally: she opened the business in 2014. She met her then-boyfriend, now husband, at 14 years old. Her husband's number in football when they were in high school was 14. While 14 is a special number to Bri, there are way more than fourteen steps she had to take in creating her business from the ground up.

Bri knows a number (pun intended, again) of things about having the courage to take the leap when we know we want something, when we know we want to use our voice to make an impact.

Now, this may be triggering for many, especially for myself—I can feel anxiety creeping into my brain.

How do we know if we actually want something?

How do we know what to choose, when to choose it, and when to take the leap?

How do we know when to ask for help?

The answer is: we don't always know the answers. Frustrating, right?

Well, despite not knowing or having control over the final result in every situation, Bri took her dream-jump anyways, starting her business straight out of college.

Bri can teach us so much more than the logistics of starting and owning a boutique at a young age; she teaches us about connection, appreciation, and the drive it takes to move forward.

She explained that the first year of starting up No. 14 was a complete whirlwind. Creating her business was followed by a ton of pressure that was certainly overwhelming at times. On the other hand, Bri never fails to rearrange each negative viewpoint with a positive spin.

She makes sure to acknowledge her appreciation for the success of her business and how she has the opportunity to live her passion every single day. Even if she is surrounded by a ton of tasks, she still told me, "I am so thankful that I get to live my dream. Thank God I have the ability to do this. When I feel overwhelmed, I also realize how grateful I am for the opportunity. And when I get stressed, it's because I care so much." She said time and time again how thankful she was to own her voice and follow her passion.

The stress that arises from following your passion is inevitable, especially being that Bri started her venture right after graduating from college. I was curious to learn about how she gained the confidence to take the leap and make the decision to start her business, despite all the hurdles and despite 2014 being such a crucial time in her life as she was searching to find a full-time job. She was young.

She immediately said to me, "Taking the leap is intimidating." She realized when starting her business that everything would be her job, including social media management, marketing, and getting everything set in its place to reflect her vision. "Taking that leap is an intimidating thing to do, but you have to do it," Bri affirmed. "To get to where you want to go, the only way to move forward is to take action, to take that first step and see where the rest of the journey leads you, even if it is different than the idea you expected."

When Bri talks about the excitement of following her dream, her dedication and passion sounds effortless. She makes following her dreams look easy, even though it's far from that. She says the look of ease is because, "It's up to me to make my vision happen, and I've found that the journey is rewarding." Even though she acknowledges that it gets hard and the process has its ups and downs, the reward is ultimately greater than the struggle.

"The pressure can be a lot, but I chose to do this. I knew I could do this if I really set my mind to achieving my goals." She grows each and every day, learning and improving from her experience, truly setting a beautiful example of how the thought of starting a boutique could transform into a beautiful reality.

She also shouts out the incredible people in her life who continue to support her vision and helped both build her up with encouragement and transform the idea of No. 14 into the boutique that it is today.

"It is very important to have people that lift you up," Bri said immediately. "The people in my life never asked anything of me other than for me to be myself. It was never a 'you will do this'; it was a 'we will do this together.'" Bri then shared that the people in her life are supportive in every way, especially her parents, the No. 14 coworkers/team, and her husband. Through the support of these incredible individuals in her life, she finds encouragement, humor, and the ability to channel her inner calm when needed. This truly is a whole recipe to create a space for vulnerability.

Bri's success may look easy from the outside because she feels she always has more to offer, and her purpose shines through. She owns her passions, and when she talks about her business, she does not doubt her truth. It is important to remember, though, that working toward our goals and owning our truth *is a process*. That's what her words help us understand. She lets go of all doubts when she talks about her business, and that mindset and tone are irresistible and inspiring.

Bri looked at me once more and said, "If you don't have critics, you're not doing anything." Bri sets an example to look at criticism in a positive light. When people disagree with or criticize our choices and actions, we can open up the conversation to a new perspective. When people want to bring us down, our dedication and curiosity should engage with that, finding ways to improve and understand why others do not agree with the path we are taking. We do not have to believe someone's opinion, but we can work to understand the people who think differently than we may.

What does this all have to do with vulnerability?

We can learn so much from Bri's story and translate it into the process of speaking up when we know that we want something—when we know that we feel something within us that we are meant to follow.

Bri shows us that we have permission to take the action needed to try on a dream that we've been wearing in our imagination. And when trying on our dreams, we can find one that fits just how we like, one that leaves enough room through the seams for growth and improvement.

Bri also shows us the power of accepting that part of us, that little voice, which holds so much authority to create a vision we are excited to try out. Like Bri said, the people in her life never asked anything of her other than her to be herself. Are you doing the same to yourself? Are you giving yourself the encouragement necessary to kick-start your own motivation? Are you telling yourself, "I *can!*" rather than doubting yourself?

We may feel afraid to take a step into the unknown, whether speaking in front of parents, significant others, the whole family, friends, teachers, bosses—proclaiming that we feel something within us that needs to be said aloud.

It's important to trust yourself and own your voice, giving yourself the credit and encouragement.

It's important to make the decision to speak up when needed. So many of us make big decisions before fully understanding the situation because we stay quiet. When building her business, Bri asked for the support of her parents who had experience with entrepreneurship, financial planning, and starting a business.

She acknowledges people who criticize, knowing that these hard times are the ones that prove we are making progress.

After hearing Bri's encouraging words that it only takes two seconds of courage to get to where we want to go, I paired it with a similar quote from the movie *We Bought a Zoo*:

"You know, sometimes all you need is twenty seconds of insane courage. Just literally twenty seconds of just embarrassing bravery. And I promise you, something great will come of it."[17]

If we just take those two seconds of courage to decide to take the leap, and then sit with the next twenty seconds of excitement, fear, discomfort, and unknown, we can move closer to the drive we need to keep us moving.

The process of following our dreams is hard. The process of speaking up to own our purpose is difficult. Overwhelming. Full of pressure. Full of mistakes. Fast and slow. Scary at times.

But the process is also beautiful. Unique. And full of learning opportunities.

We are too used to doubting ourselves as a habit. And when we think about gaining the confidence to channel our vulnerability, we have to practice loving ourselves over and over again until self-care is a habit you look forward to.

**

17 Crowe, Cameron, Julie Yorn, Rick Yorn, Aline Brosh McKenna, Matt Damon, Scarlett Johansson, Thomas Haden Church, et al. 2014. We bought a zoo. Beverly Hills, Calif: Twentieth Century Fox Home Entertainment.

Picture yourself sitting in the mall, ready to grab a quick snack you ordered minutes prior. Your friend is standing beside you, fishing around in their pockets to make sure their phone is still with them. You two stand there and wait, and when your food finally comes out, you head to a table to gobble up everything on the plate before you resume shopping. When you get to the table and sit down, you realize you forgot ketchup, which you absolutely need to make your food taste that much better.

"Hey, I am too nervous. Can you ask the cashier for an extra packet of ketchup? Oh and while you're at it, can you ask for barbecue sauce just in case? Please, please, pleeeeeease?"

We want that ketchup. We want to feel that warm and fuzzy feeling we get when eating something that makes our taste buds explode (if ketchup is gross to you, maybe pretend you like it in this scenario or replace it with a condiment you love). But we are nervous to go up to the counter and ask, so we try and get our friends to do it. We spend our energy convincing someone else to get what we want for us.

Maybe the friend refuses to get up and you respond by saying, "Well, *I* can't ask! I don't wanna! Do it yourself!" so you sit and eat the rest of your food, wishing you had those extra ketchup and BBQ packets to add flavor.

Have you ever asked someone to call a pizza place to order the pizza, or take up the money to the cashier, because you were too nervous to do it yourself? I can think back to so many times when I was a preteen, hanging out at the mall or a movie theater when my friends and I would have a five-minute-long debate about who would go ask for the popcorn and candy. The worst feeling for me used to arise when calling a doctor's office, making an appointment. "Mom, can you do it?" I would constantly say, hoping that I could continue getting out of making phone calls for the rest of my life.

Isn't it interesting how even in situations that seem so quick or small to many bring us the most anxiety? When we have these feelings, we either run away from the situation or stay and conquer. I think of taking the leap, just like leaving a message over the phone. Picture this: I was sitting in the library about to make an important call (a phone interview!). As I sat thinking over and over again of what I could say on the phone and how I can make sure the phone call goes well, I realized there is a point when I have to stop overthinking and take action. There comes a point when I stop talking about it and just do it, dang it! When the voicemail machine comes on, and the beep sounds, I can either hang up or stay and commit to what I want to complete, instead of running away from yet another form of connection due to fear and insecurity.

Maybe we don't make a move because we are trying to protect ourselves from embarrassment. Or maybe we think we actually do not have the capability to complete tasks as well as others. "Mom, I can't call the doctor's office myself! I don't know what documentation we need and all the details of the insurance, etc., etc., etc." But as the years pass, we will need to learn to call the doctor's office ourselves. As time passes by, we will need to leave that important voicemail. As new experiences arise, we will learn more about insurance and all those "grown-up" concepts that seem to hit us all at once. As the years go by, we will have a choice to use or not use our voices. And the situations will grow larger and larger—you'll have to not only speak out and embrace your want for ketchup, but also embrace what you need, too.

Another example that crosses my mind is the salesperson. Let's think about the salesperson who has to cold-call a company and pitch it an idea. If their pitch is rejected, they may take the rejection personally, thinking it was something they said wrong, the way they worded the pitch, or any other scenario that pops up in their mind.

In one of my favorite books, *Rejection Proof*, Jia Jiang shares research that explains that "the pain of rejection is actually a chemical experience in your brain: Opioids. When humans feel physical pain, our brains release natural pain-killing chemicals called opioids into our system to lessen the pain."[18] Thus we can make the connection that rejection pain = physical pain. In grade school, I remember randomly asking out one of my friends over text message, checking the phone again and again to see if he replied. When he finally replied with, "No, sorry," I thought I was going to puke and

---

18 Jiang, Jia. 2015. Rejection Proof: How I Beat Fear and Became Invincible Through 100 Days of Rejection. Potter/Ten Speed/Harmony/ Rodale. [2015]

I swear that I felt my chest tingle and my muscles tense up. I thought those initial feelings sounded too dramatic, but when I learned about the connection between rejection pain and physical pain, it made a little bit more sense.

Fear, the pain of rejection, shame and guilt—all of those terms we've discussed can easily try to stand in the way of our self-confidence, and we can get way too used to giving in to these seemingly uncomfortable feelings.

Will We Run Away or Stay?

The moment you start writing a book on vulnerability, there is this expectation you will be vulnerable, all of the time. And heck, is that hard. When someone is considered an "expert" in something, or the "best" in their field, even if that's a popular store or the best doctor in the world, that's a ton of pressure on one human being.

If you become an expert in something, you must be perfect!! You must know *everything* there is to know, and if you blank, you'll fail forever! If you fail once, you're sure to fail again, and that's not an option here. Once you do well, you have to keep topping yourself. Are you ready for the challenge?

Wait, that does *not* sound like reality.

I am an expert in being a student. I've been through sixteen years of school, tons of different assignments, class topics, and learning styles. I am not an expert in supply-chain management. I am not an expert when it comes to traveling.

But with experience, if I set my mind to it, I could learn supply-chain management or grow in my knowledge of successfully planning a trip across the world. Expert is defined by the Merriam-Webster Dictionary as "having, involving, or displaying special skill or knowledge derived from training or experience."[19]

The point is, even when we know what we are doing, we may feel this immense pressure and feel overwhelmed at times. We may beat ourselves up when we make mistakes. We talked a lot about when things get hard, how do we react? Do we give up or keep going? Is improvement possible? Once we reach our goals, is there ever more for us out there to accomplish?

One thing many of us probably know all too well: public speaking. Whether you are a communication major like me or you are asked to speak at family events or in front of your coworkers all the time, many of us have felt the pain of public speaking when we do not want to. Have you ever been in a situation where you had a required speech to give to a room full of people? Have you ever volunteered to read at a friend or family's ceremony? Or how about those dreaded school projects where we can only have one notecard of small notes for a ten-minute presentation? And the teacher says, "Okay, make sure to prepare for next week's presentation, it will be 40 percent of your final grade," your stomach flips?

19   "Definition Of EXPERT". 2019. *Merriam-Webster.Com*. https://www.merriam-webster.com/dictionary/expert.

Or maybe at work you have to step into your boss's office to ask for a raise. Any speaking outside of the corridors of your bathroom may give you the chills when you are trying to convince the public that you know what you are talking about.

For as long as I can remember, I would look at a rubric after rubric, filled with criteria I had to meet when speaking in front of the class. "Steady eye contact"—worth ten points. "Smoothness of speaking," 10 points. "Presence of 'um's or 'uh's in the speech": failure if you use more than three "um"s.

In my high school freshman year public speaking class, one of our assignments was to memorize a children's book and bring in props so we could read to the class in an interactive and fun manner. I chose the story of Cinderella and tried to memorize each and every single word, attempting to find a cool way to incorporate props and convince a room full of fourteen-year-olds that this assignment was "no big deal." I arrived in class the day of the speech, not feeling fully confident I knew the story of Cinderella word for word. I knew the story well enough that I could paraphrase but was more worried about not messing up any single word that I read in the children's book when presenting. I wanted to do it perfectly.

Our teacher allowed us to hand someone else in the class our short story book just in case we were stuck at a certain part of the story and forgot the words. The helper was allowed to whisper the next line to us, but we couldn't overuse the privilege if we wanted a decent grade. When it was my turn,

I thought someone else holding the book would distract me and I would overuse the privilege, so I put my book in my backpack, zipped it up, and carried my props to the front podium.

The minute I started to talk, my mouth went completely dry, and I began stuttering. Not even four lines into my presentation, I totally forgot who Cinderella was.

What the heck is the story of Cinderella again?

Did I skip a word?

At this point, the students in my class were staring intently, silently encouraging me to keep going.

Wait, no, not everyone.

My eyes nervously scanned the room as I muttered out the last couple words I could remember. My eyes stopped when I saw two girls to the right of me chuckling. I had no clue if they were laughing at me, but their faces when they looked at me, holding back that deep belly laughter, made my mind completely blank. I skipped half of the story; my hands shaking, I raised my magic wand and coughed out, "Bibbidi … Bobbidi … Boo."[20] My voice fell as I kept focusing on the laughter, and I ended my presentation right there.

Tears welling up in my eyes and my face so hot that I could dunk my head in a bucket of ice, I ran to the teacher's desk, asking for a bathroom pass. I took the pass, tried to hold in my already falling tears, and hid in the first bathroom

---

20 *Cinderella*. 1950. DVD. Walt Disney Productions: by Clyde Geronimi, Hamilton Luske and Wilfred Jackson.

stall that was open. When I finally let my emotions flow, my tears poured out and I started gasping for air, nervously checking under the stalls to make sure no one's feet were by me so I would not completely embarrass myself.

Footsteps.

"Julia?" I heard.

"Hello? Julia?" I heard again, but this time, the voice had a slight chuckle. I knew that voice.

Since the teacher was sitting in the back of the class and could not see the view I saw, she had no clue why my mind went blank. She sent someone to check on me, but it just so happened to be one of the two girls who was laughing.

"Are you okay?" the voice said, trying to contain her laughter.

"Yeah, I'm fine. I'll be back soon," I said quickly.

I was mortified.

At the end of the year, when that public speaking class ended, I was absolutely thrilled, and never wanted to speak in front of an audience again. I told myself time and time again that I was an awful public speaker, and would always be.

But that wasn't the end of school presentations. Year after year, I had loads of class presentations in history, English, Spanish, math… And every single time it was my turn to speak, I felt like I was going to pee my pants. My stomach would drop and my teeth started to chatter. My mouth would go completely dry, and I always lost my breath from talking too fast in the first minute of presenting.

When I graduated from high school, I had this small bit of hope in me that I would either dodge the infinite number of presentations that had the possibility of popping up in college, or somehow be the best speaker on planet earth. Little did I know, one day I would major in communication.

Sophomore year of college, I took my first communication research class, which was honestly the most challenging class I'd ever taken in my life. Toward the end of the semester, I went into class one morning with an awful stomachache, trying hard not to let my group members down for our presentation that day. I walked out of my dorm fifteen minutes early, made it halfway down the hall before I walked back and sat in my blue plush foldaway chair in my dorm, trying to heal from deep breaths and sips of ginger ale. For the first five minutes it worked, and when I finally made it to class, I felt lightheaded and my stomach was churning. I was so anxious. I wanted in A in this class so badly. I wanted to come out strong.

When our group went up and started to talk, I felt like I was going to puke. I was putting way too much pressure on myself for one speech. My stomach started to hurt more, and I felt a bit dizzy as I stood by my group. I was placing so much weight on a seemingly small moment in my life, just like the lettuce story.

No, no, no! This cannot be happening. Julia, hold it together! Ten minutes, that's all I need to make it through. You don't want to screw this up! It's not that hard, I thought.

When it was my turn, I got through about three minutes of content and then asked the audience a question. The student who chose to answer (thankfully) had a long and insightful remark to share with the class. As the student was talking, I whispered to one of my two team members, notifying them I was about to faint as I gripped the side of the chair, face completely white.

"Oh geez, okay. I got you; don't worry," he said. By the way, Ryan—if you are reading this, thank you so much, because that was easily one of the most embarrassing moments in college, looking my teacher in the eye during my portion of the speech and completely booking it out of the classroom. I staggered down the hall and ran to the bathroom.

I ran away. I ran away when I was anxious. I put these high expectations on myself, got stuck in a spiral of overthinking, and doubted myself. I ran out of the room, not finishing what I started. And I felt the anxiousness. I was not only overthinking, but physically felt the anxiousness crawling inside of my body. And I chose not to give myself compassion and work through the difficult times, but rather run away.

I've run away during tough conversations with family members. I've run away during disagreements with friends. And not just to take time to collect myself—I ran away and told myself I would never be able to do it again. I told myself I was incapable and a failure.

I would rather run away than stumble on a word, or say the wrong thing in front of more than one person. I chose to run away from everything possible because I did not think my voice was smart enough. I did not think my voice could handle it.

This may seem pretty over the top for public speaking. But think about it: are we running away from something we committed ourselves to finish? Why are we running?

Know What to Expect

Think about something that seems impossible to do. Think about something you've always wanted to do but tell yourself that you can't. Think about something that brings you pure joy, but you're afraid to move past the hurdle and take on the challenge.

What do you feel you were meant to do in life? Who do you feel you are meant to be? What is holding you back?

Whether that is speaking in front of others, or even telling your family you've decided to move across the globe. Maybe it's starting your own business that you feel called to, just like Bri. Maybe it's improving your lifestyle or moving past a breakup or parting with a friend.

We tend to tell ourselves, *I can't do it. I can't get past this. I can't be myself. I'm wrong for being me.*

I personally struggled with improving my lifestyle in my deepest stages of depression; I struggled to care for myself. I would stay in my bed past 1 p.m. and watch television, play games on my phone, and refuse to drink water or wash my face. You may have heard the advice to keep your cell phone on the other side of the room every night and get up in the morning to turn off the alarm, make sure not to snooze the alarm, and immediately drink water and wash your face to fully wake yourself up and emerge from the morning slump. Some may say to immediately go to the gym right after you wake up, or do some kind of physical activity, then follow that by showering and taking an hour of downtime for yourself. Where this is all advice I challenge myself to implement into my routine, I want to dedicate some time to talk about how much we do not want to do these things, no matter how easy they sound written down on a piece of paper. I want to highlight how difficult it is to love ourselves, how difficult it is to encourage ourselves at times.

It is absolutely going to suck at times when we follow our passion. It is absolutely going to be difficult when we make a commitment and have to shoo off other temptations. In my case, when trying to improve my lifestyle by drinking more water, getting out into the sun more, and taking care of my body, even if I woke up one day energized and ready to improve my lifestyle, I found that it will likely suck the second and third day. Maybe even for two weeks. Or a month.

You may cry when working out after ten minutes, feeling like it's impossible to go on. You may walk away from the treadmill because you are so tired you do not want to fall over and hurt yourself on a run. You may play it safe for amazing reasons. And it's okay to feel that way. But you are either thinking about improving or you're actually doing it. Working out for the first time, and the second time, and the fifteenth time can feel hard, so freaking hard, and even when it's refreshing sometimes I still don't want to be there.

Hal Elrod, who wrote *The Miracle Morning*, suggests going to bed with the intention of being excited to get up in the morning.[21] But I also want you to expect that it is going to be so hard. When it gets hard, raise your voice in your mind saying, *YES, THIS SUCKS. THIS SUCKS, AND I HATE DOING THIS, AND THAT'S THE ONLY REASON I AM DOING IT.* Nothing will have power over you anymore when you keep going despite how much it sucks.

I am constantly working and improving to make sure my anxious thoughts and fears do not have power over me anymore—whether that is to improve my lifestyle and work past the laziness and depression that tries and holds me back, or even if it is Bri starting No. 14 right out of college, working past any barriers that arise.

Just know that yes, it's normal to feel like you can't do something. Just think of how great it will be to say, "I did this," instead of "I can't do this."

Notice If You're Judging Yourself

When I was in junior high, I was so excited to attend the sixth through eighth grade school dances that would pop up from time to time. When my friends and I arrived on the

---

21 Elrod, Hal. 2014. The miracle morning: the not-so-obvious secret guaranteed to transform your life before 8AM.

dance floor, we would immediately let loose, jumping up and down for hours. In eighth grade, one of my friends came up to me and tapped me on the shoulder. "You are one of the worst dancers; it's so embarrassing!" she said with a smile, still patting me on the back.

I have since gotten over some of the crippling embarrassment I felt when having to dance in front of others, but that one comment was something I fixated on, telling myself because of that one time, I can't dance again without ruining my reputation. I was distorting what could be; I was distorting any possibility of fun that I could feel from letting loose and dancing. Cognitive distortions are exaggerated patterns of thought that arise especially when we feel nervous or upset.

I struggle with self-confidence and fueling cognitive distortions in many areas of my life, and work to improve these struggles day by day. I have a mantra from the movie *She's Out of My League* that helps me put into perspective all the pressure I throw upon myself on a daily basis. One of the characters says to her ex-boyfriend, "You were plenty good enough for me—you were never good enough for you."[22]

When I heard those fourteen words, it immediately clicked in my brain that I am not accepting of myself. I do not give myself credit, and I do not encourage confidence to tell myself that "I *can*!!! I *am* capable!!!" We may think people hate us, will abandon us, or will try to one-up us, and we fail

22 Smith, Jim Field, Jay Baruchel, Alice Eve, and Mike Vogel. 2017. *She's out of my league.*

to always appreciate the love we have surrounding us every day, even from that stranger who smiles at you and gives you a wave on the street.

Are you good enough for you? When I tell myself that "I can't," I now immediately challenge myself to follow-up by interrupting my self-deprecating thoughts and asking myself, "Why *not* me?"

"I Can't Do It" ----------> "I Can"

When you want ketchup for your food, what's holding you back from doing it yourself? Why do you believe that someone else, even if it's a parent, sibling, or friend, is more capable than you are of getting up and asking for the ketchup? Apply this question to situations in your life when you ran away rather than choosing to stay to complete what you started. Have you ever run away when you wanted to express your true feelings to someone? Why or why not?

I am currently waiting for my class to start as I am finishing up this chapter, and we just filled out course evaluations. The professor popped his head in the room asking who was still writing and only two people out of seventeen raised their hands. There was an envelope sitting on the table that we were supposed to put the evaluations in but no one got up to place it inside. My friend turned around to me asking if we should go and put it in the envelope now, and she stood up and walked down to put hers inside. Immediately, the rest of the class followed her.

Why, in such small situations, don't we think we can be the first? Why are we waiting for others to start for us to work up the confidence to get to where we want to go?

What to expect:

- You will think you can't do something that you are more than capable of completing. You may want someone else to complete a task for you, doubting your own abilities. It's bound to happen that self-doubt will present itself in one way or another. It's part of the process; it's part of growing. Remember Jordin Sparks' infamous lyrics, "one step at a time"[23]? If you can continue to tell yourself that you *can* finish what you started, you will gain so much power and experience along the way. It's just as sweet of a feeling knowing we finished something, looking back and reviewing our hard work, than it is sitting around waiting for someone else to do it. You will hit barriers in life, but the secret is to keep going. It's that simple.

- You may not want to do something. Heck, I'm lazy at times. But there will always be things you do not want to do, even in a life of complete lavish. Once you work past those hard parts, you can conquer anything. You've always been able to.

What you can do:

- Be gentle with yourself and still remember that you've got your back. You have a connection with you. It may sound

---

23 "Jordin Sparks – One Step At A Time". 2019. *Youtube*. https://www.youtube.com/watch?v=PIE5QtkxzvM.

cliché, but really listen to that. Be gentle with yourself. We beat ourselves up the most through self-depreciation and excessive doubt. My professor always told me, "Done is better than perfect." When you are writing, speaking, preparing for something, practicing—first work on completing the task. You do not need it to be perfect. Get done with the task; you have time to actually finish it later. Writing this book took a long while to complete, but I had my thoughts finally all on paper, all in one place. We focus too much on doing things perfectly to show others we have worth.

- When speaking up or being in front of an audience, don't be afraid to stand up and admit, "I am extremely nervous right now, but hey, I'll give it my all, and I'll try to save both myself from embarrassment while I am presenting and you from secondhand embarrassment for me."

- One of my communication professors, Dr. B, one of the most intelligent men I've ever met, always had amazing words of wisdom hidden throughout our senior year capstone classes. I remember when he was giving us tips to present to the class, he told us that when we feel nervous or like no one is listening to our voices, we should "find the friendly eyes." He described how there are always friendly eyes somewhere—eyes that want you to succeed rather than mess up, eyes that care about what you are saying. He told us to build a connection with those friendly eyes when nervous.

- Motivational coach Tony Robbins teaches about how we can move toward our discomfort and excite ourselves in times of fear. He appeared on an episode of the *Dr. Oz Show* and was teaching the audience different ways they could break negative patterns of thinking. One of the most noteworthy moments I took away from the episode came when he helped the audience channel their inner excitement. "Focus on that moment you are proud of. When you are a little kid, what happens when you are really proud?" Then he said, "Think of something you can really be grateful for, excited for. A person, a moment—or something if you wanted to you could be excited about." He then asked them to close their eyes and redirect their focus to something exciting. He had the audience focus on how they breathe when they are excited and continued, saying, "When you were a little kid you probably made noises for the hell of it and people told you not to. Make a noise of excitement, a sound in your body."[24] The audience proceeded to scream. I challenge you, and Tony would as well, to close your eyes, and let out a sound of excitement for yourself. Let out a sound of excitement for the person next to you to complete what you started, to encourage yourself to use your voice without the barriers of shame, doubt, or guilt.

---

24 "Motivation – Tony Robbins On How To Break Your Negative Thinking". 2019. *Youtube.* https://www.youtube.com/watch?v=GyqrYmjjqVk.

- Mel Robbins, one of my favorite speakers and authors, is known for her five-second rule technique. She writes, "If you have an instinct to act on a goal, you must physically move within five seconds or your brain will kill it." She continues by writing: "When you feel yourself hesitate before doing something that you know you should do, count 5-4-3-2-1-GO and move towards action."[25] I use this technique every single morning to simply get out of bed. Where can this technique be helpful for you in your life?
- Most importantly, don't let your beautiful, unique self go to waste. Don't be afraid to own your imperfections.

---

25 "The Five Elements Of The The 5 Second Rule". 2018. *Mel Robbins.* https://melrobbins.com/blog/five-elements-5-second-rule/.

CHAPTER 4

'I'm Too Much
to Handle'

———

Have you ever felt like you've lost a grip on yourself?

Have you ever felt that others think you are just looking for attention?

Do you ever feel invisible?

I am going to take you back to a time I felt at my absolute lowest.

Working through obsessive-compulsive disorder and depression that later accompanied my anxious feelings heightened from senior year of high school and almost came to a complete crash by my sophomore year of college. I had constant obsessive thoughts that kept me lying in bed, too afraid to get up. I would get stuck on thoughts and fuel them so far that I would convince myself I was a bad person, that

I had the stomach flu every day, and even that I had every single disorder and illness on earth. I obsessed about my body image. I obsessed about pleasing everyone. I obsessed about almost any uncomfortable thought that popped into my head. And I tried so hard to control the many compulsions I felt I had to do that accompanied my obsessions, including obsessively Google-searching to check if I had every illness under the sun, taking way too many Tums to "fix" any rumble of my stomach, washing every surface, even spraying my rug, when people left my room, and praying a certain prayer a certain amount of times so that I could go to sleep.

As hard as it is to describe how severely these feelings affected my life over the years, I will share a story with you where every feeling that I was holding in caved in at once, sending me over the edge.

**

My mom is an incredible woman who dedicates her life to caregiving. When I was born, she stayed home to take care of me while my dad worked two jobs. She spent her free time taking care of my great uncles, as well as my grandpa and grandma. She stuck by their side nearly every day for years and was alongside their beds when they passed. To this day, she dedicates a huge portion of her life to caregiving for family members and friends. She has a huge heart and means well. I appreciate and admire her so much every single day, but I always felt like I could *never* express these feelings and bring myself to say it to her face.

My mom and I also had the hardest time getting along for as long as I could remember.

Growing up, I felt that each time my mom and I were in the same room, I would eventually be blamed for something. I would often wake up and make it a goal to not argue with my parents. Sitting in the car as we drove from place to place, I tried so hard not to say something that would send us into an argument. No matter how hard I tried, we ended up in a screaming match.

There were many times when we were trapped in the confines of the car, my mom in control of the wheel, me in control of the music. The music in my headphones was not loud enough to drown out our constant screaming. I knew I was in the wrong and immature in many of the arguments that surfaced. Friends and family would notice the tension in the room each time my mom and I would talk. Our relationship continued to shatter after years and years of breakdowns and misunderstandings.

Over the years, I assumed my parents never fully understood my thoughts and feelings. Over time, when I was in the presence of my parents, I felt as if I lost my voice and all the wind in my body. I felt numb and awkward when trying to get along with them, expecting an argument to arise in some way, each and every day. Instead of talking to them when everything was calm, I started to hide my emotions, not giving myself or my parents the chance to talk things out.

I would beat myself up, blaming myself for the relationship that my parents and I had. It always turned out to be my fault somehow, two against one because I'm an only child. I always wished I had a sibling or someone else in the house to talk to who understood how I felt, being that my parents always had each other's backs. I knew how much my parents cared for me and appreciated how much they wanted me to succeed in life. But I silenced my appreciation. From a young age, I was bitter toward them and felt like I could not open up and explain my feelings, positive or negative. I always felt like a bother and a dramatic drama queen. And I refused to talk anymore.

Throughout high school and college, my mom and I were both trying to balance loads of stressors present in our lives.

**

Flash forward to the fall semester of my sophomore year in college, I felt like our relationship was hanging by a thread.

Nearly every day, my mom would drive to and from my grandma's house to make sure my gram was fed, situated, and that the nurses' aids were greeted and notified about how she was feeling each day. My mom was also balancing the stress that my dad was carrying, as well as making sure I was functioning well after my hospital visit just weeks prior.

I was in the hospital early in the semester due to constant nausea and rapid weight loss after catching the stomach flu, a process I was very used to at this point in my life. I had trouble leaving my dorm room for months after the hospital visit, in fear that I would throw up the minute that I walked out into the open. I was also coping with other strong forms of obsessions and compulsions that kept me up at night, unable to go to sleep early, in fear that I would lay awake thinking and spiral out of control. I developed a habit of staying up late until I could not keep my eyes open any longer, just so I was guaranteed to fall asleep the minute I hit the pillow.

I was having a hard time explaining my thoughts and feelings to others, and for the first time felt like I did not want to go through life feeling this way anymore.

I felt like no one in my life, even the closest people to me, would take me seriously when I felt upset. I came to this conclusion by judging myself. Every day, I obsessed that I had the stomach flu, stopped going to events, had trouble getting up for and staying at school, and constantly needed to clean the space around me, looking for germs at every second. I would express my fear constantly; it seemed to be the only subject I could talk about. By the time my obsessions kicked in full-force, people never believed that I was sick, they thought it was always anxiousness until I had physical proof, like a 101-degree fever, to back up my pain.

I started by suppressing my anxiety. I never understood myself and why I was so fixated on my thoughts. Looking back, I think, *Maybe it was not the people around me who did not want to understand me, but I could not properly depict what I was feeling myself.*

I felt like the girl who cried wolf and started to refrain from sharing any of my depressive feelings and thoughts. It did not take long for these thoughts to spiral so fast that my grip from reality started to slip faster and faster.

Those assumptions pulled me out of reality.

**

On a chilly winter night during my sophomore year of college, I was back home in Pittsburgh, leaving the house of a friend I hadn't had the chance to see since school started that semester.

Although I knew how to drive, I was relying on anyone out there who could drop me off and pick me up due to my overthinking and anxiousness, which hindered me from getting into a car by myself. The thought of being alone when I was in this mental state petrified me. I begged other people to drive me to and from events. Even trying to talk myself into getting off my butt and driving to the grocery store down the street was too much of a struggle. It felt highly embarrassing for me to admit that I, a sophomore in college with my drivers license, wanted my mom and dad to drive with me to and from work, friends' houses, and other activities.

As I was talking with my friend and her parents while standing by the door, my mom pulled up to the house to pick me up. I was inside, finishing up the conversation while my mom waited in the car. When I got into the car after making my mom wait a long time, a fight ensued.

On this specific night, my mind was not in the right place. I was not only exhausted from the emotional strain on the relationship with my mom, but also completely worn out by my anxiety and obsessive-compulsive thoughts. In the car, I was trying to explain how I was feeling at school, but my mom and I were not listening to one another. I was gasping for air, screaming at the top of my lungs, wanting to be heard. I chose this time, when both parties were unhappy, to talk about something serious. I remember trying so hard to explain how I felt extremely unhappy in my life and that no one was taking me seriously. Each time I would try to bring up my feelings, I was guilted into knowing that someone else had it worse.

I had to then try and tell myself that what I was going through was not that bad and convinced myself that I was just going crazy.

I kept apologizing and trying to make a point. My mom kept fighting back, saying:

"Julia, I'm not wrong in this situation!"

She halted at a stop sign just minutes from my house. I opened the car door, attempting to catch my breath and get out of the car to walk the rest of the way home. As I started to remove my seatbelt, my mom kept driving at a slow pace, trying to make sure I did not leave the car. The door was open just a smidge, and we were both screaming at the top of our lungs, interrupting each other every second.

"You're acting like a teenager, Julia! You're acting immature!"

Bickering quickly turned to screaming, where both of our voices were raspy from trying to get our feelings across to the other. My mom and I were back in a situation we both knew all too well: trapped in the confines of a small vehicle, forced to stay together and try to work things out.

I was worn out and exhausted, unsure if she would hear me out. And I sure as heck was not ready to hear anyone else out. Unsure if she would truly listen to what I had to say. Unsure if she valued my thoughts and my voice.

I've never thought so far as to end my life, and feared that if I brought it up, I would be labeled as dramatic and merely looking for attention.

By the time we pulled to the next stop sign, I was out of breath and soaked in tears.

My thoughts spiraling and my body out of energy, I let out one more yell as loud as I could. I yelled something that I will never forget, that chills me to the bone to relive the memory:

"I'm going to do it—I am going to hurt myself and no one is going to care. I can't do this anymore!" The words that ejected from my mouth did not even stun me. I felt like I was coming to a firm decision to end my life.

My mom, thinking that I was just being dramatic and looking for attention, called me out for going overboard. She kept saying she did not have time for this argument, and quickly dropped me off while she drove over to check on my grandma before bed.

I stood in the driveway of my house, mind racing and tears of anger, confusion, frustration, and sadness spilling out of my eyes. I ran up the steps, slamming the front door behind me.

I am worthless, I thought. *All I am to anyone is a dramatic girl crying wolf every second of every day. Who am I to think I am depressed? There are people going through so much right now and I am bitter. This is all my fault, my feelings are stupid. My own mom does not even believe me. There is nothing left I can do.*

I felt like my world was crashing down. I was alone and hated myself.

I sat in the entrance of the house, leaning against the chair, sobbing, coughing, hysterical. I paced around the house, trying to think of who I could call and talk out my feelings with. I opened up my phone and scrolled down my contacts, passing my closest friends and family members, too scared to dial any number. I knew that each of my friends and family members have heard me complain about my stomachaches and anxiety before, and I feared calling anyone, scared that no one would take the extent of the issue seriously. I did not want to lose any more friends from complaining too much.

No one will believe I feel depressed. I have a good life. I have a roof over my head. I am not worthy of feeling depressed. My mom thinks I am seeking attention. Am I manipulative? Am I even depressed?

I ran up to my room, shut the door, and sat on the bed. Across the room, there was a completely full jar of pills.

My mind, which had been whirring with thoughts a moment prior, started to feel numb once again. My house was completely silent and my head was pulsing as I tried to calm down.

When I started trying to reason my way through the situation, my obsessive thoughts popped back up again. I was disgusted with myself, and ready to give up, accepting that my voice would never amount to anything.

I replayed moments in my head when I felt confused and alone. I replayed the comments others made to me:

"You're wrong!"

"You're being dramatic!

"Grow up!"

"You're too sensitive!"

"Stop worrying!"

I felt exhausted from trying to find acceptance from others and assumed that others were exhausted because of me.

After what felt like hours of sitting down on my bed staring at the wall, I got up, grabbed the jar, and sat on the floor.

What would happen to me? I thought.

I'm too scared to see what happens, but I am too scared to live with myself.

I tried to hold back tears as I laid my head back on the wall and tried to stop myself from overthinking, attempting to talk myself down from making a huge mistake.

I started to panic even more when I thought of the people in my life.

I don't want anyone to find me like this.

I don't want anyone to blame themselves for an action I did myself.

Is this really the only way others will understand how I am feeling?

If I tell anyone else, will they even take me seriously?

I was conflicted, thinking the only answer was to hurt myself instead of putting others through any more trouble with my obsessive, anxious thoughts.

I thought people would not care unless I actually made a move and changed somehow.

And for the first time, I agreed. But not in a malicious way, discounting anyone's feelings. As I was sitting on the ground, about to give up, I said out loud, "I wish that someone would take me seriously. I wish that someone would give my feelings attention without judgment."

No, I did not want to scream to the world that I was about to end my life, but I wanted to feel like my life was worth living. And in the state of mind I was in at the time, I felt like there was nothing left to live for, when another part of me, somewhere, knew that was not true.

I felt immature. I was hurting, but kept talking down to myself instead of talking myself down.

My mom may be sick of me. My friends have to be sick of me. I'm childish, a complainer, and everything is my fault, I thought to myself.

I opened my eyes, took a breath in and thought, *Is this the end?*

Stuck in the Feelings

My mind was going back and forth as I stared at the pill jar in my hands. I felt dizzy, overwhelmed, and afraid.

More conflicting, anxious thoughts ran through my head.

Don't do it Julia; this could be bad.

But no one seems to care anyway, because no one thinks I am actually feeling upset. It's the only option.

But think about everything that could go wrong.

What if you decide you don't want to hurt yourself and it's too late?

I felt exhausted battling these thoughts. I was confused and conflicted, not sure how I could make a decision. I forced myself to stand up, walk to the bed, and lay down to collect my thoughts. I turned off the lights, pulled the covers over my head, and slept.

Hours passed and I was asleep in my room, still in the same clothes from the visit to my friend's house. I awoke to the sound of my dad's car pulling up in front of the house. He walked in, headed upstairs, and went on the computer.

Minutes later, I heard my mom's voice as she entered the front door, asking if anyone was home. After my dad said hello, she frantically asked where I was.

"I haven't heard her; I think she is sleeping," I heard him say as I removed the covers from my head.

"Well, can you check on her?" I heard her say.

My dad slightly opened the door and when he saw my lights off, he whispered to my mom, "She's asleep!"

That's when I snapped back into it. *What if I wasn't sleeping? What if I can keep fighting and get help? What if my anxious thoughts didn't arise and I didn't go lay down and fall asleep? Maybe my mom was concerned?*

"I'm here," I said.

My dad said goodnight, closed the door, and started to walk down the hall.

This is my chance to tell them how I feel, I thought.

I waited and waited, still afraid that my voice was worthless and that I was too much to handle.

It wasn't until the next day, as we traveled back to Cleveland after a long weekend, when I finally tried to tell both my mom and dad how I felt.

"Mom? Dad? I really don't want to go back to Cleveland today. I feel like something is wrong with me. I don't feel like I want to be here anymore."

"Julia, if you want to transfer, we aren't forcing you to stay at this college if that's what you mean."

"No, that's not it. I mean, I think ... I don't think I want to live anymore."

Making Sense of It All

I think back to that time in my life often, trying to make sense of the way I was feeling in those exact moments. My scarcity mindset, the constant focus on perfecting the end result of every situation, pulled me so far into moments of panic that I lost control.

When I felt as if I was losing a grip on my life, I was in a different mindset, one where I could not rationally make decisions. I was afraid and chose to run away when I felt myself hitting my breaking point. This story is just one small moment that I've been alive, but the domino effect of choices I made that weekend had a huge impact on my life that I am living today.

Why did I feel like suicide was my only option? I remember feeling that I did not want to inconvenience anyone else, that me experiencing severe bouts of OCD was too much, too stressful, for others to love. I remember thinking it was too difficult to live with the thoughts, and the only way to make sure I was no longer suffering and no longer a burden was not being here at all. And, sadly, people seeing suicide as the only option is very, very common all over the world.

When I close my eyes and look back to the days I felt my worst, I see a girl who thought that she tried hard enough.

I see a girl who thought she spoke up for a long time and felt that she never found the answers.

I see a girl who, through years of living in the same routine and pattern, felt stuck.

Even though I was simply stuck in a dry place that I desperately wanted to break out of, I somehow felt like I was sinking.

All I wanted was for someone to really listen when I felt like I was losing my grip on my life, without them trying to fix me or quickly transform me into someone I was not. I felt like many of the people closest to me, the ones I thought I trusted most, shut my voice down by not taking the time to understand how I was feeling.

I would wonder how the heck anyone can let their voice shine when everyone else in the room is shutting them down, when the people shutting them down are the ones who need to hear it the most.

Many of us know by now that life's most complicated questions, like the one above, do not always have a clear answer. But we can choose what speaks most to us as we learn new lessons everyday. I searched long and hard for answers through counseling sessions, my faith, research, and talking with peers and adults. All of these things helped me immensely, but I fell into a habit of taking in so much information that I held close to me as valuable, and somehow lost my own voice in the process. I listened to others give advice but would rarely question the things that confused me or continue speaking up when someone was not really listening to me.

I had a hard time choosing what messages I identified with most because of the possibility of either me or someone else playing devil's advocate for the choices I made. I was afraid of failure, embarrassment, loss. I came to the conclusion that I would rather lose myself before someone else.

I was afraid of vulnerability. I was afraid of others challenging the way I truly felt, challenging my vulnerability.

On my trip to Utah (yes, the infamous lettuce trip), I was one of tens of thousands sitting in a convention center, listening to incredible humans share their inspiring messages of motivation, wellness, and the process behind success. After multiple days and hours sitting and taking in information, a woman named Kristin Van Wey won the company Elevation Award for the immense passion she has shown for helping people around the world. She was congratulated by the crowd and offered a few words of thanks. Her words replay in my head to this day:

We don't raise our voices to scream. We raise our voices so those who don't have one can be heard.[26]

When I heard Kristin say those words, my eyes lit up. I immediately asked myself again the question that confused

---

26 "Doterra Awards Kristin Van Wey With The 2018 Elevation Award". 2019. *Prnewswire.Com.* https://www.prnewswire.com/news-releases/doterra-awards-kristin-van-wey-with-the-2018-elevation-award-300729720.html.

me for much of my life, "How the heck can anyone let their voices shine when everyone in the room is shutting them down?"

**

We can let our voice shine when we also allow and encourage others to use their voice. We speak up so others feel empowered to share, letting each other know that there is a place in this world for every single person.

We speak up by helping others understand perspectives that may be different from their own. We speak up to connect with one another.

We connect with each other by finding out that we have so much in common, way more than we may think. Not just surface-level qualities like our favorite colors and music. But from our thoughts, feelings, passions, and emotions. From the wise words of Mandisa, "we all bleed the same."[27]

Why do we determine what our voice is worth by the reactions of the people closest to us, the reactions of the ones who are "in the room?" Why do we tend to fixate only on the people in the room, when there is someone out there in this gigantic world you can identify with? By using our voices, there is someone we can help and someone who can help us if we don't give up on searching.

---

27 "Mandisa – Bleed The Same (Official Lyric Video) Ft. Toby-mac, Kirk Franklin". 2019. *Youtube*. https://www.youtube.com/watch?v=UEzCQBwQkdA.

When I felt like my life was at its very end and I gave it my all, all I had to do was continue speaking up and owning my voice. Even if I raised my voice 5,000 times and received no response, all I had to do was say something one more time, and speaking up was the first step in a process that may have just saved my life.

I once felt like it was impossible to express my feelings to my parents. I tried over and over again growing up, just to be shut down because we all misunderstood each other. My parents and I were all trying to change each other for what we thought was the better, to force our voices upon each other, rather than collectively coming together and choosing to not only speak, but really taking the time to listen.

I had to realize that it would neither be easy nor comfortable to speak my mind in high-pressure situations, and it may become so hard that I may doubt my own voice for a moment in the process.

I had to realize that it would neither be easy nor comfortable to also listen without speaking, making sure I also understood my parents' perspective.

Speaking up extends farther than just positivity, affecting my own life. My choice to keep speaking and living through the rejection, failures, and struggles helps instill hope in others.

When I started writing this story to share in the book, I kept deleting my words and doubting if sharing this part of my life would be a good idea. I kept anxiously thinking about the possible criticisms in my head: *You're seeking attention. You're immature. You're dramatic. You're making a huge deal out of nothing. What you're feeling is fake.*

But I am better than that. I am rising above the statements that shut each other down. I know that the fear of sharing my voice was how I got close to my breaking point in the first place. During my sophomore year, I was not sure exactly how to process what I was going through and too scared to take up someone's time to explain it. Chances are, there are many out there who feel the same way.

What are some other factors that kept me going? I'm a friend; I'm a daughter; I'm loved and cared for even if I lose sight of that for a time.

People may not believe you if you feel like you are on the verge of a breakdown. People may talk up a big game and say that they are in it for the long haul, in it to help each other, but shut each other down when help is needed most.

We have to remember that we know our own experiences. We have to keep sharing our voices.

Not just speaking at people, but *sharing* our voices.

We have to own our truth. People will try to pull that away from us, many times without even knowing what they are doing.

But we know what we've been through, and we have a part of us that could change someone's life.

We have permission to be vulnerable, because without it, we can lose ourselves.

Changing the World or Forcing Ourselves to Change?

One common question we may have all heard at some point in our lives, whether it was directed toward us or our favorite celebrity in an interview: "If there was one thing that you could change about yourself, what would it be?"

In our heads, many of us may pick ourselves apart and say, "Oh, maybe my arms. My stomach could be a little smaller," or "I am content with the way I look, but my eyebrows need trimmed."

To the audience, many may say that they would not want to change anything because they are thankful for the process. And I would definitely agree with that answer. I am very thankful for all the lessons I've learned and joys I've experienced throughout my life.

But, the "negative me" who tends to self-depreciate would say something different.

I am really fixated on changing the way my teeth look.

Remember when I mentioned that I sucked my thumb for years? Well, that is one of the major reasons why my teeth were all over the place and I needed braces in middle school. After the dreadful but necessary expander and rubber bands and tons of pink retainer molds later, the braces were finally removed after my eighth grade graduation. The braces were worth it—my teeth looked great. I cried at first, resisting the change and actually missing those metal teeth accessories for a hot sec, not sure if I liked how the "new me" looked.

Shortly after my braces were removed I was told to wear my metal retainer every single night for the rest of my life.

Whoop-de-do.

I swear I tried to wear them consistently at first, but they made me gag, and we all know by now how I feel about the possibility of puking or anything of the sort that resembled what could happen when germs attack. The feeling of wearing the retainers was new to me and I was afraid of what could happen. So I stopped. I stopped wearing my retainers, and yes, I continued to suck my thumb.

As a result, I was heading right back to the same place I was in before I was told I needed braces. I tried almost everything I could think of to stop sucking my thumb but eventually stopped making the effort to sustain what both I and others had worked so hard for: a new smile.

Months after the braces' removal, I would look in the mirror as minutes passed by while I analyzed my shifted teeth. I used to replay the times when I screwed up and did not wear my retainer.

If I just would have worn it that one time…

What if I wore them that night? Would I look better? Would things in my life be different?

I just cannot stop sucking my thumb. I am trying so hard, but I cannot stop.

The thoughts and fixation on my teeth would spiral over and over again. I would take an iPod and abuse the front-facing camera taking pictures of my mouth, making sure I captured the uneven look of my teeth and thought about everything I could have done right to avoid the shift.

I started to constantly mention how much I wanted Invisalign to bring my teeth back to their proper form. If I could change anything about my physical appearance, I knew darn well that I would choose my teeth.

As I reflect on this long journey, I actually think it applies to life in a pretty spectacular, spot-on way.

Yup—all this teeth talk has a point, surprisingly.

Reality Check

Our teeth may be uneven. Misaligned. Out of place.

Other people's teeth may be uneven. Misaligned. Out of place.

We may be critical of ourselves and others and seek change.

We may want to better ourselves and straighten out our life (or rather our teeth). Someone else may even notice those teeth that are not exactly in the spot they were meant to be. And they may want to help us by working those teeth to move like crazy.

There will be hard parts. When we get those braces on and those gears start turning, we may experience pain.

We may resist the feeling and our daily actions may have to change to flow with the process. Yup, that means no more bubble gum or popcorn for a while!

There will be the fun parts, where you might get to pick out colorful bands to spice up the metal brackets.

There will be times where you move fast. Bands go on the brackets and those teeth shift at the blink of an eye if we keep at it.

There will be times when everything is slow. When that doctor says, "Four years and your teeth will be back in place!"

There will be times when others are moving at a different pace.

There will be times when others have the same situation as you do. Expanders going on at the same time?! Heck yeah—twinsies!

There will be the removal: the rebirth. The results.

Then there will be the choice to sustain the work we have done. The improvement. Choosing to keep or let our teeth move to wherever their little hearts desire.

The grand reveal took time. It was a process with tons of highs and many lows.

The process is beautiful, not because everything will go perfectly, but because you are evolving and feeling in the process. Although you may feel pain, you are also feeling relief. You are ultimately feeling the change in your life.

You are gradually seeing the change.

You hit points where things may shift and things may stay the same.

These feelings mean we are alive, people!

Feeling pain and sadness is still having that ability to feel! And that's a gift!

To my surprise, having the means to wear braces was a gift, even though to me I once thought it was torture.

In our lives, we may feel out of place and stuck. We may go through a long, grueling process to get to where we want to go. And we get there, we may want to change paths or things may go unexpectedly! My teeth aren't exactly where they were when I got my braces off, but they can still continue to stand where they are planted.

We have the luxury to keep going in whatever we choose to do in life.

We have the luxury to choose what we do next. We have the choice to embrace our voice, passions, choices, or rather—emBRACE who we are!

Others may not accept the way that we look. The way we think. The way we feel. The steps we take and the way we take those steps.

And we also may not accept ourselves either.

Life might not be a straight path. Recovery from where we ended up before is not a straight path. With dedication and determination, we can get where we want to go. We may change our course and hurt in the process. Things may go wrong. Things may get confusing. But these are just small moments. Make the collection of moments worth it.

Maybe one day I will get Invisalign. Who knows? But if I want that for myself, if that's the route I choose to take,

I have to find the means to get to where I want to go. I have to save up that money and trust the process. I have to work with others to see those results. And I have to dedicate myself to my decision. Whether it turns out to be a bad idea or not, I am going to keep on moving forward. I will emBRACE who I am.

My wonderful developmental editor, NeKisha Wilkins, wonderfully said, "Even wealthy people with straight teeth, long beautiful hair, and/or awesome pecs and glutes; have vulnerabilities. Vulnerability is a double-edged sword; it can be negative and positive. It can be negative in the fact that you never display it – so you are shut off, in a box, distant from people and yourself, not facing any truths in order to progress in a variety of areas in life. It can be positive in the fact that it helps you to make changes in your life and it can help others to make changes as well."

So, if there was one thing you could change about yourself, what would it be? Why? And instead of saying nothing and ignore how you are feeling, try to find the value in it. EmBRACE your feelings and find the positive in vulnerability.

"I'm Too Much to Handle. I've Had Enough." ----------> "I Am Enough."

Think of a time when you wanted to give up. Think of what kept you going, and if you did give up, what tore the progress apart. Think of a time there was something about you you wanted to change because someone or something else made you feel like yourself was not good enough.

Some questions to keep us thinking: Do we feel like we are annoying to others by constantly telling them how we feel? Do we feel that we drive people away when we are our true selves?

Remember, someone out there hears you. Don't lose sight of knowing that "When the whole world is silent, even one voice becomes powerful," as Malala Yousafzai said.

What to expect:

- Relationships are important. We have to keep in mind that yes, relationships with others are important, but we cannot forget about the relationship we have with ourselves.

- Talking about ourselves may seem easy at times, but sharing parts of ourselves when we are in a dark place, no matter what the situation may be, is a lot harder to admit. Trust me, this chapter petrified me to publish. But I've made it past this hump, and once again, we are not immune to new experiences. And hey, the point of this book is to push past the stereotype that we always have to show up perfect to be considered someone special. So I couldn't not include this story.

What you can do:

- When you are feeling in a funk, turn on a motivational video. Pump yourself up by finding the things that really take you to a place of excitement and pure joy. Turn on a song that really excites you, start dancing around, close your eyes and let loose, unapologetically. You may feel uncomfortable at first, but try and focus on what's happening rather than on how you look, how you feel, or how you are supposed to be.

- See not only others but also yourself as more than your thoughts or your mistakes. Show yourself that unconditional love that you can show to, let's say, a pet golden retriever (that's my dream dog, so if anyone has an English cream golden retriever puppy, send me pics!), who barks, whines, and needs you to assist them outside to pee every day. The same pet we may cuddle and love even though they hide our socks and shoes, while occasionally eating our belongings. Show yourself the discipline to not give up on you, learning to embrace the parts of yourself that are imperfect.

- "Remind yourself what you started with," as Marie Kondo said[28]. We get so lost in the clutter that we forget to appreciate how much life we've experienced and how much more we have to go. Challenge yourself to remember that joy you may have misplaced. Progress is important. Progress takes time. Progress leads to healing. Remember, you are improving. You are aware.

---

28   "Tidying Up With Marie Kondo." 2019. *Netflix*.

CHAPTER 5

'I'm Crazy'

———

Yup, I wrote this chapter you're about to read, but I will need to reread it over and over and over again, because I too forget that my anxieties and obsessions do not define me at times. It can be dang hard to believe that we are worthy and ABLE.

Raise your hand if you consult Google to answer burning questions you've had in your mind.

Maybe you want to know what year and day the Nickelodeon show *Rugrats* aired. More importantly, maybe you are curious to who voices the many characters in your favorite cartoons.

Maybe you want to learn how to play piano or guitar.

Then you try searching more opinionated posts, like "best places to travel around the world." Or "how best to stick to a budget."

What about those questions that have to do with health? Let's say that you go online and search, "I have a red bump on my arm. What does that mean?"

Then all s*** breaks loose.

The answers somehow lead you to the conclusion that you are going to die, specifically in five minutes.

Let's talk about those times where we try to find answers; let's talk about those times when we think we are crazy because of the way we feel, trying to convince ourselves that there is a way things "should" be at all times or else we are doomed. Thinking we *should* be a certain way or people will abandon us, look at us differently—judge us.

**

Thoughts will pop into our minds that we cannot control. Say that we hear about a tragedy in the news. Naturally, our minds may try to process how something or someone can wreak so much havoc on others. Our thoughts may drift, trying to process the news of current events, and our mind may go all the way to wondering if we are crazy ourselves and what defines crazy. We may wonder what we are capable of. And sometimes we get stuck on certain thoughts that drive us up a wall. Whether we think our partner is cheating because they did not call us back when they should have, or we think we have a life-threatening illness because our back hurts, every human may get stuck in a cycle of overthinking and finding evidence at one point or another in their lifetime. It's like watching a video with the topic "how to edit photos on Photoshop" and we somehow, hours later, end up on a whole different side of YouTube, watching cats dance to famous hip-hop songs or the classic "Charlie Bit My Finger" video[29]. Keeping up with our thoughts is hard. If we did everything our thoughts told us to do, we might not even have time to blink.

But maybe, just maybe, if people made mistakes and did not feed into the reputation others gave them, knowing there was a chance to learn and improve, would these toxic situations minimize?

Many people get stuck in an assumption that what they are thinking or saying is crazy. The definition of the word "crazy" can come across as unsettling: mentally deranged, wild, aggressive. Crazy is also used to describe high enthusiasm and someone who acts, in many circumstances, unapologetically, against the perceived norm. The word crazy is used in multiple negative and positive ways, but our mind has the ability to drift to thinking we are crazy for thinking, feeling, or acting a certain way. Many times, when we notice a thought or feeling we think is "crazy," there are resources available where we can talk and work through triggering thoughts. But when we are nervous being vulnerable, about opening up to others without judgment, afraid of coming across as crazy, we continue to put ourselves down in our mind, often feeling lost and confused in our own life. Some

---

29 "Charlie Bit My Finger – Again !". 2019. *Youtube*. https://www.youtube.com/watch?v=_OBlgSz8sSM.

may be afraid of earning a label, thinking they are monsters because of a thought or emotion they cannot control. Someone could then become scared that they will lose control of themselves.

It's not uncommon to be afraid of sharing our authentic feelings, to have a fear of making connections. We may fear abandonment, fear exposing unacceptable or questionable behavior, fear what people will think of us. We tend to focus on everything wrong with us instead of what's right.

My dad once said to me when I was panicking, "Different people do different things in their life; what you exhibit is not any worse. You are so focused that you are somehow 'wrong,' that you put this immense pressure on yourself because you want to achieve." That leads me to the question: what the heck are we basing the notion "I'm crazy" on? I was curious to explore this in my own life, as well as others who often feel similarly.

**

We are curious human beings. I may not be as curious about cellular molecular biology, but I love learning about animals (find me watching *Planet Earth* at 1 a.m.). I am not too curious about wrestling, but I do want to know how to dance and sing. You may feel similar, or have a differing opinion of what you are curious about.

Something else that I am curious about is what the heck is wrong with me. When my dad was diagnosed with cancer, we both had swollen lymph nodes in our armpits at the same exact time. Little did I know, a case of the sniffles was going around our house, and we were all coming down with a cold. But in my head, swollen lymph nodes were a life-or-death scenario for both myself and my dad. When my leg itches, a thought may cross my mind that I have a dangerous rash. And when we start Googling specific scenarios and symptoms, I am never prepared to deal with the thought of having every single illness on earth.

I realized over time that I am spending more time trying to find the answers, trying to find out what's wrong with me, rather than spending time experiencing my life and accepting myself for who I am. I was wasting hours upon hours Googling with time I will never get back. It's okay and necessary for something to take time, just as we talked about before. But are we spending hours after hours each week thinking about what could go wrong?

You can find almost any answer now on the internet. You can find every opinion that you can think of. You can even search and search, trying to find someone with the exact same situation as you, freaking out when you cannot find anything you that identify with. It's terrifying.

But seriously, let's think about that for a second. It is seriously bizarre. There are *so many* opinions, so many "experts" online confirming why we are or are not a certain way. Almost any viral YouTube video, Facebook post, news article, movie review will have comments saying why something is or is not wrong. And some may be right in the end, but to minimize black-and-white thinking, let's move into the gray. Some can be wrong. And I will share with you some examples of times I was wrong when I was *sure* I convinced myself otherwise with "proof."

My OCD acts up especially in high-stress situations, when I start to fixate on what is wrong with me. I've had debilitating obsessions accompanied by compulsions for days on end, that would last for weeks, even months and at times years. These obsessions were so bad that I could not get out of bed to sip water, let alone walk out of my room. I would be tempted to act on my compulsions, to keep trying to find answers by testing out my fears.

Here are just some of the fixations I've had growing up:

- Thinking I was pregnant—as a virgin. Yeah. I seriously convinced myself I was pregnant, calling some of my friends to break the news to them. Yes, they were just as confused as I was.
- Thinking my friends were mad at me or sick of me because they forgot to reply to a text or any other scenario I could think of at the time for proof.
- Having the stomach flu or food poisoning. This fear lasted daily for *years*. Years. Years, years, years. I woke up every single day thinking I was sick.
- Convinced I was contaminated by germs on every surface that I would touch.
- Making sure that my eyes weren't crossing.

- Thinking that the pimples on my lip meant I could never kiss someone, even on the cheek, because I had a disease. I stared at my lips in the mirror for *hours* panicking. I have to admit, it was not the best use of my time.
- Convinced that I was a bad person.
- Convinced that my boyfriend no longer wanted to be with me.
- Convinced that I randomly didn't love my boyfriend.
- Thinking I had multiple psychological disorders.
- Etc. etc. etc.

The pain of OCD is at times indescribable, which I will go into more later in the book. OCD or not, though, every human has had a thought or thoughts that made them anxious. Every human has a worry here and there in their lives. Most of my friends relate to that surge of fear when their period is late, even if they are virgins. Sometimes we clench our teeth as we try to guess when we will catch the stomach flu when our whole family has been sick for days. Some of us may relate to feeling a bit confused in a relationship that is maturing.

What do we do to relax these thoughts, to rest our minds and bodies?

We have rituals, habits we've formed that we need to do to relax. Healthy rituals include brushing your teeth, taking a shower, maybe even brushing hair, or washing retainers at the same time every night. Those activities that get us to think, "I can't go to sleep without completing this action!"

Janet and Chris Attwood explain healthy, empowering rituals that we can adopt into our lives such as quiet time, setting intentions in the beginning and evening, as well as "finding something that you can give away each day."[30]

Self-Diagnosing

On the other hand, one of my unhealthy rituals was Googling or asking friends and family members for reassurance, making sure I did not have a stomach flu or that I did not have every single disorder listed on the internet. These thoughts would take over my everyday life, preventing me from focusing when talking to friends, from finishing my homework, and from attending to my self-care.

After multiple therapy sessions and educating myself on different ways to work through fears and obsessions, I was always told to "name my uncomfortable thoughts." When these harmful thoughts, these thoughts that try to bully me, pop into my head, I label them. I hated naming my thoughts at first, but I started to label my thoughts as Jerky Julia. Every time my thoughts would spiral, I would acknowledge that Jerky Julia was just trying to bully me. My thoughts were louder than my actual voice. I was creating awareness.

I needed to practice patience with myself instead of trying to find answers every single second. I always wanted to be completely in-control of my life that I held myself back from

---

30 Atwood "finding something that you can give away each day."

experiencing so much. I would always anticipate something bad happening to my health, happiness, and success.

Tough love advice: something can go wrong at any minute of any day. When my obsessive thoughts act up, my friends and boyfriend try to use humor to make me feel better. Hearing some of my thoughts said back to me makes me giggle, knowing how much I am overthinking, because thinking is one thing and saying them out loud is another. When I get caught up in a negative pattern of "what if"s my boyfriend usually says, "We can all die right now. Seriously. A meteor can drop from the sky on us in 3 … 2 … 1 … Oh, look! It didn't! But it can. If we spend time waiting and waiting and worrying, we won't give ourselves the opportunity to take care of ourselves, make a move, or grow in confidence."

My friend Addie Macioce perfectly describes feeling stuck in an anxious cycle, not knowing what is wrong with herself or what could happen. When stuck in this cycle of anxiety, she describes feeling helpless and powerless, putting so much pressure on herself: "Thoughts take over our minds. I fall into these extreme panic attacks where I get extremely hot, especially on the back of my neck. The heat spreads down my back and my heart rate increases. I start too look everywhere, my thoughts running at what seems like 100 miles a minute. Sometimes I will even start to shake and look at the goosebumps that appear all over my arms. Between the stomach aches, constant thoughts, and confusion, my focus changes from living my life to fixating on my anxious thoughts."

When we are in the midst of panic, it is hard to tell what is going on with our mind and body. How we are feeling can be hard to describe to others. But when we are in a state of panic, we may not be as nice to ourselves in our own mind, fixating on everything that could go wrong and everything that could be wrong with us.

One of the most powerful moments is when we connect with people who feel similarly in their lives by fostering authentic connections. Instead of trying to search for what is wrong with us, we can invite others to see the good, the bad, and the ugly. Addie continues to say, "People inspire me when they speak up about things that are not easy to say. They encourage me to be transparent because it became too difficult for me to think 'I'm not strong enough' or that 'others won't believe how I feel.' Speaking up and sparking change starts with people who are brave."

When We Think We Are Crazy Because of Our Thoughts: Disappointed in Ourselves

Thinking we are crazy because of our thoughts hinders us from telling people how we really feel.

As I started to speak out about topics such as vulnerability and mental health awarenesses, a number of people would reach out to me and share their stresses and anxieties with confidence. As friends and I would talk for hours, discussing the reality of our thoughts and feelings, I felt more and more connected, empowered, and confident to speak up, not always feeling ashamed of my thoughts and voice.

One night in college, I was lying down, stuck in a spiral of thoughts that made me feel as if I were spinning out of control. I was having a breakdown, one of the many I experienced throughout college. I was clicking around on my phone trying to find ways to distract myself, and I felt a buzz, looking down to see my friend calling my phone. I wanted to continue lying alone and crying, even though this cycle lasted for days. I kept thinking if I held everything in and stayed by myself over and over again, all the stress in my life would somehow improve. Without even seeing where my thumb was pressing, I picked up her video call. She saw tears streaming down my face and immediately came to visit me in my room.

She first asked me how I was feeling. Knowing that I was in a panic, she understood that it was hard for me to easily explain what I was feeling at that moment. She listened intently, allowing me to explain how I was feeling at that moment. To my surprise, she would nod her head, saying that she feels the exact same feelings and experiences some of the same thoughts that I was experiencing at the time. She explained that she also overthinks when she's alone about some of the same topics I brought up. Before my friend came to visit me, I was under the impression I was completely alone and nobody could relate to how I felt specifically.

I was shocked to hear that she had similar thoughts and struggles as I did. As we connected more and more, my shoulders did not feel as tense and the tears were dried from my eyes. As long as we had been friends, I never knew she felt the same way that I felt.

As we continued to talk, something in our conversation stood out more than the rest. After I was done talking, and she was done sharing with me how she was feeling, she looked at me and said, "But please don't tell anyone about how I've been feeling."

"Of course!" I said to her.

She continued by saying, "There are a lot of people in my life, even some of my closest friends and family members, who would think I am faking, crazy, or simply misunderstood. Some of the closest people in my life do not believe in anxiety as an illness. They see it as an excuse: a dramatic, exaggerated illness."

I paused and replayed those words in my head.

I knew exactly how she felt. I identified with her words when she said she was in fear of talking about her struggles with others who think that anxiety and other mental health struggles are fake and annoying.

I felt the power of my friend's words as she shared her feelings with me. I felt like I understood her more, and that we were learning about each other in a way we never knew before. Knowing that she feels like she has to hold these raw feelings back from some of the closest people in her life made me want to empower her to embrace the way she feels.

When conducting interviews on vulnerability, I continually hear people share with me the times they felt unsafe, unaccepted, unable to voice their feelings with others. The more I heard these stories, the more I wanted to give people a platform to speak out about the reality of their struggles, and how they manage their stressors day by day. How they cope when things feel difficult.

After years of sharing my voice and speaking out, I started to own my feelings and connect on a deeper level with so many people. I learned that every voice matters, and each and every person is going through something we are not aware of.

Secrets

Secrets are okay from time to time. I'm sure you do not always plan to tell your friends and family the gifts you got them before it's time to open them. Surprise parties, surprise announcements, surprise wedding proposals—all of that fun stuff. Hey, I am writing this book, but I still have secrets, just like you! Keeping secrets may not always mean that we are afraid. Keeping secrets may not always be deceiving. But I know in my life there were many times when I was not ready to tell someone something about myself out of fear. We are going to discuss the dangers of holding in secrets when it is something that we want to release.

In my college ethics class, we learned a great deal about keeping secrets. In my business ethics textbook, *Honest Work: A Business Ethics Reader*, a couple of lessons stood out to me when we were learning about the differences between secrecy and privacy. The purpose of secrets and privacy "is to become less vulnerable, more in control." Author Sissela Bok goes on to say that keeping secrets also has its dangers: whether we let something build up in our own minds, or keep secrets that could harm someone else. On the contrary, "With no control over secrecy and openness, human beings could not remain either sane or free." Bok goes on to talk about how people can hold back reality by keeping a secret, therefore influencing how others see them, gaining control on their image. When we try too much to become like "everyone else" and choose not to embrace parts of us that may be broken or a work in progress, we let our thoughts and feelings build up until our brain reaches what feels like a maximum limit.

This last quote really screams why people may have a fear of vulnerability: "To have no capacity for secrecy is to be out of control over how others see one. It leaves one open to coercion."[31]

Ethics class was fun for me, knowing that I could think outside of the box and debate with others about the meaning of Immanuel Kant's universalism principles, but ethics is also

---

31 Ciulla, Joanne B., Clancy W. Martin, and Robert C. Solomon. 2014. *Honest Work : A Business Ethics Reader.* New York : Oxford University Press, [2014].

overwhelming, because it's a lot of analytical work, as well as bringing in various opinions on morals. When talking about secrecy and privacy, there is a bit of a hard line to draw on the rightness and wrongness of keeping a secret.

But let's think about secrecy in our own lives. Are we holding the way we feel inside because we are afraid of something? Are we hearing others tell us secrets that they make us promise not to ever speak about because they feel afraid of judgment?

Yes, I do have secrets. One of them I will reveal right now for an example: my mom caught me sleepwalking when I was in middle school, and I peed in my hamper thinking I was in the bathroom. Now this secret may not hold much importance or make a huge impact on the world, but there may be someone out there who has a huge fear of doing something stupid in their sleep. If that happens to be you, always remember—your fellow friend Julia peed in her hamper.

I have way more embarrassing moments that I am still nervous to share. And that's okay! We do not need to share all parts of our lives that hold a sacred importance to ourselves and others. You do not need to overshare to be vulnerable. You may not always be ready or clear on what you're feeling to share what you are thinking. Secrets are not always considered negative or deceptive; they can be something you tell someone in confidence that increases your connection and understanding of one another. Not everyone needs to know how you are feeling and what you are thinking at all times.

But even if you are telling someone a secret, it still may be hard to let loose something you've been holding in and trying to process all by yourself. No, I am not telling you to go on Facebook and post all of your biggest secrets to be vulnerable. My goal is to help us realize what we are holding in and how it makes us feel, thinking about why it would be hard to talk about, even in a therapy session.

When I am fearful of sharing my vulnerable side when I know I want to say something, I think to myself:

Sharing our voices can make a huge impact in more ways than we may realize.

Sharing our voices helps others feel at ease—people who may be going through the same struggles.

Sharing your voice can help you make a move toward something you want. Think about someone working up the courage to ask their crush on a date.

Think about the power when someone says, "I love you" to their significant other, parent, or friend.

Think about when you start dating someone and you work up the courage to share with them your biggest fears. Think of the courage it takes not to lie just to come across as "normal" or "desirable."

Why do people regret saying they love someone? Why do people regret telling their best friend that they feel depressed? These moments carry true value, and they are just merely feelings that have the ability to grow, flourish, or even change over time.

Your voice is important even if you don't think so. The message you carry is important, even if you don't think so. Remember, this applies to everyone.

'I Regret Sharing My Vulnerable Side'

In college, I attended a retreat at which I observed a friend sharing a big part of her life with both me and a small group of others whom we had just met the day prior. It was an intimate setting where everyone was supportive and present with one another, really listening and embracing everyone's unique voices. When my friend shared a personal story with the group, she immediately opened the conversation for the other people in the room to feel confident in sharing their feelings, too. Her openness and trust in sharing with the group helped spark that trust in others, and the process of seeing everyone come out of their shell was truly amazing.

Later that day, the same friend approached me and shared that she regretted her vulnerability. She did not want others to take pity on her or think she was weak. She did not want people to treat her differently, such as acting nicer to her, just because she experienced adversity.

We worry that we have to act a certain way to matter. We may feel that we have to hold our feelings inside 24/7, in fear that our voices and feelings won't be accepted by the people around us.

I frequently talk about why I suppress emotions, and my therapist always says to me, "Why should we gain the whole world when we lose ourselves in the process?" Why do we have to work hard to impress others when we have so much more to offer?

While I totally could understand and relate to my friend's fear of pity, I also wanted to point out that whether or not someone thinks differently of her, she helped others realize that they do not have to hold their feelings in and that every voice counts. She may never know who was inspired by her message and how her words impact their lives from this point forward.

One of my favorite topics Brené Brown shares with her audience is about "vulnerability hangovers." Oh my goodness, when I first heard that term, I finally felt understood. I will word-vomit to a new friend or freak out to my family about a way that I am feeling, then wake up the next day feeling like I have a hangover that will last for a good hundred years. In her Ted Talk, "Listening to Shame," she shares the petrifying feeling of knowing her previous "the power of vulnerability" TedTalk, which was all about vulnerability, would be on YouTube for people to view when she was talking about personal moments and breakdowns in her life. Brené joked that she was thinking about breaking in and deleting the video so no one else would hear her story.[32]

Sometimes we want to erase the times we were vulnerable with others.

---

32   Brown, Brené. 2019. "Listening To Shame". *Ted.Com*. https://www.ted.com/talks/brene_brown_listening_to_shame?language=en.

Why the heck did I say that? you may think over and over again, maybe going as far as telling someone, "I didn't really mean what I just said!"

One misinterpretation about vulnerability is that we have to explain how we are feeling, in detail, to anyone and everyone, every single second of every day, to experience true connection with one another.

No, I don't want to have to explain to every person in the world that I am feeling depressed each moment that my depression kicks in. Although I may not talk about my depressed feelings 24/7, in order to work through it in my life, I do not want to be afraid of admitting when I need to talk about them.

I don't want to keep holding back my voice when I need to talk about something.

If I feel a need to share how I am feeling, I do not want to immediately feel fearful or shameful for admitting how I feel.

I do not want to be afraid of admitting I need help.

I now developed enough confidence in my flaws to speak on stage so others can have the confidence to do it too, to show them what they can do when they don't yet have the confidence to do it, even if I think I am crazy and doubt my vulnerability.

And when we have the opportunity to be vulnerable, we may even feel like we are forcing our feelings because we have to, not because we are appreciating the process. Are we truly asking each other how we feel, on this day, at this moment?

Are we engaging and learning about moments in our life that hold true importance to us?

We try to live up to this perfect image. We hold ourselves to standards that either make us feel important or break us to feel less than and worthless.

It's difficult to be vulnerable, because in our heads, we don't always accept ourselves. I still find it hard to share my emotions in front of certain people, as did Mike Veny.

Elephant in the Room

I had the chance to speak with the wonderful Mike Veny, speaker, author, and drummer, who is recognized as one of the top 100 influential speakers in the healthcare industry. Mike was very open with me, as well as with the rest of the world, in describing his journey with depression and OCD. He discusses the pain that sometimes accompanies telling his story and reliving the hardest moments of his life.

In 2011, Mike was having a breakdown. He was once walking down the busy streets of NYC, having another meltdown, screaming, angry, and talking to himself. He decided to call a woman named Cheryl, who worked in the mental health field. He wanted to inquire about how to find a therapist. "I needed help and was becoming suicidal, self-harming again," Mike admitted.

She picked up the phone with a cheery voice, as he asked for help finding a therapist. Instead of answering his question, she asked him if he would like to be a speaker at her mental health conference.

"I don't want to speak to those people, those mental health people. I think speaking is stupid," he said as he hung up the phone.

The next day, Cheryl emailed Mike and cc'd a ton of other people he knew on the same email, formally asking him to be a speaker at the upcoming mental health event.

"If I put the date on the calendar, it's something to look forward to. 'I won't kill myself,'" he described.

On the day of the event, although he does not remember much of what he said, he started to cry onstage in front of everyone. Next thing he knew, he got a standing ovation and people approaching him from all over to speak at their schools, events, and more.

"Someone taught me to look at your gifts and surrender to those gifts, even if you do not see them as such. Maybe this mental health thing is a gift and I don't know it. I am in a lot of pain, but I feel something in my body when I speak about it because I've been there," he stated. He makes it his mission to heal emotional pain instead of avoiding vulnerability. Normalizing mental health takes work, and he knows he has to keep spreading the message to educate others who may not yet understand. He then said,

I used to care what people thought of me. I cared until around thirty years old. Even my parents suggested for me to keep my mental illness quiet. But there came a point in time when I couldn't just hold it in anymore. If I don't say I am feeling upset, others in the room may pick up that you do. When we speak up, we take that elephant out of the room. It takes a lot of effort to try and hold everything together. Sometimes we need to talk things out before we make decisions.

If we really think about it, holding in our feelings is uncomfortable, and often speaking about our feelings is uncomfortable. But there is way more internal harm in constantly keeping our feelings in, letting these thoughts eat away at our minds.

"Vulnerability taught me to be very honest with myself," Mike explained. "People are stuck in a prison and sometimes not even aware. Mental health can be confusing and we do not like to feel confused. Vulnerability does not mean you have to throw all of your dirt out there. You can just admit you are going through a hard time. Stories are what touch the heart." There are people out there who will help you take your mind off everything. They are everywhere, even if you haven't noticed yet.

**

Chris Ulmer, a special education teacher, started a nonprofit organization geared toward spreading awareness and "normalizing the diversity of the human condition"[33]: Special

---

33   "SBSK – Normalizing The Diversity Of The Human Condition". 2019. *SBSK*. https://sbsk.org/.

Books by Special Kids. Chris's organization is well known for the hundreds of YouTube videos that feature people from around the world sharing their life stories of the neurodiverse community.

Chris interviewed Cecelia McGough as she described her life with schizophrenia. This interview in particular is extremely powerful, a video that I watch time and time again when I feel in a panic because I am able to relate to Cecelia, knowing that even though I think differently than another, that does not mean I have no worth. She said to Chris, "I often say, 'I am just someone who can't turn off my nightmares even when I'm awake; that's not a reason to be scared of me." Cecelia started to hallucinate the vision of a clown in her junior year of high school. She talked about the fear paralyzing her before she knew what her diagnosis was. She described, "At first I thought I was possessed and, let me just tell you, that's a lot more scary than realizing you have a chemical imbalance inside of your head. That's why I promote education so much, because it is often said you fear what you don't understand. So me understanding more about my diagnosis makes me less afraid."

In her lifetime, Cecelia has attempted suicide, and she discussed why she started to believe that suicide was her only option:

It's because I didn't feel like I could be the person I wanted to be, and that people wouldn't accept me as a person, wouldn't accept my diagnosis. I hear voices in my head, but it's really the fear of real people, like what real voices have to say than the ones I hallucinate in my head. Those are the ones that matter to me more.

Chris then asked her: "What do you fear others saying?"

She bravely proclaimed, "I am afraid they will think of me as a freak. I have been called a freak, I have been called crazy. I've been called deranged."

He then asked, "What would you prefer to be called?"

"Cecelia."

She then powerfully stated: "But, do we really know what is going on in anyone's head when we are talking to them? You have that fear of people thinking that you are crazy but getting that help is so important—don't let anyone get in your way of that, especially yourself."[34]

"I'm Crazy" ----------> "I Have Permission to Feel"

Do we frequently say to one another, "Don't tell anyone I said that!" Do we think about why we do not want certain people to know how we are feeling? Is it because we think we are crazy or different from everyone else? Make note of what you can do to release your feelings apart from the immense pressures that shame and guilt can exert. What would you do if you didn't have to worry about acceptance from others?

---

34 "Cecilia's Life With Schizophrenia (Living With Hallucinations)". 2019. *Youtube*. https://www.youtube.com/watch?v=7csXfSRXmZo.

What if you were the last person on earth? I saw a beautiful quote the other day that said, "You are entirely up to you." What would you do if you believed that you were entirely up to you?

Now, let's think about this: have you ever told a friend, or even someone you just met, something about yourself that you don't usually publicly share with the world? Then did you wake up the next day and instantly panic, asking yourself why the heck you revealed that part of your life at that time?

What does that person think of me now?

Will things go back to the way they were before?

Do I want things to continue the way they were before or do I want to stop holding in my feelings?

If I had a penny for the amount of times I heard, "I regret saying that," I would be paying off my college loans at a rapid pace. And even though I really would love to pay off those loans ASAP, I would politely reject the pennies pouring in, in hopes of helping the world become more comfortable with vulnerability.

Some reasons why people regret being open and honest with others:

- We don't want pity.
- We don't want to be labeled, especially as negatively "crazy."
- We fear someone misinterpreting our voice.
- We fear a lack of control.
- We fear change.

- We fear someone's reaction.
- We don't want to publicly admit something.

And the grand finale: we do not have everything truly figured out ourselves and often fail to admit that. We tend to hold in how we feel, rushing to make decisions before thinking things through and talking them out.

We are allowed to feel!!! Just like we are allowing others to feel when we put ourselves down for the sake of others. Even the world has ups and downs with weather and times of the day. It fluctuates and forms habits. Things change quickly at times depending on situations. It's possible to move to safety in many situations. Just because you think you are crazy does not mean that defines your whole being.

What to expect:

- We try to find answers all of the time. When we do something wrong, we think we are wrong. When we make a mistake, we think we are failures for the rest of our lives. It's common for people to say to us, "Why would you ever even *think* that!" Know that we are not defined by our thoughts, and if we are having trouble controlling our anxious thoughts, there is help available. We have the ability to take action, and if we gain power over the disturbing and uncomfortable thoughts that are bound to pop up, we will gain power over our thoughts before our thoughts hold power over us. We don't give ourselves time to improve and don't give ourselves much credit. Personally, for me, writing this book has been rewarding but difficult, having to relive the feelings that shape me into who I am today, the good, the bad, and the ugly. Expect the journey to creating connections with others to be difficult—but rewarding.

- We may compare ourselves to others and feel jealousy arise when we see people we think are "normal" and "have it all together." It's okay to feel that way. Stay aware, and remember that everyone is fighting their own battles.

- It will be difficult to speak up when we are going through a tough time mentally, and that's okay. Anxiety and nervousness tend to stand right in front of us, blocking our vision from relaxation and serene feelings. When I was hung up over the effects of my OCD and the challenges I work through day by day, one of my professors told me that OCD is a "life sentence, but not a death sentence." We have the ability to improve over time, and although we aren't defined by our struggles, we hold them so close and sometimes fail to try and release our pain. I still have old obsessive thoughts that pop up in my head. They still arrive, but I've stood up to them, making it easier to pass. Just because we relapse does not mean that we can't try again. When my old obsessive thoughts arise, I use that opportunity as a challenge to stand up to myself, for myself.

- As I was listening to a meditation by EasyPiece Mediation, the narrator said, thoughts "do not define you. If you have a bad thought, does that make you bad? What if you have a good thought? Does that make you good? What if you have a stupid thought? Does that make you stupid?"[35]

- We are all crazy to someone else. Whether we are wild and upbeat, or serene and introverted, someone will naturally judge us in their heads, trying to separate us from whatever they perceive as the norm. Think: are our actions empowering people, even if others think we are crazy?

What you can do:

- Make this your mantra when you overthink: "It's okay to be happy. It's okay to feel confident. It's okay to feel upset and confused. I am capable of working through it." Don't just *say* those words, but focus on what they actually mean. We forget that every single human being is flawed and we all have emotions that are up and down at times. I may have to reread this book myself to remind myself that it's okay when I am lost in my thoughts. Study your worth so you don't lose sight of it. Hold yourself close. You are still deserving, and always have been.

- Sometimes things seem like they will never get better until they actually happen. We have to keep going. When I had the stomach flu, my biggest fear, I would say: "this too shall pass and will soon be a memory." Count to three: 1 ... 2 ... 3 ... let that feeling pass.

---

35 "Guided Meditation For OCD/Anxiety – Detachment From Intrusive Thoughts". 2019. *Youtube*. https://www.youtube.com/watch?v=e5sI6qujzIs&t=423s.

- Have you ever watched the show *Impractical Jokers* or read an art history textbook? Humor helps lift my mood immensely, and when I am in a panic, sometimes learning about something new or reading something that does not try to "fix" me helps me gain a grasp on my life, giving myself time for relaxation and self-care.
- We do not have to feel ashamed of going to therapy. Therapy sessions are some of the most rewarding parts of my week. Attending therapy does not ever mean we are crazy, inhumane people. It means we are dedicated to ourselves, giving ourselves the time to focus on us and learn methods that help us relax and focus on the moment. My senior year of college, a friend of mine walked up to me with tears in their eyes, and said to me, "Hey Julia, I'm not sure if you remember, but in the beginning of college I went to the school's therapist for the first time. I was so nervous, not sure what to expect as I was struggling. When I entered into the building, I saw you sitting in chairs waiting for your appointment, and for the first time in a while, I told myself, 'I'm not alone. I'm going to be okay.'" You never know when your actions to better yourself are making a mark on others. Sometimes you can simply take care of yourself and influence others more than you or they can ever imagine.

PART 2

'YOU CAN'T DO YOUR OWN LAUNDRY'

"We realize the importance of our voices only when we are silenced."

—MALALA YOUSAFZAI

One of the most daunting tasks for me was doing my own laundry. Why? Because I was afraid of messing up, ruining something, and embarrassing myself.

This obstacle dates back to my youth, when I would scurry around the house finishing chores so I could make paper cell phones or ride on my tiny Razor scooter. Every time I would think about throwing my load of laundry into the wash, I was afraid of shrinking my clothes, overflowing the washing machine, or even turning on hot water when it needed to be cold. There were so many instructions that went along with washing clothes that I had trouble remembering all of the specific details given to me by my parents. "*Always* wash your underwear in hot water! Don't put too many clothes in at one time! Hang dry as much as possible so you won't shrink your only pair of leggings! Do separate loads rather than throwing lights, darks, sheets, towels, and underwear together! Make sure certain loads are with hot water, and others work better with cold!"

With the presence of my anxiety and overthinking, I would seek perfection through my chores. I did not want to make my parents upset, knowing that they were stressed out and I knew my chores were one way to help them relax. But the problem was: I always needed to ask questions.

"What water do I soak my lights in again?"

"Is this considered a light or a dark?"

"Will this pink tint go away?"

"How long should I dry these running shorts?????"

Even if I did my laundry on my own, I still needed to bother my parents. Growing up and going to college in a different state with no car meant doing my laundry at school, and I still needed to ask questions.

It was a habit to Google, call my mom, or consult my friends before I threw a load of laundry in. I did not trust myself and my own judgment, so I had to keep asking for approval before I completed this weekly task.

I started to hop on any leggings or jeans sale available, supplying enough clothing items to last me weeks so I could avoid doing my laundry up at school. I didn't want to look stupid. I didn't want people to keep coming in my dorm room, commenting on how big my pile of laundry was. I didn't want people to look at me when they saw me carrying two full bags of laundry to the car when I would travel back home. But all of the above happened.

People would comment on my laundry saying, "My goodness, you need to do your laundry," or "You *never* do your laundry!" It is a bit hard to justify my anxiousness surrounding the concept of dirty clothes.

First, I strongly dislike doing laundry anyway—sorry to my future family. I'll try my best, promise.

Second, I was anxious about it.

If I would admit this, the common response would be, "Suck it up! It's not a big deal; work on it."

When I was vulnerable, explaining the way I felt to others, I was more often than not shut down. And when we are shut down, our perception is clouded by other people's attitudes. Critical words made me upset because I thought others were upset with me. And when I was in a vulnerable state, I knew from hearing this "negative" word vulnerable, that I would be easily influenced.

We may think something is wrong with us, want approval, or crave acceptance. When these thoughts and fears pop up in our minds, it sure as heck is hard to be our most authentic selves. When we are critiqued for everything we do, judged and hounded, it is sure dang hard to be vulnerable. And we look for other people to give us answers in life.

And that is where the reputation of vulnerability is jaded. Have you ever...

... landed a job for first time, doubting your skills and fearing you wouldn't be able to perform well enough to impress your boss?

... been nervous to speak on stage, sing, perform—afraid you'll mess up and embarrass yourself in front of everyone?

... been in a situation where you wanted to speak up but felt judged by the majority if you used your voice to express your unique opinion?

... changed your actions just to dodge the possibility of judgment from another person?

... filtered what you truly wanted to say because of how others make you feel? When you are feeling at your worst, has someone ever said to you, "Just relax. It's not a big deal," or "You're so dramatic"?

Has someone else made you feel like it was impossible to even show your vulnerable side comfortably in the first place? Is your authentic being, your authentic voice, held back by judgment? We want to pay attention to different perspectives and welcome them into our lives, but what if others don't encourage us to express ourselves?

In Part 1, we first explored personal fears, assumptions, and judgments we throw upon ourselves that hold back our authentic being. In the coming chapters, you will notice how others may talk to us and influence our vulnerability.

You carry messages that you are meant to share with the world. Your unique voice is truly beautiful, whether it's through the way you act, the way you look at the person next to you, or the way you speak. Why are we so afraid to use our voices? Do we have a fear of someone's reaction to what we have to say and what we truly feel?

We must keep in mind that your voice can be greatly influenced by the people around you. We will explore how comments others make to us either hold us back or push us forward to become comfortable with vulnerability.

This is how we can understand others' voices, and how to keep our own voices in the process.

It is difficult to open up when others try to shut you down. Let's talk about that.

So, ask yourself, are you working for others' approval? How can we notice the influence harsh words have on our vulnerability?

This is what laundry means to me: having the strength and courage to step into vulnerability and speak up no matter what others are saying to me. Laundry symbolizes the strength to throw the dirty clothes in the washing machine, washing away my fears, completing the process how I want to do it without the fear and pressure of messing up, relying on other people's reactions to make me feel motivated.

I invite you to step into the pile of laundry in these coming pages, exploring the many challenges that accompany vulnerability, and pick up some tips on how we can influence ourselves and others that we can clean those nasty criticism stains once and for all.

CHAPTER 6

'Calm Down and Let It Go'

———

"This is so hard. I wish that I could just memorize all of the answers," I whispered to myself as I sat by Ms. Lavery, completing a practice test for the annual middle school TerraNova's.

"Wanna see something cool?" Ms. Lavery exclaimed as she moved the answer sheet closer to her side of the table. "I bet that I can memorize all of the answers for one of the test sections in less than twenty seconds."

"No way!" I said, hopping up from my chair.

"Sure can! I've had a photographic memory for as long as I can remember. Count to twenty and tell me when to stop!"

I counted to twenty as I studied her technique. She didn't take her eyes away from the page. *No way could anyone remember that many answer choices!* I thought to myself.

"Stop!" I chirped after 20 seconds.

She quickly looked away from the answer sheet and slid it over to me, making sure that she couldn't see the answers anymore. I peeked up from behind the sheet and cheered, "Ready, GO!"

She quickly named each letter in the exact order on the answer sheet.

"How'd I do?" She said curiously when she finished.

"Perfect! How'd you do that?" I said while looking back and forth at the sheet, trying to memorize the letters myself. *Ms. Lavery is so cool!* I would always think to myself.

"I wish I had that talent!" I said to her.

"You don't need it!" she said to me, handing me my pencil back and turning to a different practice test where the answers weren't already obvious to me. "You can do this!"

The Perfect vs the Realistic

I remember always thinking that teachers had the perfect life. *They know so much!* I would always think as a child. *They know the ins and outs of life! Nothing could go wrong for them!*

Katie Dombroski, whom I always knew as Ms. Lavery, was both my tutor and teacher in middle school. I remember my over-the-top excitement to go to her classes and tutoring sessions every week. She always made me feel capable as a student, especially when I struggled grasping various math concepts. At a young age, I felt that Katie was someone who had my best interest at heart and neither judged nor gave up on me. She inspired me to be myself and always voice my concerns.

Over the last 8+ years since I have seen Katie, I learned that she has been through many ups and downs. Various tragic moments were present in her life such as her dad's passing, her divorce, and losing her job due to the downsizing of the middle school where I met her. She also has many happy moments: she met the love of her life, recently welcomed her baby girl into the world, and began teaching once again at the same middle school.

Although there were many ups and downs, there was one defining moment that stuck with Katie that helps her to help others by encouraging people to use their voices. Let's take a peek into Katie's life through the years.

Katie was diagnosed with panic disorder and anxiety when she was just twenty years old in college. Her father was very ill at that time, and she would constantly experience panic attacks, worried she would come home one day and find her father dead. These distressing thoughts continued over time, and she felt as if no one took her seriously when she was in a panicked state.

She grew with her anxiety and often felt that her panicked feelings controlled her life. To cope with her panic disorder, running was her therapeutic outlet. Hearing the gravel crunch below her feet as she finished each mile encouraged her to continue running to clear her mind. This activity helped her focus, stay positive, and set goals. When thoughts would arise that made her uncomfortable, she would throw on her running shoes and go.

She continued to run through the tough times that came later in her life such as her divorce. She started running so much that she lost over thirty pounds and couldn't keep weight on. She was not eating enough and burning too many calories.

As time progressed, she met her current husband and started to gain a stronger grasp on her happiness. Katie's husband could relate to her struggle with mental illness and knew how to help calm her down any time she experienced any sort of panic attack. He would bring Katie cold cloths to relax, leave any event or activity with her if she was feeling uncomfortable, and ultimately did not try to fix her, assuring her that her struggles were not out of the ordinary.

One thing that I always remembered since I was her student in middle school was that Katie always wanted children. A couple of years into her current marriage, she was pregnant with her baby girl. The majority of her pregnancy, she felt great. She was appreciative and ecstatic for the welcoming of the newest member of her family.

Unfortunately, in the last weeks before the delivery, she experienced pain and discomfort that quickly increased. She took trips to the hospital multiple times to make sure that she and the baby were okay. Katie's heart would race day after day, and she knew she wanted to make sure that the baby was safe at all times. She wanted to be reassured that everything was going to be okay at such a crucial time in her life.

In addition to the pain, Katie feared that her anxiety diagnosis would get in the way of the doctors believing that something was really wrong, and that a serious health problem would go unnoticed. She had a recurring vision that, when anyone at the hospital would type in her name, her panic disorder diagnosis would flash up as if she was forever labeled one way in the system. She feared that once someone saw the words "panic disorder" on the screen or on paper, they'd say, "Oh, it's just in her head." She felt as if she had never been taken seriously in the past, experiencing her fair share of health professionals who tried to contribute anxiety to everything else going on in her life.

Her due date was quickly approaching and the pain in her abdomen continued to worsen.

"How does your pain feel, from one to ten?" doctor after doctor would ask Katie.

"Ten. It's been a ten," Katie would confidently say, hoping that she would finally find out if everything was going to be okay.

When Katie was induced, the hospital had to see if a bed was ready. They asked her over the phone if she could wait and come in the next day. Katie, still in a ton of pain, began to cry, saying, "No, I can't wait!"

She will never forget what the doctor said next, a comment that sticks with her to this day:

"Well, if you're in that much pain, I guess come in." The doctor hung up the phone.

Katie felt deflated and afraid. She tried to tell herself, "If you're in pain, you just go; don't worry about them." She kept worrying that something was wrong. She knew something in her body felt different. She experienced times of panic, feeling as though she was having a heart attack, but another part of her tried to ignore it, feeling as if she was annoying the doctors.

To try and ease the pain herself, she would take a heating pad and lay it on her side. She felt judged and forced herself to stay home. Almost everyone around her thought the pain was all in her head.

The date finally approached when she would meet her baby girl. Although she was once very excited, she arrived at the hospital in loads on pain, with a ton of worries on her mind. She went to the ER two or three times within a month and the doctors told her that she was fine over and over again. In reality, she had a cyst the size of a tennis ball and had to have an emergency C-section. The cyst was so large that she ended up losing her right ovary, losing a part of herself.

Katie reflected on her time in the hospital, saying, "If I had not been afraid or worried what the doctors and nurses thought of me, I may not have had an emergency C-section, followed by a one-hour surgery, losing an ovary."

She was afraid to go back to the ER, afraid that no matter what she was experiencing, she would be told, "You'll be fine; just go home. Understand that you have anxiety. You're a first-time mom—things will get better." She felt ashamed of the way she was feeling, afraid of what others would think of her.

She felt that, when she needed reassurance, she was continually put down or blown off for the way she was feeling. Even though she was certain that she felt uncomfortable and in pain, she started to base her actions on the assumption that every health professional she encountered was judging her. As a result, she forced herself to stay home when she felt uneasy. She felt like she was never taken seriously and that she was annoying the people who were there to help take care of her. She thought everyone was just trying to put a bandaid on her struggles instead of helping her understand herself without shame. Fear took over. "I tell people all the time that I don't want to feel this way when I am in a panic. I cannot control it."

Defined by Diagnosis

Katie is another example of someone who used her voice speak up, explaining to others how she felt, and still was not taken seriously. She spoke up so many times but was continually shut down. She started to hide her feelings, despite the pain running through her body. Even after her daughter was born, there was still fear within her that her voice and the way she was feeling did not matter.

After the delivery, she could not snap out of her worries and truly felt depressed. She struggled for weeks and months to find happiness within herself. She would often cry, thinking, *I have this beautiful baby, home, and family. Why do I feel so sad?*

She would stand in the confines of her shower and cry to let out the feelings she held in her mind every day. She did not know why but she could not leave her house, even to get to the grocery store. Driving petrified her, and her depressed feelings worsened over time.

Her husband quickly encouraged her to get help when she was afraid. With postpartum depression, women do not always have the support necessary to get back on their feet. As time passed by, she started to notice more and more the lessons she learned through the process, the support she had within her family, and the impact her voice can have on the world.

Katie reminds us that the pain we feel is real, whether physical or emotional. "It's okay to feel this way," Katie reflected. "I appreciate every moment someone helps me realize that it's okay and not my fault that I experience panic attacks. Just like someone who has diabetes and has to take insulin, panic disorder is a disability that I have. I am continually learning and practicing ways to work through difficult times in my life."

We may often feel that we must keep our thoughts to ourselves, because we do not want others to label us as crazy or unstable. No one may ever know you are in pain and hurting unless you say something. Many times, we nonverbally communicate how we feel—the way we take care of ourselves, our posture, the expressions on our face. But until someone truly asks us what is wrong, they are assuming how we feel.

When people try to dismiss your feelings, saying, "snap out of it" or "suck it up," we have to remember that feelings of panic or anxiety are neither something we want nor choose to feel. We don't even always know why they're there in the first place. Others may not fully understand what you are going through in the beginning. You may feel stuck. Trapped. Afraid to continue when it looks like there is no clear path ahead. Katie shared her powerful words of encouragement:

> We should not have to be afraid to say how we feel or what we are feeling. Vulnerability should be accepted. If you know something is wrong, fight 'til the end. Do what you need to do. You know your story. If you know something is wrong, your voice is enough to carry that message. You have the right to figure out why you feel the way you feel. You have the right to get the right help. I lost a part of me when I had my baby because I felt that others neither listened to me nor believed me. If you know something is wrong, keep fighting until the end. I personally am becoming more comfortable with myself as I work through the process of

panic. This is who I am, and I am not ashamed of it. She continued, saying, "The doctors knew my diagnosis and chose not to listen to me. It was always the 'what if's going off in my mind that tried to hold me back from consistently moving forward, trying to stop me from embracing my voice. It made me feel like I was going crazy."

She knows that if she had not been afraid to keep going, things could have turned out differently. Opportunities are missed because people see a diagnosis of an anxiety disorder and make a judgment. She leaves us with this message:

Stop trying to put a bandaid on the way people feel. Figure out *why* others are feeling the way they feel. In my case, the hospital is not Disneyland; people do not always want to go there and many cannot afford to stay there. No matter who you are, listen to others, try to get them the help they need. Reach out to a resource that can help, that can provide help to them. No one wants to feel ignored. Neither do I.

It's hard to relate to someone if you have never experienced what they experience. Yes, it sure is hard to understand why someone cannot go outside to get the mail because of depressed feelings shadowing their life. In some people's eyes, anxiety is just another word for drama. But in Katie's eyes, in my eyes, and in the eyes of many others, whatever someone is going through is a real, valid part of their life.

We may feel like our voice has no worth. For example, we live in a world where social media tries to show us worth by numbers. By likes, comments, followers.

One new notification: our voices carries the same worth as the person next to us. Even if our voice reaches one person, it carries more worth than we give ourselves credit for.

Sometimes it's too late to fix the result of a situation, as we see in Katie's example. But when we use our voice to speak out, it can truly help other people, whether they are the patients or the doctors. It can help that doctor to realize how the patient is actually feeling. It gives the doctors a second chance to understand you.

You are not defined by your thoughts. You are not defined by your diagnosis.

If you lose a part of yourself, you're still valuABLE. I used to assume that certain people, such as teachers, lived a perfect life. I used to assume that the people who helped me find myself had already found themselves.

With this new lens for life, not even nine years later, I see Katie even stronger than before, when I thought nothing went wrong in her life. I see her as the influential woman that she is, who can power through anything because she learned from her experiences and chooses to share her voice in hopes of helping others. She allows herself to be vulnerABLE and feel the vulnerability. And you can too.

How Vulnerability Can Inspire

Along with Katie's vulnerability, I want to give an honorable mention to my friend Taylor.

Taylor's vulnerability inspired me from the moment I met her. She's the kind of friend I can disagree with and we move forward with the conversation about each other, learning where we differ and where we stand together. She can express openly to whomever she is around when she is feeling happy, frustrated, annoyed, sad, or confused. Again, just like Katie, I thought Taylor had it all together her whole life. To my surprise, she shared with me multiple times when she felt like she needed to cover up her emotions just to move forward in her life amid the rest of the world.

She bravely said to me, "My relationship with myself was not always stable. I was always in my own head hiding it from the world. I thought I was nuts and felt alone. There are of course certain instances I was afraid of the reactions and repercussions to speak up in multiple situations, and how that would go down because I was not considered important."

Even though Taylor has grown and continues to grow in embracing her vulnerability each day, she describes that "I do feel the urge at times to cover up my anxiety. Especially when I need to have serious talks, interview, or speak in front of a crowd. My jaw immediately starts shaking as I talk. I start shivering even though I am not at all cold, and multiple feelings spread around my body at once."

She taught me an important lesson in vulnerability: "You don't need to say specifics and overshare all of the time because we are all humans." She also described that, when people do not understand our feelings, she does not take them having a chip on their shoulder personally. She just remembers they might not understand.

"It is very empowering to me that I have my own voice and my own opinion and the person I am talking to is going to hear me whether they agree or not." Sticking up for yourself is hard to do, and Taylor improves upon this every single day. She makes it a commitment to stay true to herself, not letting people push her around. "Stand up for yourself and stick up your yourself. That's what my mom always taught me to do at a young age, and it's led me to where I am today. My mom's vulnerability inspires me, and I hope to inspire others."

"I know how it feels to hold stuff in," Taylor said. "I allow people to open up by creating a safe space for vulnerability. I convey to others that I wear my heart on my sleeve. I am human, I am here for you, and I am here to talk about it with you. It makes me feel good that other people feel like they can open up to me and release something that holds them back. I always try to be that person for somebody. I get people to talk to me by setting an example and opening up to them."

"Calm Down and Let It Go." ----------> "Take Time for Yourself to Feel and Recover but Don't Stop Yourself From Taking Action."

Think of a time when you used your voice over and over again and you were rejected. Think of a time you were told to "let it go" or to change paths. What criticism sticks with us and why?

What to expect:

- There is *so much more* to the words, "I feel depressed" or "I feel immense pain." These aren't just words: we can't just push them aside. These are not statements representing one second—rather a prolonged time of pain and suffering that you experienced. When people try to discount your feelings, know you're a damn trooper, because you are not just a statement or a "complaint"; you are improving.

What you can do:

- Whose vulnerability inspires you? Think of them. In other words, whose openness, curiosity, and honest persona inspire you to authentically live your life? Whether it be a parent, friend, teacher, singer, motivational speaker, author, who builds you up and makes you feel confident to spread your passion? Because someone did not just "let something go," what impact did they make?

CHAPTER 7

'You're Too Dramatic'

———

"Julia is perfectly fine."

"There is nothing to be worried about."

"Julia, I think these worries may just be part of your personality."

"You seem fine to me."

"Julia just has anxiety—keep up the therapy and mindfulness."

"People with OCD are affected in severe ways, Julia. It sounds like you just have anxious tendencies."

After thirty – to sixty-minute intake conversations with multiple different doctors and therapists from grade school all the way to my last year of college, somehow my whole life was summed up into one end-all statement: "Julia will be fine."

Years ago, my mom reached out to doctors when she noticed that I would randomly shake throughout the day, as well as make slight noises, and as embarrassing as it once was for me to say, those "slight noises" were swear words. She thought these were considered tics and that I may have Tourette syndrome. She thought I did not notice what was happening, and pointed out every single time I would flinch. After a couple of months with these repeated actions, I was tested for epilepsy.

I never knew what triggered these actions to begin with and could never pinpoint why I felt the need to shake or make a high-pitched squeal. The part I personally found confusing is that I was completely aware every single time I would shake or make a noise. Strange enough, most of these compulsions would happen at home, and only occasionally in front of friends and family members. Thinking back, I tried so hard to hide what I thought were tics when I was in public. If I kept it in long enough, I would have to go to a corner and quickly shake, or try to do it slightly enough that it was not overwhelmingly noticeable.

As time progressed, I fell into the habit of constantly winking. Often, as I was sitting in the passenger seat of the car, all I wanted to do was sleep. Instead, I felt the need to look out the window, blinking one eye every time that we would pass something, whether it was a telephone pole, a sign, or a car. I would turn my head so far toward the window to make sure no one could see how rapidly my eye would wink as the car passed by each mile marker. I never knew why I felt the need to wink, but everyone told me I was fine, so why bother asking over and over again when the answer was already clear?

I started going to a therapist and a psychiatrist in late junior high. My mom would walk into each session with me. We would start the sessions talking a bit with my therapist about what was going on in my life at that time, then would end by learning lessons about what was going through my mind and how I can stay organized and focused as a student. Not long after meeting with my therapist and psychiatrist, I was diagnosed with generalized anxiety disorder (GAD), as well as attention deficit disorder (ADD). I then started my first medication, which was recommended to improve my attention span.

Every morning in my eighth-grade social studies class, my feet would shake uncontrollably and my eyes were wide open. One part of me felt exhausted, but another part of my body felt like it was moving a hundred miles per hour. I remember waking up and having to take a stimulant medication with breakfast before school, as well as multiple over-the-counter medications to help my nervous stomach. At a young age, both my family and I were well aware of my constant stomachaches and anxious feelings.

Other parents would tell my mom that I was not my usual peppy self when taking the medication. Even though I was just entering my teenage years, I knew that something felt off when I took the stimulant each morning. After much trial and error through the years, I was on and off different medications geared toward ADD, GAD, and depression. Some doctors would describe me as stubborn, or not following rules, since I did not feel right taking the stimulant medication.

I constantly felt like I was crazy. I thought this anxiety diagnosis defined my whole being. The minute anyone knew I had anxiety, the rest of my struggles were not taken into consideration. I felt trapped, even when I was speaking out. The obsessions and compulsions I was having—but did not know that is what they were called at the time—affected my everyday life. I wanted to feel understood by the doctors and the people who claimed they could help me but did not even know how to describe what I was experiencing. I lost my trust in many health professionals at a young age due to feeling they did not know me well enough before medication was thrown into my lap that would help me function better even when they would say, "Nothing is really wrong with Julia." I could not comprehend what others thought of me, and most of all, I felt continually misunderstood.

Therapy Through the Years: Misdiagnosis

Click. Click. Click.

My eyes would intently stare at my iPod touch screen at 1 a.m., way past my bedtime on weekday nights before high school classes the next day, as I clicked the home button and the buttons on the side of the screen simultaneously. I was trying to lay down and sleep, but felt the need to screenshot the time, multiple times, before I put my device down on the floor. When listening to music, I would even screenshot the songs to make sure I remembered to listen to them again. My camera roll consisted of thousands of photos, many of them the screenshots. These types of habits started to increase over time. When one habit went away for a while, another would progress. Hundreds upon hundreds of screen shots would live on my camera roll from random times throughout the day and night.

These habits developed into compulsive shopping and long wishlists that I felt a strong need to complete in order to relax. My friends would describe the items in my bedroom as an "eye-spy game." There was clutter everywhere, all the time, and so many people would comment on it the minute they walked into my house.

I then started to fixate on organizing everything in my room, in my academic planner, as well as the thoughts in my head. I went through periods of staying up late and fixing everything that wasn't in its exact place.

My frustration increased when I would work on improving one fixation but yet another one would arise and crash on my life just as hard. But, as always, I tried not to complain to one person too many times because, like I was told through the years, "Julia will be fine; she just has anxiety." I didn't want to make the mistake of talking too much.

My experiences at a young age—attempting to talk about my struggles with others but never feeling like I identified with the actions I was being told to take—moved me into a stage of hiding my feelings and lowering my voice for a number of years.

Over the years, my obsessions seemed more difficult to handle, such as my fear of germs living on every surface, preventing me from even leaving my bed some days. Every time my parents drove away when they would leave the house or drop me off places, I had to say a specific prayer to ensure in my mind that they would be safe. Every time I sat in a car, and every time I prayed, I had to physically do the sign of the cross for it to "count" as a real prayer and ensure I would be loved and safe in my mind.

I never knew that my obsessive thoughts, organizing, and rituals were going to become so hard to handle, let alone thinking I ever had obsessive compulsive disorder. I always put myself down thinking if I spoke more openly about these rituals in the beginning, I would have had an opportunity earlier to know how to cope. I was always quickly told I was "fine" from the get-go, but I knew something felt off in my body.

As I started college and receiving more help for my obsessions and compulsions, I found it even harder to be understood by my peers and people in the media. The infamous assumptions that OCD was just a repetition of cleaning or washing your hands made me feel like I was dramatic and crazy when I would try to talk about my other fixations.

Other people may make it hard to use your voice. Other people may doubt you, and you are on a path of discovery every single day. Some people will try to convince us otherwise when we are in a vulnerable state, desperate for answers, that our own emotions may go unnoticed or overlooked. It's sometimes hard to hold to our word when we are in an emotional state, and other people may notice it or accidentally miss it.

Even though I struggled greatly with my mental health before knowing the proper way to handle my anxious thoughts, I learned different ways to continue and cope with my OCD. I also challenged myself to stop letting OCD define me, and to stop waiting for others' approval to improve.

'You're Ditsy and Annoying'

Remember in the beginning of the book when I said that I was a professional, some may say an expert, in feeling anxious every day in my own life? Well, if that's not already apparent, I'll share some more with ya.

I am a nervous talker. When the room is too silent, I talk and talk and talk, hesitating, stuttering, stumbling upon my words. I am also very outgoing, bouncing all around and giggling at everything I hear. When I am giddy happy-go-lucky, I would ask my boyfriend why he was quieter in social settings, and how he stayed so calm a majority of the time. He turned, looked at me, and said with a smile, "I don't talk a lot because I say only things that I mean."

I admire Michael for being so open and honest, while still recognizing the importance of everyone's voices. He helps me practice appreciating silence vs. talking too much when I feel nervous... when I try to force connection by attempting to find the perfect thing to say to someone else.

It all started with the questions. Whether I am nervous or not, I love to ask questions.

Imagine me in a classroom setting: I've always asked a ton of questions that circulate my mind. My thoughts are scattered a majority of the time, and asking questions helps me buckle down, understand more, and organize my thoughts on a personal level. I asked so many questions, staying after class and attending tutoring sessions throughout grade school and high school to grasp subjects like geometry, algebra, trigonometry, chemistry, history, Spanish, and English. I was always told in my family to "keep asking questions! Everyone learns differently and asking questions helps you understand and apply what you are learning."

Sometimes I asked even more questions than usual because I doubted my own ability to perform well. I felt nervous and as if I always needed approval when completing a math question or writing a passage in a thesis paper. I would ask questions even if I knew the answer, wanting to clarify.

I asked question, after question, after question, until one day one of my teachers said to me, looking frustrated, "Julia, you have to learn to do things on your own. No more questions until you finish." Time after time, I was shut down in certain classes for asking too many questions, making me too scared to ask any more. When I asked more than two questions in a class, I would try and hold my tongue, whether or not I understood the material fully. From time to time, people would crack a smile when I would raise my hand, and other people would call me out, expecting me to have a question when I didn't raise my hand.

In social settings, I would ask questions, even if I knew the answer, because when I would nervously talk, I would frantically search my brain for something to say.

With my nervous talking, outgoing personality, and constant question-asking, I used to be called "ditsy" or "naive." "Airhead" was another common nickname, as well as "klutz," "spacey," and "dumb." When I was looked at as ditsy, I felt weak and unable to recover from being perceived by that word. I was treated dumb before anyone gave me a chance and was afraid to speak up. Many would let the word "ditsy" define me.

Growing up, I was almost always the last to be chosen and made fun of when playing trivia games. And when it came to sports and online games, people would "let" me win.

Once at a birthday party, the partygoers and I were playing a casual game of football. Where football is *not* my personal strong suit, I still wanted to attempt to play. When I finally got a hold of the ball and started to run, I noticed that the other team was hardly blocking me, slowing down and letting me run right through to our designated touch-down line. Keep in mind, I was well into high school at this point and far from gullible when watching people of all ages spread out instead of attempting to grab the ball from me. As I passed some of the players, I heard a slight whisper from one of the two people running behind me, "Go easy on Julia."

One of my biggest pet peeves, which started from a young age, is people letting me win. I always wanted to earn it, and if I lost while doing something will all my effort, I knew I at least tried.

I started to feel completely weighed down by other people's assumptions of me that I gave up and would play into the ditsy persona assumption. I started to believe that I was incapable because I wasn't smart enough for others. I started to act like I didn't know facts when I actually did, afraid that I would mess up if I owned my voice and intellect. I was not aware of this until one day I asked Michael where I can improve in my life to develop as a confident role model for others.

"You do this thing…" he started. "You tend to pretend you're stupid and allow yourself to be the laughingstock of a group. You are fun and outgoing and have an awesome personality, but you don't seem to allow yourself to speak up." I was rejected because of people's assumptions when I was being my true, comfortable, fun self. I was rejected, even in casual scenarios, before I was given the chance. And Michael noticed that I play along with the assumptions by not just laughing them off, but actually feeding into this ditsy label I was given from a young age.

It seemed easier to let other people define me than for me to speak up.

When I heard Michael's words, I reflected back on all of the times I talked nervously, asking questions I already knew the answer to, just so others feel smart and capable. Being perceived as the least experienced, youngest, and dumbest in the group made it incredibly hard to speak out. I started to act ditsy just to fit the stereotype that I felt like I could not back away from.

I was a people-pleaser, not allowing people to listen to the real me, sacrificing myself to be the "dumb entertainment."

Sometimes we rely on others, and think we are less than the rest. Some were shocked when I succeeded and treated me like a child when I did not.

After years and years of buildup, I started to become obsessed with getting good grades and achieving big heights to feel appreciated and nurtured. I wanted to show others I could earn things myself. I made it a goal to hit the dean's list every single semester of college and would completely break down when I got anything less than a A– on an assignment. I was not competing against anyone, rather pushing myself to work hard and have proof to show just so others in my life would change their mind about me.

Sophomore year of college, a friend of mine was walking past me when I was dancing around, talking to people in the hallway, and he looked at me, stopped, and said, "Julia, you're great. Never change."

Those words.

That was one of the very few times in a long time someone complimented my silly persona. Those words snapped me out of it, realizing, *Why do I have to wait for others' approval to be myself? Why can't I just drive myself to do the best I can without pushing myself to these extreme limits? Why am I living my life and not taking myself and the way I feel into account?*

I tended to act ditsy growing up and earned myself a reputation for that. I earned myself a reputation in late junior high for not speaking up. People won't give you a chance to change sometimes. So how do we work past that?

'Who Can Relate?'

Maybe you've felt prejudged or talked down to in your own life, someone constantly labeling you as gullible, ditsy, or incapable. Maybe people do not believe what you have to say, thinking they are always in the right. Maybe people think you are acting too dramatic or annoying when you are your true, authentic self.

Just like we reflected on earlier in the book, have you ever sat in class or a seminar, confused and stressed, wanting to ask a question but feel like you'll look dumb in front of everyone else? You may be that person who asks a ton of questions, or someone who is annoyed by people asking questions. But how do you feel when someone else in the class speaks up and asks that burning question that you want to ask but don't? Do you feel relieved? Thankful? Calm? Inspired to ask next time?

People shut me down for being ditsy, but I show them what I am capable of through action. I don't only talk about vulnerability—I live it. I live being myself and embracing myself. This is real. This is me. This is honesty. I make mistakes, but I am vulnerability. You can be, too.

If I'm stumbling upon my words, anxiously muttering and asking 1,000 questions per hour, it's okay if I don't have the "perfect" words at that moment. Vulnerability takes time, and we have to step up and work to grow in confidence, even if it is a long and uncomfortable process.

Duh, experience comes with time! But everyone's voice holds value. Michael often reminds me, "Don't confuse age with experience. Just because you are younger or treated like you do not matter does not mean you have nothing special to share with others."

From me to you, please never change who you want to be based on someone else's opinion. Like author, blogger, and speaker Rachel Hollis says, "Someone else's opinion of you is none of your business."[36] YOU have something to offer to the world. It's inevitable that someone will doubt us in life, whether that's to protect us, change us, or deceive us.

---

36 Hollis, Rachel. Girl, Wash Your Face: Stop Believing the Lies About Who You Are so You Can Become Who You Were Meant to Be. Nashville, Tennessee: Nelson Books, an imprint of Thomas Nelson, 2018.

People may treat you like your old experiences. They will treat you how they remember you acting in a situation. Keep showing them that you have capabilities. I kept in my feelings to the people who I thought needed to hear it the most; I didn't know how to use emotions, thinking I was abnormal for feeling frustrated, and labeled as ditsy.

One of my other favorite quotes from the movie *She's Out of My League* is when one of the main characters, Stainer, described why he earned that nickname in the first place. When he was a child, he peed his pants and was forever labeled as "stainer." So he said, "I called myself stainer so nobody else could hurt me with it."[37]

Words hurt. We all interpret meanings of the words thrown at us in different ways. How can you embrace your imperfections, without focusing on the past, giving yourself the chance to grow in confidence?

When I feel like I am the underdog, about to give up, thinking no one else notices my worth, Michael would say a quote that I wake up every single morning reminding myself.

When I was about to quit one of my passions as a college upperclassman, Michael said to me, "If you saw someone suffering and you had a special message that could help them, why wouldn't you share it with them? Don't withhold what you were meant to share with the world."

---

37   Smith, Jim Field, Jay Baruchel, Alice Eve, and Mike Vogel. 2017. She's out of my league.

'You're Childish'

Another criticism closely associated with a ditsy personality is when someone calls you childish.

I always connect the word "dramatic" to my childhood. I probably at some point begged my mom to stay up a little later at night, asking my mom to read me just "*one* more story! Or two more stories!! No!!! Three! Can I have some water? Can you grab my doll for me?" Sometimes we act very dramatic and entitled. I definitely was as a child when I would hear the word "no" every second of every day. "Can I have a pony someday? Can I have a phone like all the other kids???" We may throw fits and lose our cool, but we grow and learn over time.

How about when people label us for being dramatic or annoying when we are acting as our most true, authentic self?

I had the opportunity to speak with the wonderful Dr. Jiani Wu, who taught me about embracing our inner child. Dr Wu's business, The 4th Space, helps others channel their creativity through various creative outlets such as painting, filming, crafting, and more. When I asked her what the words "4th space" meant, she described it as the space inside of you born from personal experience.

When we are children, how did we pass time? Did we read? Write? Sing? Volunteer? Act? Dance? Draw? Hang out with friends and family all of the time? Whether we were the world's greatest drawers or the worst? What did we enjoy?

What is still "childish" about us?

As a child, I loved to read, would always start to write silly books, as well as create websites and cell phones with pieces of looseleaf paper. My friend and I created "Club Z," where we made poster advertisements to sell McDonald's toys. We were convinced that we would set up signs outside my house and run the business through my room, allowing strangers to come up and into my family's house to pick from a small selection of trinkets. We knew, even though we had about ten products that were only worth twenty-five cents each, that we would put smiles on a ton of people's faces and somehow profit.

When I was in high school, and teachers asked all of the students what we were interested in when heading off to college, I just knew I wanted to help people. As vague as that sounded, I knew that's what I wanted to do.

Late high school to the middle of college, I was so hung up on wanting to get a job that was prestigious. I was conditioned to believe that if I did not major in business or any of the sciences, I would not succeed.

Today, I write, speak, and create in hopes of spreading positive messages about mental health, self-care, and vulnerability. I majored in communications, channeling my passion for content creation and advertising, which I also loved doing as a child. Little did I know I would major in communications, despite my prior fainting during public speaking classes. When thinking of my major and how happy it makes me, I think back to my childhood when writing and creating were my favorite pastimes. And I think about Dr. Wu's initiative through The 4th Space.

Dr. Wu teaches us how we can reframe the negative connotation of acting "childish" into a positive: "I am reviving my life! The life within me that is begging to be released."

Before Dr. Wu created The 4th Space, she worked in a company doing door-to-door sales. She encountered tough people and dealt with negative reactions when she approached the door of someone who clearly did not want anything to do with anyone who had a promotion to offer. "You expect kindness from other people, and entitlement comes up," she told me. "Even though I felt angry at times, I accepted that I could not control others, but I still needed to use my voice elsewhere. When you are vulnerable, people may be rude to you because maybe they were treated that way when they were vulnerable."

There are people out there who feel the need to always protect their voice as a defense mechanism because one may feel threatened or unsafe when speaking their truth. It may even be you. It sure has been me before.

We make things happen by continually speaking up and showing up. People will shut our voices down, and we have to sit with that and realize that others do not define the worth of our voice. We are shaped over time and our opinions may change, but forcing our beliefs on one another is not an option. No matter how hard anyone tries to bring us down, we will not give up because we believe in ourselves.

I stopped being myself because of my own fears. I halted my progress on passions because of constant rejection. It's always been like a little person in my brain needed to continue growing but was held back by anxious thoughts and critics, when she just wanted to run free like a child.

Dr. Wu shared that "vulnerability is ongoing. It's a gradual process to make a change. I want my values to contribute to this world."

When I was exploring Dr. Wu's content online about The 4th Space, I stumbled across a review that one of the participants posted: "I used to hide my artistic talents, but now I am excited to show them."[38] Dr. Wu helps others find confidence in activities and talents they truly enjoy. Let's think about her mission from a vulnerability standpoint. How will you use your voice to help others find confidence in proclaiming what they truly enjoy?

'You're Looking for Attention'

Put your hand wayyyyyy up in the air if you can relate:

Have you ever been walking with a group of friends, family, coworkers, students, etc., and felt like you were pushed behind the group?

Have you ever been talking in a group and felt constantly interrupted or ignored?

---

38 "The 4th Space". 2019. *The 4Th Space*. https://www.the4th.space/.

Have you ever tried to tell someone something, and they either did not listen or did not believe you?

Have you ever tried to talk to someone about something, and they flip it back on you, using your words against you?

Have you ever felt left out?

Above are all situations in which we may feel ignored, afraid, stuck, or confused.

Sometimes people don't speak out because they think their baggage will be used against them. They think no one will believe the way they feel. They may be afraid they are looked at as annoying, faking, or childish, needing attention and attempting to expose other people.

An example that comes to mind is from one of my favorite childhood book series Lemony Snicket's *A Series of Unfortunate Events*.[39] Recently, Netflix released multiple seasons that take us through each story in the book series in a visually pleasing and captivating manner. To sum up the series in a couple of sentences: three main characters—Violet, Klaus, and Sunny Baudelaire—are orphaned after losing both their parents and their house in a fire. An agency takes them to the house of a "family" member, Count Olaf. When they arrive and meet Count Olaf for the first time, they quickly realize that he is plotting to ruin their lives and steal the family fortune that the three children inherited from their parents. Each time the three Baudelaires escape, Count Olaf disguises

---

39 "A Series Of Unfortunate Events | Netflix Official Site". 2019. *Netflix*. https://www.netflix.com/title/80050008.

himself to find a way back into the children's lives to capture them to steal their fortune once and for all.

In the entirety of the series, the three Baudelaires are very clever and gifted individuals who attempt to prove to others that Count Olaf keeps showing up in their lives, trying to steal their money, and possibly their lives. When watching the series, especially the very last episodes of the third season, I was greatly reminded of the struggles that may accompany vulnerability. Finally, after three long seasons, Count Olaf was put on trial so that they could convict him as a criminal. When the Baudelaires were called to the stand, Count Olaf flipped the switch and started to pull evidence on the Baudelaires of destruction they've caused when trying to escape, so that everyone started to see them as at fault once again. It was bad enough that very few people believed the Baudelaires when they were trying to tell others that Count Olaf is trying to destroy their lives, but then they got blamed by Count Olaf himself as he highlighted every mistake they made.

A Series of Unfortunate Events is an example of people not listening to each other and manipulating others into thinking everything is one person's fault. It is an example of people not taking time to understand others, merely thinking about themselves. It shows the struggle and long process of criticism and adversity.

I deleted so many passages in this book and rewrote them, afraid to write some of my embarrassing stories where you are reading them, right now. I've lost my breath, shook before

I was about to speak, and cried before I had to confront some-one about how I was truly feeling because I was afraid of others' reactions. I was afraid of the exposure that comes with vulnerability.

Do not let anyone tell you that your voice does not mat-ter. Remember when we discussed that you do not have to be someone widely perceived as important to be someone special in this world? I am writing a book right now, and if you ask me for my prior experience, I will not say I have worked in corporate for the last eight years or published seven other novels. I will not be saying right now that I built up an audience of millions on social media. But I will tell you that I overcame the fear of standing on stage, staying in the moment, and finishing what I started. And not only finishing what I started, but staying true to how I feel and being honest with myself and others.

I will say, "I am Julia Ruggiero, and I have a lot of drive and a lot of myself to offer. I love to write, and even though my work is not yet featured in the *New York Times*, I have a message that can help someone. Would you take a listen?"

Experience is important and comes in handy. We learn from it; we often learn from trial and error. But stop doubt-ing your own drive, capability, and experience. We mature and learn over time, and we always have something to offer whether we realize it or not.

Again, always remember: don't withhold what you were meant to share with the world.

Yes, people will try to manipulate us and make us feel less than for our opinions and thoughts. And sometimes it is just a matter of maturity and others recovering from their own life experiences. That's why I am writing this book—to help educate both myself and others that not only our voice matters, but also that of the person next to us too. Just imagine if everyone in the world lived that way!

When watching an interview with actress and model Cara Delevingne, she shared a snippet of her experience with anxiety and depression, highlighting the impact that other voices can have on people's view of themselves. She acknowledged that there are models who "don't stand up for themselves because they feel like they should be used because that's what models do." Cara teaches us that if you are a model, you are also [insert your name here]. You are not a replica of the person before you.

She went on to describe her journey being discovered and plunging into the public atmosphere: "A year into it, I was discovered; I did Burberry and then everybody wants you. You know, after so long I've been like, 'Nobody wants you' suddenly like, 'Oh my God, who is that? You're pretty.' You sure? You didn't want me two minutes ago." It makes people feel that they are defined by a specific moment in their lives, like they need to be on top to be considered a valid person.

She said that it's important to find "people around you who have your best interest at heart." It doesn't matter if one person has ten people like that in their lives, and another has one or two people. "Flaws are the things that make us special The cracks within us are the beautiful parts that need to have light shed on them otherwise they are just left."[40]

When Others Hinder the Confidence in Our Voices

I know in my life, the people who embrace their imperfections are the ones who appear unable to be defeated. When the imperfect human dances like no one is watching and sings like no one else is listening, that's one of the most powerful and impactful moments to experience.

We may not speak up because we don't even think we can or have a place to do so. We may not think anyone will be affected by our messages.

I will share my voice, as dramatically as I want, right here, right now.

Whoever is reading this, thank you. Thank you for helping my dream come to life—you are visibly a part of my dream coming true right now as you read these words. And it was all because I sat at my computer (currently at 1:53 a.m. on a Sunday night) and did not delete these words. I did not hold them back for one more second. Whether you read this in 500 years or 50 days from now, you are reading what is in my heart, and I thank you for that.

---

40 "Cara Delevingne's Powerful Life Advice On Overcoming Depression And Anxiety (MUST WATCH)". 2019. *Youtube*. https://www. youtube.com/watch?v=CfvYlWG1cAo.

To any critics, think what you want. Take my words and run with them in whatever way you please, but when they ask you to explain further, you'll be telling your story, not mine. That's why I am not afraid of putting my voice out there anymore. Because I know my experience, and you know yours. We both have something unique to offer to the world; why shut it down, why cover it up, why push it aside?

And the credibility I needed was to be Julia Ruggiero, at now 1:55 a.m. on a Sunday night, sharing my experiences and thoughts with you.

What message do you believe lies within you that is waiting to be released? How can you impact the world? Proclaim it. Own it. Practice proclaiming it; get used to the sound of your voice. Because you have something special within you, and I do not need to know you for years and years to confidently say that.

"You're Too Dramatic" ----------> "You Show Emotion"

Have you ever doubted yourself, thinking you have lack credibility to help others through sharing your voice and experiences? Have you been labeled dramatic for explaining how you truly feel? Have you been laughed at and shut down just for being yourself? Have you ever been told, "you're so ditsy," "you're being dumb," "you're weak," "you need more experience," or "you're wrong"?

I am clumsy, spacey at times, a nervous talker, and scattered when I lose focus. I am calling attention to my downfalls. I am human, and thus not always perfect. But I am capable, committed, and curious. Do people make you feel less than? How can you reframe the negative comments into something that everyone experiences, that we all feel at times, a lesson we can all benefit from and improve upon? Whose words will you let define *you*? Why? Who says who you are?

What to expect:

- We just need to talk things out. Not talk negatively about others (see: gossiping), not talk down to others, but rather talk things out with the people we need to talk to. We may think texting is easier; we may think avoiding any personal interaction is easier, but over time, it sure gets harder. If you are in a misunderstanding with someone, try to talk it out together and understand each other's perspectives. Yes, it is a hard way of doing it, but it's the only way.

- Just because one person sees one part of you as "ditsy" or "average" or "clumsy" or "annoying" does not mean that is your full self. Just because you are a writer doesn't mean you don't have the capacity to learn math and master history. Because I am considered ditsy, I also look at that as silly, fun, and naturally imperfect. I am a natural at being imperfect, and proclaiming that is one of the most impactful phrases we need to hear!

What you can do:

- If you are anything like me when it comes to nervously talking and not always feeling confident in your own intellect, it can be hard to do tasks on your own. It may make you come across as childish, even though you are still working through our fears and insecurities. One of the best lessons my entrepreneurship professor taught me about asking questions is to ask a question with a solution in mind so that you can discuss actual action plans and goals: "I'll figure it out and ask along the way."

- Think of what makes your approach to vulnerability unique. Are you labeled ditsy? Is one of your strong suits your outgoing and contagiously hyper personality? Call yourself "Stainer" and find a creative way to use those criticisms for good!

- You don't have to pressure yourself to come across as the smartest person in the room. You are always learning, and have something special to learn from everyone. I was so worried about others seeing me as ditsy, when in reality, the more questions I asked and the more thought I put into my work, I was learning more than I ever imagined!

- Reflect on the times you've heard critical comments said to others, or even times you've labeled others as annoying or ditsy. Rather than letting these experiences define you, ask yourself, *How can I grow from these experiences?*

CHAPTER 8

'You're Wrong for Being You'

––––––

"You do not have enough experience."

"Your life isn't as hard as that of the person sitting next to you."

"You are experienced in this but not that, so you have no worth here."

"You are too privileged. You have no worth in the real world."

"You don't have enough resources, so you'll never make it."

"You can never improve."

"I've done this in my lifetime, so I can tell you to do that, not caring about your worth."

"You made this choice."

"You made a mistake."

"You support this side of an argument and not my side."

We can easily mistake all of these statements to an end-all-be-all statement: "I have no worth."

Yes, we have voices of authority in our lives.

Yes, these voices of authority can help us see what benefits our health, safety, and growth.

But what voices are we letting determine our worth?

What voices are we letting influence who we are?

Growing up, my dad always said to me, "You do not need to change schools or jobs or any part of your lifestyle just because someone is not acting in your favor. You will see this everywhere you go. You will encounter barriers, but the trick is to not let them define who you are."

Even though my dad always reminded me of this, it was somehow so hard for me to remember in the most important moments. Sometimes the obvious, the greatest life lessons, can slip our minds when we need them most. And that's why I want to give you this chapter, just in case you forget like me (and every other human that walks this planet).

One example that reminds me of my dad's lessons can be found in one of my favorite movies, *Matilda*, produced by Danny DeVito, based off the novel written by Roald Dahl. My own interpretation of the character Matilda is someone who sees through the bulls***.

Matilda Wormwood is an extraordinarily gifted young individual who is unfortunately mistreated by her parents and brother. Her father is a car salesman who sells what one would call "lemons"—aka defective vehicles—which Matilda knows is wrong. When she tries to confront her dad and ask why he sells cars knowing they are defective, she is immediately shut down.

Matilda: This is illegal.

Mr. Wormwood: Do you make money? Do you have a job?

Matilda: No, but don't people need good cars? Can't you sell good cars, Dad?

Mr. Wormwood: Listen you little wiseacre. I'm smart; you're dumb. I'm big; you're little. I'm right; you're wrong. And there's nothing you can do about it.[41]

We talked earlier about how people may perceive someone being vulnerable as someone who can easily be taken advantage of. Matilda teaches us that even if you're smaller than the person next to you, even if you are not as educated as the person across from you, that does not mean you have no worth. Someone else's size, education, or opinion does not always mean you're wrong and that you have no worth.

Through all the obstacles in Matilda's life and all the people who try to hold her back from embracing the intelligent young woman she is, she sets an example for children (and for me, who still watches as an adult) all over the world that, although some people may try to make it seem like you have

---

41 *Matilda*. Directed by Danny DeVito.

absolutely no worth, no matter how many bad examples are set, you can continue to find happiness by powering past the adversity in your life.

There are countless examples in our own lives that tear us apart, big or small, making us feel like we have no chance to move forward.

Let's brainstorm:

- Someone chooses a favorite person within a group and it's not you, and you automatically think you are not enough.
- You get rejected from ten out of ten jobs you applied to, making you think something is wrong with you and that you have no worth.
- Someone breaks up with you and you claim you will never find love again.
- You earn a low grade and believe that mark defines your future worth.
- Someone accomplishes more than you and you direct your anger toward them for taking away your worth.
- Someone copies you and you think that was your last great move.
- Someone critiques your work and you think they are saying that you have no worth.
- That girl/boy doesn't pay attention to you, so you have no worth.
- You were fired from a position.
- You didn't get that raise.

- You were laughed at by the group over there.
- You didn't block the other team's winning goal.
- You are in the middle of a fight with a loved one and now feel like you have no worth.

Especially today, with the overwhelming presence of media, we feel that we are defined by our mistakes. People attempt to define us because of the things that we like and dislike. We are connecting so much on different media platforms but not connecting face to face. Just take a look online at how people treat one another when someone makes a mistake. Take a look at how people treat one another when they disagree on a concept. It is so easy for someone to type behind a screen, "You have no worth." And those four words can do a heck of a lot of damage.

It's easy now to prey on others' vulnerability. It's so easy to miss someone else's voice through all of the clutter. We may not notice someone else's feelings or may not even see our own worth ourselves. When thinking of how my perception of my own worth has affected me throughout my whole life, I can think of many big and small examples.

I remember cheating on a test in my grade school music class. Although I cannot remember what we were tested on, I do remember that insane guilt and shame that accompanied me the minute I walked out of the classroom. Later that day when waiting for the bus, I remember seeing my music teacher standing not too far away. Not being able to hold it in any longer, I burst into tears admitting that I was a cheater—and truly thought I would always be a cheater.

I remember thinking I needed to cheat because I was not prepared enough myself. I did not think I was capable enough. I thought a good grade was what sustained love and acceptance in my life. The feeling after cheating on a test *is not* worth the aftermath; grade school Julia can attest to that.

Thinking about cheating brings my mind back to my senior capstone class. One day in class my professor was talking about the dangers of plagiarism. "I know when a voice changes in a paper," he said to us.

We talked about when people feel the need to use someone else's voices because we are too lazy, or because we feel we are not capable enough to do well ourselves, or when people want to take credit for something they think is genius even though it's not their own. I beg of you to embrace your voice so the person next to you can realize this space is safe for them too. Show up for other people, and they will show up for the rest of the world with you. Let's set an example, together.

**

We live by messages and mantras that we were taught growing up, some that end up holding us back from valuing each other's worth and emotions. For example, there is a stigma surrounding men that they should be tough and suppress emotions because "they are better than that." And that's why I went right to the source. Men.

Are men wrong for being vulnerable? Of course not.

Let's discuss.

David Hatfield gave a TedTalk on men and vulnerability starting off with a powerful short story.[42]

Hatfield was talking with his friend who described a man she was talking to earlier, saying that he was "crying like a baby."

Hatfield immediately asked her, "Wait, how old is he?"

"Thirty-three years old" she replied.

He responded to her by saying, "He wasn't crying like a baby; he was crying like a thirty-three-year-old."

Why do we have to fit a certain image to be vulnerable? Why is it only okay for a baby to cry and not an adult? Why is the concept of speaking up about our true selves such a daunting, scary process?

Have you ever been afraid you would lose a job, a position, an opportunity for showing emotion? For struggling or making mistakes? For going through a rough patch?

I spoke with an author (Brian) and he shared a difficult part of his journey with me—a time his vulnerability was challenged. A week before he graduated from 8th grade and went to a new high school, Brian experienced assault from one of his now former best friends. Over the following decade, he found himself struggling for others to see him apart from his past.

42 "Honoring And Working With Male Vulnerability | David Hatfield | Tedxedmonton". 2019. *Youtube*. https://www.youtube.com/watch?v=rotwI8lSyQo&t=75s.

He found himself losing opportunities after he showed his vulnerable side.

In college, he applied to be a retreat leader and then eventually he applied to be a student coordinator for that same program. In his interview for student coordinator, afraid but willing to be vulnerable, he shared the story of assault. Brian's vulnerability was integral in landing him this great opportunity. Not too long after, Brian was pressured to leave the job because, "he still had emotional work to do before he was ready to continue showing up for others." He described that moment:

> My vulnerability made people think that I was not ready to handle the challenges of the job. My assault was one thing – that taught me not to be vulnerable. This retreat program showed me that maybe I could be vulnerable, and that that was a good thing. I then was open and shared myself with other people. And although most were receptive to my vulnerability, the program's leadership didn't think I was ready and held that against me. The same people that hired me turned around and used my experiences against me because I didn't share myself in the ways that would have wanted me to. I learned that you either withhold your vulnerable side, or leave yourself open for critique. In other words, I had to be strategically vulnerable. I had to use vulnerability in "the right way"

or be told I wasn't ready, whether it be in a passive aggressive way or outright animosity towards me.

At first, he looked at covering up his true self as a simple task because he did not have to worry if he was making himself too open. Brian's fear is common, thinking that when we share parts of ourselves that are difficult to talk about, we may lose opportunities.

A perfect answer for reframing the mindset of not only men, but everyone, sparked when I sat down with my friend Owen Wolf to talk about how we can notice the ABLE in vulnerABLE. He first described to me the stereotypes that have been thrown at him as a man in society. He explained the difficulty men have going against the "strong, powerful, tough, steady" stereotype that follows them day by day, and how he is expected to put up a front and "suck it up and move forward" in times of fear, sadness, and anger. "I tried to play out that I was seamless for a majority of my life," he told me.

He then shared with me these powerful words of wisdom: As a man who shows emotion, people may lose sight on my "toughness," but to me, being tough is standing beside others who feel like they are standing alone. To me, courage is the definition of vulnerability, and I want to relay that to others. Our power is channeled through empowerment. The ability to speak up is within all people—it's just allowing them to see that. When I am vulnerable, I am taking all the glamour out and acknowledging that, 'This is who I am and this is my truest self.' We live in a world where we set these standards for ourselves that are unrealistic. We have so much pressure and so many expectations... deadlines... The more we focus on perfection, the more we crave the experience of simplicity.

When Owen would share his vulnerability, he feared that other people would doubt him. He feared the thoughts others would have about him. Just like Brian, he once felt that he was not allowed to show his vulnerable side to succeed in all areas of his life. He ended by saying:

As humans, we all share similar baggage yet we are all so embarrassed about it. We don't always have to 'fix' ourselves. You need to constantly care for yourself, but do not need to look at everything as a fix. Life happens. ... You have the capability, tools, and resources. We don't have to take every positive thing in our lives and crush it. We tend to follow our negative thoughts. We just need to channel that inner courage to quiet that negative voice. We let that voice tell us we are screwed up and wrong. The power that you have through your words and actions will multiply. Grow with the courage and make sure you pay it forward and passing it on. Once we let our guard down, we see that everyone is in a similar boat.

Let's not associate vulnerability with gender. Let's not shut one another down for struggling. Let's let other people speak, and speak life into one another.

**

When thinking of people I look up to who speak life into me, I immediately think of Leslie Sansone. In college I had the pleasure of working alongside Leslie, the creator of Walk at Home, a well-known fitness program geared toward simply walking for an effective workout. When I met Leslie for the first time, I was instantly intrigued by her positivity and infectious energy. If I could share with you every single word that ever came out of Leslie's mouth, I would, because that woman inspires the heck out of me. One of the best lessons she ever taught me was that when we don't believe in ourselves, we are acting just like the critics, but to ourselves. She said to me, "Criticism can hurt. We *cannot* pretend it doesn't hurt. It does. All criticism takes you steps backwards. Eventually, it just stops you if you let it define you. Now I realize that I am fine with people's viewpoints: it's just not my view. It's okay if their criticism is directed at me. People are not always trying to be mean-spirited—it's just their opinion. They may be trying to express something."

Leslie has been a thought leader in the fitness industry for years, but before her passions developed into the success they have today, she encountered her own barriers to creating the now sensation Walk at Home. She described how some of the people closest to her in her life did not agree with the path that she was taking to start her own business.

For example, one day Leslie and her mom were discussing her education options after she graduated from high school. "I just finished four years of excellent grades in mechanical drawing and she hoped I would be heading into architecture. My mom then blurted out, 'Aerobics is stupid!'" Leslie recalled.

She described that "the woman who loved me the most, my mother, told me aerobics was stupid. She didn't know that comment could set me back! She did not mean to hurt me! She wanted to see me reach my potential, and had a different viewpoint than I did. I knew she loved me, and I did not forget that." All criticism can give us an uncomfortable feeling inside, confusion, and sometimes what feels like a sting to the heart. But Leslie teaches us that we can decide what we are going to do about it with her words: "I was not going to let someone else's views or perception hold me back from helping others understand what I want for myself and others."

Another amazing influence in my life is Stephanie Martin, a successful entrepreneur and a wonderful role model. When Stephanie and I were discussing entrepreneurship, criticisms, and advancing in your career, she highlighted the importance of realizing that we have to make the most out of the present, not always waiting for happiness in the future or dwelling on the past.

She taught me the power of the statement: "New level, new devil." She said to me, "When we reach a new milestone we think everything is going to be better, but there are new challenges we have to work through every day." Every decision leads to more decisions. Every advancement brings new challenges. I personally had this expectation throughout my life that people who are happiest in life always feel perfectly content and experience no pain, sadness, or inconveniences.

She continued, saying, "The amateur thinks that fear will leave in time. The professional knows that it won't; they lace up their shoes, and are ready for the challenge. You have to believe in yourself more than other people do. When you speak up, people will likely try to tear you down."

She then said to me, "I heard Tony Robbins speak and he told the audience that he has 30,000 working for him right now. Ten are probably upset at him. He proceeded to say that there will always be one human being who is upset at you for no given reason or who does not align with your beliefs. I almost did what they wanted me to do: hide. But that's the last thing we should be doing."

Make the most out of your now; make the most out of your experiences, because no matter where we are in life, there is always room for other opinions.

No, I'm not advising you to sit on your bum for the rest of your life and claim "I'm right" in every scenario. I am rallying for you to keep fighting hard for what you want and staying true to who you are. When we fail to speak life into others, as well as ourselves, we are missing a ton of potential. How are others, our close friends and family, making us feel? Are we making those around us feel like they have to be a certain way to have worth?

What to expect

- One of the most powerful practices that we can allow into our lives is patience with and for others. I frequently wear a bracelet that says patience. I write the word on sticky notes around my room and set reminders on my phone to stay patient. It's hard as heck to remember that darn, freaking concept. Patience is imperative when someone is trying to make you feel like you have no worth. Just know that when you stand by your word and stay true to who you are, you are paving a path for others to feel stronger in their fight to be who they want to be.

- "It is hard but essential to face the wounds within," Kiyomi LaFleur once told me. Sometimes people's comments toward us can hit us in a way we never expected. Sometimes the words said to us can make us assume that we have no worth. Don't be afraid to clean out those wounds and commit to healing.

- Owen Wolf shared this beautiful reminder that I want to pass along: "Stay aware that some days might not be the best, but every day does not need to be terrible."

What you can do

- One of my favorite ways to learn about someone new is to ask them their unpopular opinion. This was a popular school icebreaker that I personally did not mind taking part in. When you meet someone and don't know where to start, spark a conversation by asking them their unpopular opinion. Owen likes hot sauce (specifically

Frank's Red Hot Sauce) on his peanut butter sandwiches. Find the fun in your differences. Find the fun in the strange. Maybe you'll even find a commonality? This is a great way to realize that each and every one of us has something unique about us that makes us happy. And instead of making our own assumptions about people, let them show you the unexpected sides of themselves.

- Notice: do you make statements about or to other people that may make them feel like they are not, as Rachel Hollis puts it, "made for more"?[43] Do you assume people do not have worth because of their gender, race, viewpoints sexuality, experiences, and the like? Yes, others may say these things about us, *but* we have control over how we take action in our lives. If we can set an example for others, we will actively play a part in working past any judgment that tries to cloud our views of one another.

---

43   Hollis, Dave and Rachel Hollis. *Made for More*. Documentary. Directed by Jack Noble. 2018.

PART 3

'WE THOUGHT THAT LOVE WAS PERFECT'

"A calm sea does not make a skilled sailor."

—MY FAVORITE FORTUNE COOKIE QUOTE

Love.

That word is even more confusing than vulnerability, isn't it?

What does love feel like? What are relationships supposed to be like? Is this feeling normal? What about this feeling?

What am I supposed to think when I love someone? Why does that couple look so darn happy? What does love for a family member or friend feel like vs. love in a romantic relationship?

Love has taught me a majority of what I know about vulnerability, growth, and connection.

Love taught me that honesty strengthens trust between two people.

Love taught me to listen to others and to appreciate the cycle of connection.

Let me first ask you: what does love mean to you?

How do you want to be loved, and how do you love others?

How do you spread love?

How do you talk about love?

What does love look like in your life with your family? Friends? Romantic relationship(s)?

There are countless meanings for the word "love": pleasure, excitement, desire, intimacy, appreciation, infatuation, idolization...

I always imagined love as this constant feeling of excitement, bliss, and attraction. We throw this word around so much, that the meaning of love expands even further.

"I love Dairy Queen!" "I love the show *Deal or No Deal!*"

"I love my parents and siblings."

"I love you so much. You're the first person I've ever loved."

"I love you, pal!"

Hold up—what the heck does love mean if I love Dairy Queen *and* my parents *and* my boyfriend?! I mean, I like the items on the menu at Dairy Queen but am I excited to eat them all of the time? Am I always in the mood for their ice cream and meals? What about my parents? Do I have to be infatuated with my parents to love them? Ew!!!

Okay, so what about my boyfriend? Does he have to meet all of the criteria of love? Should I feel constant pleasure, excitement, and desire around him?

AHHHHHHHHHH!

I always thought love had completely different definitions. If you look up the word love in the dictionary, you'll find a ton of different specificities and variations. Love can be based on aspects like sexual desire, admiration, and affection.

Growing up, I always wanted to know:

How do I know if I am really "in love"?

How do I know when someone loves me?

How do I know how to open myself up to the unknown in a relationship?

How do you express love to people? Even parents and friends?

These questions were challenged to the extreme throughout my 7+ year relationship with my boyfriend.

He and I met when we were just thirteen years old.

Both he and I formed a close relationship with one another and both of our families and extended families. Every time a holiday would roll around, my excitement would burst off the walls knowing that I would help his family decorate their house, and he would get to come see all my cousins with me.

Truly, everything felt perfect in the beginning. The recipe for love was right there in front of me: infatuation, excitement, pleasure, desire, appreciation—everything under the sun.

As the years passed by, we were closer than ever before, forming holiday traditions, joining each other on small and large family trips, and visiting each other as we departed to different colleges in different states.

He treated me well and accepted me for my flaws. He loved me and accepted me despite my strong OCD flare-ups that would create a large dent in my sanity. I remember sitting in front of the mirror for hours, crying over the phone thinking that the cold sore on my skin was contagious and that I would never be allowed to kiss Michael again. I remember panicking and telling my mom that I thought I was pregnant because of a missed period, when there was *absolutely no way* pregnancy was possible (I constantly searched symptoms to check, but hey, at least I found some of my favorite family YouTubers because of it). I obsessed over daily stomachaches, thinking that I caught the stomach flu. Michael noticed a pattern, and started to think of cute ways to calm me down when I was in a panic. Instead of stopping, dropping, and rolling away when my OCD started to affect my happiness, he continued to stay with me and calm me down even more than ever before.

When I complained almost every single day about my nausea and fear of the stomach flu, he never once told me to stop talking but rather encouraged me to throw away complaining and take action. He remembered that his mom used to try and "cure" his stomachaches when he was little by "pulling the stomachache out of his stomach." When I was nauseated and in the middle of a straight panic attack, no matter where we were, Michael would look me in the eyes, ask me to place his hand where I felt discomfort in my stomach, and he pretended to pull the stomachache out of me. "Julia, look here," he would say, directing my panicked, fidgety face to stare at his. "Do you feel the strings pulling? Do you feel the nausea going away? Don't worry; I will keep pulling it out until you feel better."

We grew up together, experienced so much hand in hand, and both changed drastically as the years passed by.

Over time, the severity of my stomachaches died down.

The fear of an infected cold sore died down (thank God).

Other OCD flare-ups died down.

Despite some small bumps in the road, our relationship was straight out of a storybook for years. Until my obsessions and compulsions started to target what made me the happiest and most comfortable in life: my relationship with Michael.

And my comfort with vulnerability in the relationship flew right out the window. It was not until this breakdown that I was introduced to the power of love and community. I never understood love like I do now.

**

Let's review: so far, we talked about lettuce: how we talk to ourselves.

Then we talked about laundry, focusing on how others talk to us, how we internalize these messages, and respond.

Now, we are going to talk about how we talk to each other and open our eyes to how we can inspire together, and how to work our differences out with one another.

Sometimes it is dang hard to love and accept ourselves and others. It's hard to be honest with yourself, and especially hard to share that honesty with others. By now, we know it is at times terrifying to be open and honest, even when we are afraid.

One concept that society feeds more and more into is talking *at* others instead of *with* them. How do we collectively collaborate and connect with one another, even when we have differing opinions and differing experiences?

Before separation, encourage collaboration.

By focusing on how love can bring our voices together, a community of people has the opportunity to create a beautiful impact on the world with the tools we learned throughout this book. Truly understanding and embracing love is how we come together and find true connection in vulnerability.

CHAPTER 9

'We Can Talk About This'

Getting stuck in an obsessive cycle is like you're paused in a movie, not able to move forward, lagging every other minute. It's like a scratch on a DVD: not always all-consuming, but it can make a big dent in the efficiency and productivity of finishing the story. And it's pretty hard to get that scratch to disappear. How can we keep the disk moving, despite the scratches and barriers that stick with us?

My own movie was paused for years. Every time I started to move forward, I would get caught in a web of obsessive thoughts that felt like they consumed my whole being. I was defining myself by my wounds, feeling guilty and always making something wrong in situations where I felt happy. I started to follow my obsessions, acting impulsive, not able to tell what thoughts were my anxiety and what were not.

Have you ever *really* wanted to do something, like an upcoming vacation or concert that you've been waiting for? And do you think to yourself, *I hope nothing goes wrong ... I hope I don't get sick ... I hope this doesn't happen ...* and so on? And worst of all, sometimes you *actually get sick.* I have stressed so much that I was confined to my bed all day long, missing school dances, meetings, and movies because I would actually convince myself I was on my deathbed.

It even happens in small situations. For example, I kinda like shoe shopping, but kinda hate it at the same time. I found a pair of super cheap, cuuuuuute white boots and felt so confident when I wore them. Too bad every time I left my room with the shoes I was constantly freaking out, knowing that I could spill something and "ruin" the shoes in one second. And guess what? Even though I freaked out trying so hard to prevent stains, lo and behold, my shoes are not perfectly white anymore.

But I digress—let's get back to relationships and love.

I especially feel anxious in regards to the parts of my life that I hold dearest to my heart.

"I am not sure what I am feeling," I said over the phone to my friend. "My relationship is everything that I ever thought I wanted, and my boyfriend is my best friend. He makes me incredibly happy. But for some reason—well, for no reason at all that I can pinpoint—I cannot remember what that excitement feels like. I feel off, confused ... maybe bored? I guess I need to end the relationship for this to be fair to him and myself. I am so young, I shouldn't feel this way if I really love someone. My depression is probably because of my relationship."

I sat in bed, crying my eyes out, trying to process why I suddenly had a burst of feelings of confusion and change in my relationship. "Am I just falling out of love? Wait, did I ever really love him?" I would ask others. "Please help me, I do not want to break up with my boyfriend, but I may want to. But I also may not want to. Agh! I don't know!"

When these words would come out of my mouth, my friends and family were confused. Some would laugh, expressing how ridiculous I sounded. "If you loved him, you would know," some would say. "Love is easy; you'll know it when you have it!"

That triggered me like crazy.

Well, I guess that means I should end the relationship. So many people, mainstream culture, movies, and the like suggest that the spark should never die. So many people told me that high school sweethearts are rare and don't often last until marriage. I have to be sure this is what I want, I would tell myself.

I started checking. I started checking my vision of the past and vision for the future every second that I could. I was sabotaging myself, not allowing myself to feel happy, always trying to find something wrong in the best parts of my life.

I started to replay past events and interactions from our relationship over and over again in my head.

I started trying to imagine myself with other people, checking in on my feelings to see if that's what I really wanted.

I was coming across articles that listed "bad signs of a relationship that is falling apart," and "reasons you should leave your significant other if you are acting or feeling this way."

I would space out in the middle of my everyday tasks, or lay in bed for hours, panicking. I lost my appetite as the checking increased. One moment, I would think of something that calmed me down, and the next moment, something I read online or heard in a song triggered me to think about my relationship again. It felt like someone was pushing me constantly on the back of the head, a pressure that was difficult to explain to the people surrounding me.

When I first started to think my sadness was caused by unhappiness in my relationship, people would look at me like I was going crazy, saying, "Julia, you two are probably just drifting apart. You just need to make a decision. Break up with him and explore your other options."

Others would say, "Julia, if you and Michael break up, I will lose all hope of finding love later in life. You two are perfect together!"

All of the opinions and my spiraling thoughts made me feel like I had lost control of a vehicle, and I was constantly falling down a hill that was never-ending, and there was no way out. I felt responsible for other people, not only my boyfriend, but also for pleasing the people around me. My decision was not "my decision" anymore.

The thoughts continued:

What if I have feelings for someone else?

When I think someone else is attractive, does that mean I should break up with Michael?

I started drifting apart from Michael, scared to hang out with him and feeling numb when I would think about us breaking up. I was afraid that I would have to make a decision to leave or stay. Both sounded absolutely terrifying.

I had no clue how to tell him what was going on.

I started to come to multiple conclusions about our relationship that started to make sense in my head.

I must be falling for someone else, I thought to myself.

I hated lying, so I had to tell Michael the truth. But I could not find the right time to do it. So I waited and tried to cover it up, hoping the anxieties would go away.

At the same time, all I wanted to do was talk to Michael at the end of the day. All I wanted was to stop feeling anxious, and let this all blow over.

**

One day, Michael and I were out to eat, waiting for our orders. Michael kept looking up at me, flashing a big smile and complimenting me, making jokes, and having a great time. When we received our food, I couldn't even focus on our conversation.

Why do I not feel like smiling back? Shouldn't I have to smile when someone looks at me lovingly? I thought to myself, looking away. I was critiquing every single movement I made, expecting that I had to always feel a certain way around Michael.

"Jul?" He said as his smile dropped. He could tell that my mind wasn't in the right place.

I started to feel overwhelmed and afraid.

He kept looking at me, trying to make eye contact. "You don't want to be with me anymore, do you?" I heard him say.

My heart sank and my mind started to hop from thought to thought: *This is the end, isn't it? But I don't want it to be, do I? I must be falling for someone else if I am feeling this way. Or maybe I have some kind of disorder that makes me feel no emotion? Come on, Julia! Keep checking until you find an answer!*

The most random and unsettling thoughts would pop up, and my anxious thoughts were spiraling so fast that I couldn't speak.

Our waitress came up to the table checking on how we liked our food, even though we'd both only taken three bites.

"Can we have to-go boxes?" Michael said as I pushed my plate to the side and fidgeted with my hands.

The next couple of weeks were difficult. After seven years of minimal drama, fun memories, and fantastic experiences, I couldn't process why I was doubting myself and it was so hard to put my feelings into words. Maybe seven years is too long—maybe I needed to experience life more. Michael and I would try and talk things out as I kept coming up with new fixations and realizations about our relationship.

When I realized I loved Michael and was happy, I would try to find a new scenario that would drive me back to questioning my feelings.

Michael respected my feelings but noticed that over the years, I would stay fixated on certain thoughts, making myself so anxious that I couldn't leave my bed or focus on my daily tasks. Although during this time I was just starting more intensive therapy for OCD, he noticed the patterns of my anxious thoughts arising day by day. "Julia, I really think this may be an anxious thought," he would say.

Selective Attention

What is something that makes you insanely anxious? Where does your attention focus when you are stressed and upset? Selective attention is described when tons and tons of stimuli are bombarding us at once but we are only paying attention to one aspect of life.[44] When we overanalyze, focus too much on something that makes us feel anxious, we are selecting one stimuli to turn our attention to.

For me in my relationship, I started to try and find things that were going wrong, rather than appreciating anything

---

44 Cherry, Kendra. "How We Use Selective Attention To Filter Information And Focus". 2019. *Verywell Mind*. https://www.verywellmind.com/what-is-selective-attention-2795022.

that was going right. There would be people talking around me, cars passing by, dogs barking, music playing, and smells from food circulating the air, and I would still only focus on ONE nagging, anxious thought that would pop up. These thoughts would then evolve, and I continued to tell myself story after story. My habits started to morph into me. My focus felt out of my control.

Let's go back to my germaphobia for example. My friend and I were both drinking cups of water when we were out to dinner with our friends. Somehow, we switched cups and I started to drink out of hers. After I realized what I did, I would focus on everything that signaled sickness. Any time my friend coughed, any time I coughed, any time someone around me would talk about being sick—I was reminded of drinking from my friend's drink. And I was reminded of my intense fear of germs, coming to the conclusion that I would wake up the next day sick.

In my relationship, when I started to obsess over thinking I wasn't in love with Michael, every time I would see a picture of a couple or hear a love song on the radio I took everything as a sign: a sign I had to break up with him. But as my anxious thoughts evolved over time, my attention would shift, new triggers arising.

I used to hardcore panic, shake, and cry when I heard the song, "Happier" by Marshmello ft. Bastille.[45] Now, it's

45 "Marshmello Ft. Bastille – Happier (Official Lyric Video). " 2019. *Youtube*. https://www.youtube.com/watch?v=RE87rQkXdNw.

a song I can jam to in my underwear (sorry for that visual). But seriously, I would shake, cry, and panic when I would hear this song playing, especially if I was alone. But now, the fear has no more power over me. I once kept trying to look for "signs," directing me toward the decision to or not to break up with Michael. Song lyrics, certain words, TV shows, almost anything triggered me because I would try to interpret every single spoken word as a sign.

Reassurance Seeking

I previously did not know many ways to cope with my racing thoughts other than deep breathing and listening to ocean sounds.

"I really think I am just falling out of love," I would say to myself. I kept Google searching every possible scenario that I could think of, desperate to find some kind of answer or sign to lead me the right way. I thought so far into my fears that I started to believe that I had multiple personality disorders, and that my hormones were completely off. I went in to get blood tests at my doctor's office because of how tired I was day by day, obsessing that I had mono or Lyme disease. My anxieties were so extreme that I would sleep to try and make the pain go away, but from the moment my eyes opened to the moment I tried to fall asleep, my mind would not slow down.

There were no red flags in the relationship, and I truly looked forward to every time I hung out with Michael. But if I was feeling anything less than excited, there had to be something wrong, right?

Google gave me a bunch of answers:

These feelings most likely mean he is your best friend, and you don't actually have a romantic connection with him.

If your emotional or physical connection dwindles, your relationship is doomed.

Don't use your significant other while you are trying to make a decision.

Don't stay in a relationship you are questioning; you're wasting time.

Don't settle.

If you are in a relationship with your high school sweetheart, it probably won't last. You need to experience the world while you're young.

Then I found answers on the other end of the spectrum encouraging me: "Don't give up! Relationships are not always easy."

I started to ask anyone and everyone for advice. My obsessive thoughts would become so hard to control that I had to tell anyone who I was with what was going on, and that was embarrassing, being vulnerable about these thoughts I did not even understand. I would intentionally hide myself in my room, pretending I was asleep when family was over, I would try to put off hanging out with friends until I had at least some grip on my clarity.

It even got to the point when I decided to break up with Michael, try to take a break, try to ignore my phone. It was like my brain was bullying me into not wanting something I wanted, a healthy part of my life that made me giddy. One part of me wanted the relationship, but another part was finding reasons from years ago to now that may mean I am not in love anymore.

"Why can't we try working on it together?" Michael once said. "I am not disappointed in you; I feel like this is anxiety, Julia," he would tell me. Through the years, my anxieties and fixations got worse when it came to germaphobia and other fears, and Michael noticed many patterns of me convincing myself that something was wrong, believing the stories, and breaking down over and over again. But I always persuaded myself that my new fixation was the worst fixation, being that it is so hard to tell what is anxiety and what's not.

"First, I feel guilty putting you through my struggles. You do not deserve to deal with my craziness. And second, if we work on it together, that means I will have to face my anxiety, expose myself to my anxiety. It might just be better to heal and go on my own to figure life out," I said.

When I was around my boyfriend, it was as if my anxiety was standing right in front of me. I felt forced to face it every second.

My anxiety was bullying me. And I could not tell what was reality and what was not.

I was great at making up stories in my head. Brené Brown famously says in her Netflix show, *The Call to Courage*, "What is the story we are telling ourselves?"[46] How are the stories we tell ourselves making us feel? How are the stories we tell ourselves formed in our heads? Why do we need to write the end of our story just to be satisfied?

I tend to look for signs and clarity from God and any sign from the universe when we should just say, "This is enough."

I will say, "God, can this happen so I know the answer?"

I had to keep reminding myself when it comes to anxiety, "It got frustrating before I got better."

We Don't Have All the Answers

One day, I was obsessively Googling, looking for reassurance that I wasn't putting my partner through he**, instead of just talking about it with him.

After weeks of making this my usual routine, I stumbled across a video about relationship obsessive thoughts by Kiyomi LaFleur. It was as if Kiyomi was taking the words out of my mouth as she described her experience thinking she had to leave her partner because "she felt like something was off" or that "she was lying to herself" and having immense fears and obsessions about her relationship. Not only did Kiyomi talk about this, but there was a community with hundreds

---

46 "Brené Brown: The Call To Courage. https://www.netflix.com/title/81010166.

of others who shared that they were experiencing the same thoughts that were causing them great distress.

Many may argue that when we feel doubt in any situation, we should leave. We should leave a situation and stop trying. Although there are most definitely examples where this is true, I was becoming more and more aware of my history with obsessions and how I missed living a lot of my happiest life because I gave in to doubt. I believed my anxiety, not myself, and did not know I sometimes have to think a little differently to work around my anxiety. With the help of therapy and Kiyomi, I learned how to keep going, how to learn the real meaning of love, the reality of love in not only my relationship with my boyfriend, but all of my relationships.

Michael and I both made a choice to grow past the anxiety, to embrace the uncertainty. Heck *yes*, it's nerve-wracking writing this, because who knows where I will be in my life when you are reading this book? Who knows what is going to happen in the relationship? Will we push through and be stronger than we were before, something I did not think was possible when everything was going "perfectly"? But that's the beauty of life—we do not know what will happen tomorrow. I learned from Kiyomi that forever is an "illusion of control." Today will be the good old days, whether we are twenty-one or seventy-one. If we are still here in ten years, we will look back and realize that this moment, right now, is a comforting moment. Even if you are feeling your worst. You right now, with your hands wrapped around this book, feeling each page as it turns, looking at the movement of each page—this is a moment you may want back ten years down the line.

Learning about relationship obsessions, as well as learning more about my diagnosis with OCD, helped me realize that feelings come and go. Learning and working through the pain and uncertainty made me realize I am not crazy, and I am strong enough to fight.

People will also tell me to walk away and take time for myself if I really love someone or something. If we listened to all of these suggestions that are thrown at us in life, we just may very well feel crazy. When I decided to listen to myself for the first time, to be honest with my boyfriend about how I was feeling and let both me and him make our own individual choices, we both wanted to fight, even though that time in our lives was not easy for either one of us. We may be crazy for trying to work things out, and we may be crazy if we ended things.

I am learning day by day to sit with uncertainty despite the discomfort. This applies to all areas of my life, such as with friendships, career paths, schools, and a variety of other decisions. Ange Peters, founder of Holfit, a wellness community, explained on her podcast that we are scared to trust ourselves because it is easier to involve others.[47] It is easier to blame other people when we are in a dilemma. I personally

---

47   Peters, Ange. HOL:FIT Talks. Podcast.

struggled for a long time, and still do find myself struggling with trusting myself and my own decisions.

In therapy, I am frequently reminded that we all have a little circuit missing in our thoughts—it is different for many, but admitting our struggles is the good part, to build connection with yourself and others.

Kiyomi opened my eyes to the inevitable challenges that have the ability to arise when we commit to something. Kiyomi taught me to notice my thoughts as thoughts, that feelings are okay, and that there are many other people in this with us together.

Kiyomi taught me that it's okay to be different.

She taught me that patience and recovery are not a straight line.

She taught me that we are not defined by our past.

She taught me that to meet our needs in a relationship, we also have to show the other person we love them too.

These were all concepts that slipped my mind in times of crisis.

I am learning to appreciate the stimuli around me, what I can hear, taste, smell, and see. Focusing on the body pulls us into the present moment. I had to tell myself that it's okay that I am taking a different route rather than what it seems everyone else is doing.

In all seriousness, though, I swear I used to think love was perfect. I swear everything in love was certain. Now, I understand the *real* power in wedding vows. "For richer or poorer ... in sickness and in health ... 'til death do us part."[48] I know more and more what unconditional love means. No conditions. No, it's not *only* that excitement you get when you meet someone new or share a new experience with them. It's not about the perfect pictures or the perfect vacation or the constant attraction. Love is a commitment, a choice to keep that commitment, and a constant journey that evolves.

My therapist told me, "People change over time, their looks, their attitudes, their experiences, their views—but one thing I will always appreciate is the man my husband is." These words of encouragement help me navigate relationships with family, friends, and passerbys.

For the first time in my life, I finally understood the spectrum of deep, unconditional love.

Understanding Love

My dad and I were talking about how he felt due to his recent cancer diagnosis. He said to me on the way home from school, "My diagnosis has made me a lot happier in some ways—you appreciate every single second. I feel so good right now; I appreciate these moments." This made me think. How do some of the toughest times bring some of the greatest realizations?

---

48 "Traditional Wedding Vows From Various Religions". 2019. *Theknot.Com*. https://www.theknot.com/content/traditional-wedding-vows-from-various-religions.

In Kiyomi's book, *You Are Not Alone: The ROCD Journey*, she writes: "No matter what you read online, no matter what you hear … know this: There is hope, dear reader, there is hope."[49]

Because of my downfall with Michael, my understanding of love, appreciation, vulnerability, and connection clicked more than it ever had before. I learned that most of all, love is vulnerability. That moment when you can leave knowing that your vulnerability won't be used for deceit or critics, that honesty but compassion and understanding and acceptance and encouragement are what we should be looking for. In one of my favorite quotes from the movie *Titanic* (hey Leo), Jack says to Rose: "Rose, you're no picnic. You're a spoiled little brat even. But under that, you are the most amazingly, astounding, wonderful girl—woman —that I've ever known."[50] Although the movie shows a couple that falls for each other pretty darn fast, this quote is one that touches my heart when I think about my newly found discovery of love. There are imperfect parts to everyone. There are struggles within every relationship, and unconditional love is when each person sees past the imperfections, loving and accepting every part of each other. Jack does not have to love the fact that Rose acts spoiled, but he does not define her as that one imperfection.

---

49 LaFleur, Kiyomi. 2019. You Are Not Alone: The ROCD Journey.
50 Heart of the Ocean: The Making of 'Titanic'. (1997). [DVD] United States: Ed W. Marsh.

My dad would say to me, "Some guys may come up and sweep you away with their good looks and charm, but don't look out for that. Look for the person they are, not just what they look like."

You may look at someone sitting on the bench next to you, and for no reason at all, feel a sense of annoyance toward them. You may become so annoyed with your parents, siblings, significant other, friends, teachers, doctors, passerbys. You may feel extreme anger and frustration, even with yourself. You also may look at people with extreme compassion and love. One day, you may feel a mix of emotions that range from annoyance, to anger, to happiness. This will happen. And it's okay to feel. The power sparks one by one before it flickers on when you work to ignite that passion and light back into even the darkest times.

You will appreciate the beauty of others. People try to critique our feelings when every single situation is different, but we all have similar thought patterns at times, especially with things that mean a lot to us.

I went through a period of relationship-based obsessive thoughts for a long while, and when I started to work on it, the healing process started to take charge. Obsessions come back one after another, one by one, testing the surface when I buried them down before. But they have to resurface for me to show them that I can still swim. If we gave up every time we had a doubt, we would probably be sitting in our rooms. When we care about something the most, we tend to shut down our own voices and feelings.

People all over the internet—even some people I knew were professionals in various fields—try to say that there are only "certain" thoughts someone can have. There are so many answers out there, and no matter what a critic may say or their opinion, I will listen, but not let that take over *my* decision-making. Kiyomi then reminded me, "There is a spectrum to severe and not severe obsessions, but just because you have less than another, does not mean you are any less important. It's fluctuating all the time. There is so much to your life, there is so much to OCD, there is so much to anxiety and doubt—you don't have to be checked off of every box to know your answer and know your future. You have the power inside it takes to work through the feelings that you are afraid are holding you back from enjoying life."

We can talk about this. We can talk about how we are feeling with others. We do not have to take every suggestion, conform to every opinion, or think we are wrong for choosing our own path.

One of my favorite Brené Brown quotes is: "If you're not in the arena getting your butt kicked too, I'm not interested in your feedback." People may give you biased advice. Listen to the words of others but do not let them define you. "You will get your ass kicked," Brené continues to say. If we go into that arena, we cannot avoid critics. Some people will give us constructive criticism and engaging feedback. Others will just try to knock us down. Brené goes on to describe how when people are in the cheap seats "not putting yourself on the line and talking about how I can do it better, I am in no way interested in your feedback."[51] When I see vulnerability, when I see someone standing in the arena. I see life. I notice life. I notice the struggle, pain, the beauty—everything in between the cracks of a person. I see someone actually living. You know when you are reaching your hand so far behind a couch cushion that you find that lucky penny? But you may also find that melted chocolate that completely stained your white sweater. Although there is the "gross" and the "ugly," there is also the possibility of the ten-dollar bill at the bottom of the couch cushion. Bringing back a quote from *She's Out of My League*: "All it takes is one."[52] It takes one person to start a movement toward working through the rough patches and growing in unconditional love. Will it be you?

Sometimes people get taken advantage of and shut down. Sometimes people attempt to take our voices away from us, but one situation does not define all. Keep using your voice, even when you may try to take your own away from fear. It does not have to be the decision; it can be you admitting you feel a certain way and want to understand why, allowing

51 Brown, Brené. *Rising Strong*. First edition. New York: Spiegel & Grau, an imprint of Random House, 2015.Smith, Jim Field, Jay Baruchel, Alice Eve, and Mike Vogel. 2017. She's out of my league.

52 Smith, Jim Field, Jay Baruchel, Alice Eve, and Mike Vogel. 2017. She's out of my league.

yourself to go through the process of sitting with the discomfort of your own fears projected onto yourself.

Again, from my business ethics book that reminds me of advice my therapist gave me: "What are you willing to give up if you can't have it all?" Something to think about.

We CAN Talk About This

Let's review: what does a vulnerable relationship look like?

It can look and feel passionate, comfortable, confusing, painful, and hard. It is a relationship of accepting not only those perfections we love about the other, but also those annoying downfalls that we try so hard to repress in our everyday lives.

My boyfriend grew to understand me when I looked him in the eye and expressed my confusion, thinking this person or that person is attractive. He did react, and he was shocked. There was hurt, and confusion, but instead of criticism and blame, he said to me, "I'm not blind. I see beauty in other people, too." We were able to relate. He knew the emotions I was experiencing were human emotions and feelings that have an ebb and flow.

Like Jack says in *Titanic*: "When you got nothing, you got nothing to lose."[53] Why did I work on strengthening my relationship? Why did I refuse to give up? I was

_____

53 Heart of the Ocean: The Making of 'Titanic'. (1997). [DVD] United States: Ed W. Marsh.

pushing away the things that actually made me happy for a life I thought was perfect all around the clock. Because I knew that I had something, and I let that go unappreciated. I was always looking for "the next best thing." Sometimes relationships fall apart with friends, family members, and our significant others. Sometimes we really do lose sight of the feelings we had and find a stronger connection elsewhere. But just because someone else breaks up with their boyfriend or decided to stay in the relationship does not mean that defines your relationship.

Michael used to think my anxiety wasn't real. I used to think about myself way more than others. We both realized we have a long way to progress to understand each other, and we make it work. Because no matter what happens with me and our relationship down the line, I know that no time is wasted, but my time moving forward is something that strengthened me and that I truly appreciate.

No matter what happened at the end of the story with me and my boyfriend, and no matter what happens with us in the future, it does not define *you* and *your* experiences. The stories we tell will evolve in the future. What someone chose or chooses to do is not something you have to do. Me telling you my story right here right now is not suggesting that my experiences were navigated in the right or wrong way. Trust me, I've stumbled across thousands upon thousands of opinions about the story I just told when doing my "Googling research" and will no doubt encounter more suggestions in my life that may set me into a panic. I've shared my experiences here to show you that I am a person who has an outlook on life but am not forcing it upon you, but rather explaining how I experienced a form of unconditional love and appreciation at a dark point in my life. And how vulnerability lead me to feel more and more comfort talking about the darkness in my life, how it helped me and others understand the way I am feeling at points in time.

I wanted to puke while writing this, my mind thinking, *What about the future? What if my story changes and this advice evolves? How can I best control what is going to happen in the future so I am perfect and please everyone?* But here I am, being ABLE. I am typing past the feeling of puke, not letting my fear get in the way of holding down the delete button. Heck, it hurts—it hurts in my stomach, my legs, my head. But something is keeping me writing. Oh wait, that's me writing, buried somewhere deep in my worries and insecurities. The love and acceptance I have for myself and sharing my reality with others are emerging, even though it can feel uncomfortable.

Hey, wait, that's right—this is me and my life right now. This is my reality. And loving myself can be difficult at times, especially with the presence of shame and guilt tapping me on the back as I write. But love is a commitment, love is unconditional, and just like Kiyomi taught me, we are made to fall in love over and over again, every day.

What to expect:

- How do we spark change when someone may feel upset in the end? Not everyone will like what you have to say. For example, not everyone will like this book. You may not agree or relate to everything in these pages, but what I am asking you to do is notice it, and what you want other people to hear is to notice you and your feelings. Jennifer Antkowiak would often bring up the coffee analogy at our mentoring meetings. She would pretend to be a barista passing coffee around to everyone at the table. "Do you want coffee?" She would ask everyone. If someone said no, she would move to the next person and offer them some coffee. Not every human likes every single item, service, or concept there is to offer on this planet. Not everyone is going to like what another has to say. Even if you love the same color as another and have the same personality traits, there will more than likely be myriad areas of life you two have different views on. Even though we are similar, don't forget that we are all different in many ways, and this can feel extremely freeing and reassuring, to know we don't always have to do everything another person does. You are discovering and learning each day. You do not have to follow something that someone else is forcing you to believe.

- A friend may not answer your calls or text messages when they are upset. A family member may say something harsh they later regret. A healthy relationship does not mean everything is perfect, but when both parties are committed to working through the tough times before fleeing, there is room for growth, and bringing your attention back to that love over and over again.

What you can do:

- Now that we know that everyone has their own opinions and experiences, let's talk! Let's disagree and broaden our knowledge. I was always curious when my professors would play devil's advocate, whether they agreed with the students' perspectives or not. They wanted us to expand our minds and think further into something we claimed to agree with. When I decided to think differently and learn about the possibility of staying when my situation was tough, I learned so much about myself and others along the way.

- Kiyomi says at the end of her videos, "Here is to being human." Simply realize that you are human and the person next to you is human with a whole collection of life experiences. They feel; you feel.

- When you want to talk with someone else in a high-stress situation and are not sure what to say, start by asking, "What can I do right now for you that will help?"

- A friend once told me: "You'll figure it out." All those questions I was asking were leading me to an answer. Figuring out myself and always staying curious are what got me into this mess, and exactly what will get me out of the laundry basket clean, just like us as imperfect beings.

- Who is your Kiyomi? Try this by thinking of a friend, a family member, a mentor. Even try this with someone you don't fancy as much. What have they taught you? Separate it into positives and negatives, and reflect on how they have influenced your life.

CHAPTER 10

'We Can Listen'

———

My eyes were closed as I took a long deep breath in and out, holding my friend's hand. "Julia, I heard you were great at editing videos; you would be phenomenal as one of our media specialists!" I heard a voice say from the other side of the room.

It was after 2 a.m. on a Wednesday night. Sixteen individuals and I were sitting in a dimly lit room in front of a large chalkboard, deciding on who would take what position for an upcoming retreat that my college campus ministry program hosted. Each of us had class the next morning and were itching to crawl back to our rooms and hop into our beds.

Before 2 a.m. hit, fifteen out of the seventeen people sitting in the room had their positions figured out, except for my friend and me. We both wanted to give a talk to the retreatants on a designated topic, and there was one open spot left. We both had held this vision of being on the talk team for a long time, before the retreat ever started, making it a position we both truly wanted to share with the retreatants from the bottom of our hearts. We squeezed each other's hands once more as we came to the conclusion that I would be a media specialist and she would give a talk to the retreatants.

As much as I wish I did not feel this way, I walked back to my room that night deflated and frustrated, thinking that I sold myself short when trying to advocate for myself to be a talker on the retreat. I was afraid that I would not make an impact by being a media specialist. I was afraid that my voice did not have worth. I was upset because I did not get what I wanted. And I was battling my mind, wanting more than anything to be happy for my friend and stop thinking about myself.

Week after week before the retreat, the whole team would meet to prepare our roles. I tried my best to put on a brave face and accept that I was in a role I did not plan for.

Why can't I stop thinking about this darn position? Why am I so upset that I did not get what I wanted? Julia, stop! Be happy for the rest of the team!

When the retreat approached, I was filled with over-the-top excitement to be at the retreat house with the rest of the team and excited to meet all of the retreatants. I was having the time of my life, and we were so busy that I forgot that I was ever upset. The first night passed, and after a whooping two hours of sleep, we were up and ready in the morning for a new day. I was sprinting around with my media specialist partner, taking pictures and videos of the day, capturing all the emotions on each of the retreatants' faces as the hours passed.

Later in the day, it came time for my fellow team member to give her talk to everyone. I was excited to hear her speak, but as I set my camera down and stood in the room before her talk started, I immediately felt a wave of sadness.

This is so hard to say. My goodness. I can admit I sucked my gosh-darn thumb a majority of my life but these next three words I am about to type have been deleted over and over again:

I felt jealous. Envious.

I was making something that was a beautiful opportunity for someone else all about me. I was fearing that, because I was not in the role that I wanted, I was worthless. I wanted so badly to help other people embrace their vulnerability, thinking that I would never get the opportunity to again because I did not get the position I hoped for. I was letting this position define my worth.

I tried hard to deny that I was feeling jealous. I knew better than to let this jealousy get in the way of someone else's experience, but I kept refusing to admit that I was even jealous in the first place.

When she started speaking, I sat down and took a deep breath, trying my best to clear my mind. Immediately, she drew me in to the talk. Again, I forgot I was even upset in the first place, taking in each and every word she spoke. By the end of the talk, I was completely floored. Not only did she understand the topic she spoke on in the most profound and beautiful way possible, but her strength to share her story with the group so openly spoke volumes. The minute her talk ended, I was soaked in tears, feeling so much gratitude that I had the opportunity to hear her speak.

To say her talk affected my life in an immense way would be an understatement. When it was my cue to capture the scene and I raised the camera back up to my eye, I saw the reactions of the retreatants. Many of the students sitting in that room were wiping away tears, closing their eyes while extending their hands, or smiling from ear to ear at my friend as she ended her talk. I thought to myself, *I am so thankful the retreatants got to experience her voice. I am so thankful that I had the pleasure to hear her speak. I wouldn't have wanted it any other way.*

Right when I thought that my ego was taking over my whole entire body, I let my ears do the work, and my goodness I am thankful that I chose to listen. I am so grateful I chose to listen to the talk instead of only listening to my thoughts.

**

Why is it so hard to admit when we are jealous?

How will we be looked at if others knew when we felt jealous? How will we be viewed if people knew we felt insecure in some areas of our lives, if not all?

Think about a student receiving an A+ grade in the hardest class, while you are teetering on a C-? What about someone reaching a new fitness goal as you sit on your phone under your covers seething with anger, wanting to look like the person staring back at you in the photo?

All too often we don't reach our full potential because we think others have it better than we do, and only one person is allowed to be at the top.

All too often we bind ourselves to the confines of other people's opinions of us.

We spend more time complaining than working through any adversity, even if it's you projecting it on to yourself.

We may focus our time on worries about what other people think of us.

And when we feel most vulnerable—when we are authentically ourselves—people can try to one-up us.

People can try to take advantage of us.

People can go over the top making us look bad in front of a large crowd, our loved ones, and the like.

People can turn against us and push us away.

People can use our words against us.

These are all risks of living life the way we want to.

We start to care so much about what others think. We try to channel and force our inner authenticity so much that we lose track of our sanity, taking on so much in our lives and trying to be the best at it. We start to fake smiles instead of giving away real, genuine happiness. We start to gossip, and others start to spread things. We keep tabs on everything, wasting time looking at other people rather than working on ourselves, our teamwork, and individual improvement. We think fulfillment comes on this narrow definition of success. When we reach the top, we feel exhausted and frustrated, nitpicking instead of taking a moment to realize how far we've come!

We try to control everything possible to keep an image we think deems us worthy.

Everything above is a risk factor of not standing up to our own jealousy. Jealousy is inevitable. We just need to keep our patience and not let the jealousy turn us into someone we don't want to be.

**

Many people believe the words *jealousy* and *envy* do not have different meanings, but for those who do, let's explain how people view them differently.

Feelings of jealousy arise when you have something of value you think someone else will take. Envy, on the other hand, points toward wanting something you don't have that someone else does.[54]

---

54 "Jealous Vs. Envious". 2019. *Merriam-Webster.Com*. https://www. merriam-webster.com/words-at-play/jealous-vs-envious.

These feelings have the opportunity to arise when we see someone else doing something that we too want to do, and this type of thinking leads to a scarcity mindset. When in a scarcity mindset, we think that there are not enough resources—love, approval, connection, whatever it is you're looking for—to go around for everyone. For example, what may first seem like healthy competition between two people or groups of individuals can turn into sadness, anger, selfishness, and frustration with yourself and others.

Feelings of envy and jealousy can also prove frustrating, especially when another party is actually trying to get under your skin.

Do people brag, obviously pointing out how you do not have as much as them?

Do you feel unlucky?

Do you feel like no one is paying attention to you and what makes you happy?

In times of envy and jealousy in my own life, I would feel immediate pressure to create something that would gain approval, in return reminding me that I did have worth. I would put pressure on myself and assume I had to be a certain way to be accepted by a person or group. Again, just as Kiyomi said, I was "shoulding" on myself, thinking I *should* feel and act a certain way to be considered normal. But there are so many definitions of normal. There are so many ways people think we "should" be.

We may start to question ourselves, asking why we cannot be as talented as someone else, even though we already have the capability. We get stuck in a cycle of comparison.

Are we doing things for the right reasons? Why are we watching the other cars pass by, letting these feelings be one of the main reasons we are not moving forward? It's almost as if you are constantly keeping your eyes on the other car on the right or left side of you, instead of the road in front of you. Are you looking backward, toward your past, not paying attention to the present and learning how to improve despite the twists and turns? Or are you looking back at people behind you, spending your time flaunting what you have instead of spreading the excitement of your changing the world for the better?

The more you live in your authenticity, the more you embrace your talents and passions, the harder you will hit a gas pedal in your life somewhere on the road. When you finally pass over what seems like a never-ending hill of hard work, critics, barriers, and whatever else is thrown in your path, you will hit this moment of happiness for everything you've completed.

Years ago I read the book *Girl Code* by Cara Alwill Leyba, and always think about this book when I consider my journey with feelings of jealousy and envy. Yes, throughout the course of my life I've heard time and time again to stay true to yourself, and was made aware of the dangers of the actions a person could take in times of feeling jealous or envious—but reading Cara's book really sparked a motivation within me to become more aware of when envy arises in my mind. She talks about the inevitability of envy and how we can shift feelings of envy to act as an inspiration for ourselves, not as something to one-up one another or fall into the scarcity mindset.

I want to share with you one of my favorite passages in the book:

> Psychologists have identified two very distinct kinds of envy: malicious and benign. Malicious envy is bitter, resentful, and nasty, driven by a need to make things equal, even if that means bringing another person down. On the other hand, benign envy has an aspirational aspect—it often causes you to think to yourself, 'If she can do it, perhaps I can, too.'[55]

Cara's positive spin on envy reminds me of a conversation I had with Mary Hyatt, one of the most empowering women I've ever had the opportunity of speaking with. Both Mary and I were discussing what happens when we question if we are worthy, special, and loved. Mary explained to me:

> Can you accept that part of you that feels jealous? Can you accept the part of you that wants and needs that validation? Without saying 'I shouldn't need that validation' or 'I shouldn't need to want to feel special.'

55 Alwill Leyba, Cara. 2017. Girl Code : Unlocking the Secrets to Success, Sanity, and Happiness for the Female Entrepreneur. Penguin Group USA 2017.

Guess what? You want to feel special! You want feel value! You want to feel worthy! That is okay. You can work on believing the statements, 'I feel special,' 'I am worthy,' 'I am loved.' But could you radically accept even the parts of you that you might judge as not super healthy? Do you have it within you to say, 'It's okay. I'm human. I'm allowed to want some attention.' The acknowledgment and awareness when you are feeling envious or jealous to me is the key from preventing selfish actions from happening.

You may not want someone to see you as a jealous individual, thinking you'll be labeled that way for the rest of your life, like these words make an imprint on our whole being. With the presence of social media, there are lots of ways to try to cover up the way we are feeling, and lots of opportunities for comparison. Hyatt explained how she decided to take a long break from her social media account, and shared a great example how our ego can try to get in the way of our choices:

I gotta be honest: I am glad I got off of social media, but I really miss people liking my stuff. I feel like I never get any validation anymore. I feel so lonely now. My ego is really upset and not sure what to do about it! My soul is saying, *This break is great; you're being so present in your life!* But I am also part ego, and my ego is saying that this break sucks. I'm occasionally thinking, *Does anyone see me? Am*

I important? Does anyone care about me anymore? Has anyone forgotten about me? It's a big step when we are willing to admit that those feelings are okay.

This whole information session you just read through is to let you know that it is, in fact, normal to experience feelings of jealousy and envy at times. Yes, these feelings can affect our actions if we let them. Awareness is key, as is not letting shame get in the way and thinking it is bad to feel jealous or envious. We must accept that it's just a feeling that has the opportunity to arise no matter how mature we are, a defense mechanism for when we feel unworthy or afraid, and that we are stronger than these feelings.

Jealousy and envy can arise before we actually listen to a person, hear their story, what lights them up, what makes their hearts fall, and how they overcome adversity. Let's vow to not let these feelings get in the way of us listening and connecting to one another, because the more we learn about each other, the more we realize we are all imperfect and working through our own struggles, even if some seem smaller than others.

To quote Cara once again, she says, "Her success is not your failure."[56] Just because someone else feels good doesn't mean you can't. But let's think about why we can feel happy for the person who is achieving what we wish to achieve.

---

56 Alwill Leyba, Cara. 2017. Girl Code : Unlocking the Secrets to Success, Sanity, and Happiness for the Female Entrepreneur. Penguin Group USA 2017.

Think about it: why wouldn't the person next to us be working to be the best they can be? Sometimes it's hard to realize that while yes, some people do just want to one-up one another, there are some people who truly aspire to achieve their goals without approval from others. Let's continue to ask ourselves, *Why wouldn't people be living the best they can? Why wouldn't the person next to me want to reach their goals? Why do I let the feelings of anger, jealousy, and frustration take over actions when other people reach their potential?*

If we find that strength in our hearts to be someone who cheers for the person who got what we want, and keep moving and making new opportunities for ourselves and others, we will start to have an impact and offer an example to spread compassion and snap out of the scarcity mindset.

**

What can happen when we move past our own fear and jealousy and work hard on ourselves while still developing that care and happiness for others? Let's take a trip to somewhere near 34th Street.

One of my favorite holiday movies is the 1947 (original, babyyyyyy!) version of *Miracle on 34th Street*, and a specific scene brings a smile to my face every single time I watch it. Let's set the scene at the Macy's department store. The head of the toy department at Macy's approaches the newly hired Santa Claus, who is getting ready to meet the children and families standing in line to tell Santa their Christmas wishes. The head of the toy department advises Kris Kringle, the real name in the movie of the newly hired Santa (ironic, right? I'll let you figure that one out by advising you to watch the movie), to suggest specific toys from the list of overstocked items in Macy's to the kids who do not know what they want for Christmas. Kringle is appalled that someone would suggest to sell kids toys they do not actually want.

Later in the day, a little boy named Peter sits upon Kris Kringle's lap and explains how he wants a new fire engine for Christmas. His mom whispers in the background to Kris that no one, not even Macy's, has the toy fire engine that Peter wants. Kringle looks at Peter, disregarding what the mom says, assuring him that he would in fact receive his fire engine for Christmas. The mom angrily approaches Kringle after the child steps to the side, asking him why in the world he would ever make a promise that he could not keep.

Kris immediately replies, "You don't think I would have said that unless I was sure, don't you?"[57] He proceeds to explain how there is another store close by that has the exact item she wants, price and all.

Confused and shocked, she looks at him and says, "Macy's, sending people to other stores? Are you kidding me?"

He looks at her and says, "The only important thing is to make the children happy. Whether Macy or somebody else sells the toy doesn't make any difference." Kringle continues

---

57   Gwenn, Edmund, Natalie Wood, Maureen O'Hara, John Payne, and George Seaton. 1947. Miracle on 34th Street. Los Angeles, CA: Fox-Video, Inc.

to honestly recommend to other children and their families the best places to find the highest quality products if he knows that Macy's did not have the best options for what they wanted.

The scene then flashes back to the head of the toy department, who overheard Kringle recommending different stores to the customers instead of just Macy's products. He immediately tenses up in anger and confusion.

Peter's mom sees the head of the toy department and runs up to him, expressing how impressed she is that a Macy's employee would recommend another store with the product she wants to make her child happy. She states, "Imagine, a big outlet like Macy's putting the spirit of Christmas ahead of the commercial. It's wonderful." She then said she would now be a regular customer at Macy's.

The head of the toy department tries to process what is happening, even though Macy's is receiving wonderful reviews. He is afraid the owner of Macy's will not approve, as he stressfully continues to contemplate what to do.

Even though the head of the toy department was still struggling with honesty and pleasing his boss, Kringle's act of kindness and truthfulness helped build trust between the customers and Macy's. Let's revisit the quote Kringle said to Peter's mother: "Whether Macy or somebody else sells the toy doesn't make any difference." Kringle recommended multiple families in the movie products they could find of higher quality, not wanting to benefit himself but rather the families. This scene made me ask myself, *Can I overlook my own ego and offer the truth even if it does not benefit me?* Of course I can!

Another example of a story that has been an inspiration in my life comes from Rachel Hollis' book, *Girl, Wash Your Face*. Hollis shares a story from her trip to San Francisco to watch her friends run a half-marathon. She writes: "What I do not like—what I had never actually done—is cheering for others while they do something I am fully capable of doing right along with them. I kept thinking, *What if I didn't need to prove myself in this situation? What if making myself into someone better has more to do with my willingness to be of service than my willingness to compete?*" She then explains how she asked herself, "Imagine all of the things you would have missed today if you'd only been here for yourself."[58]

Hollis writes, "The first step toward getting past the desire to judge and compete with one another is admitting that nobody is immune." Remember when we talked about how no one is immune to new experiences? Remember how we talked about how feeling jealous or envious is not abnormal? Let's all come together and realize that each of us is imperfect, and if we listen to one another, we can surprisingly learn much more than we can if we just assume answers ourselves.

---

58   Hollis, Rachel. Girl, Wash Your Face: Stop Believing the Lies About Who You Are so You Can Become Who You Were Meant to Be. Nashville, Tennessee: Nelson Books, an imprint of Thomas Nelson, 2018.

Looking AND Listening

Let's discuss another distraction apart from jealousy that can get in the way of humans listening to one another.

Imagine yourself walking down the sidewalk on a breezy fall afternoon, wearing a light jacket with a deep pocket that carries your wallet, phone, and some chapstick. You hear the change in your wallet clanking at each step you take and feel the chapstick lightly jabbing into your waist. You are taking in the sounds of cars passing by and the murmur of light conversations as you look at the trees, clouds, and street signs and continue forward. You're appreciating each moment. As you snap back in to reality when you have to watch for cars to cross the street, you take a look around and see multiple people pass you by, looking down at their phones, listening to music through their headphones, and holding the phone up to their ear while looking at their feet as they walk and talk. There is one person on the other side of the road whom you begin to pass by as you both cross to opposite sides of the street. Right when you are about to pass, you and the person walking past both make eye contact for a split second, and before even offering a light smile or a genuine hello to one another, you find your hand reaching into your pocket to quickly pull out your phone, examining the screen for any missed calls or texts. By the time you look back up, you've crossed the street and made your way a little bit down the sidewalk, avoiding any human interaction or connection.

Does this sound like you? If you're like me and have trouble admitting it, let's move to blaming others.

Does it sound like someone you know?

Okay, just kidding. Let's not blame others—but in all seriousness, of course it sounds like you! Of course it sounds like me!

In all honesty, I have my days when I want to ignore the world. Especially when I am in a rush. There are times when I pretend to be on my phone just to avoid interaction instead of being honest with the people who pass by, notifying an acquaintance that I have somewhere to be if we stop to talk. Even if it is just for a small moment passing someone, it is truly important to appreciate the presence of ourselves and each other day by day, not letting our worries or anxieties always ruin the moment, and especially not letting media and devices sever human connection.

Many of us tend to avoid interaction in our daily lives, even when simply walking down the sidewalk. We create habits of avoiding situations that we aren't in the mood for by looking at our devices or creating a wall with some sort of tangible object. It's not that we want to avoid anyone and everyone, but we get used to the "norms" of technology, and over time, the habit created a comfortability in the way we go about our daily lives. Our comfort away from consistent interaction may even spark high anxiety in social situations.

For example, think of two people standing in an elevator. Let's say there are twenty floors and the elevator is moving pretty darn slow. The two people may have a slight conversation on the way up, hoping it ends soon, not only because they do not feel like conversing—they feel awkward, as if the conversation is forced. They worry about what to say next. They feel like they have to act a certain way, they make assumptions about the person based on their mood, and they bring the other events of their day into it, affecting their mood toward the other person.

Because we consistently reject human interaction, we are rejecting the pure, emotional connection we can create with someone face to face. We start to feel awkward when interacting with humans without a device in our hand to fidget with, hoping again and again that our phone rings just so we can flee an awkward situation. Constantly looking at our devices, always wearing headphones, and avoiding eye contact are all walls we put up that prevent us from stepping toward connection.

Have you ever suffered from secondhand embarrassment? The feeling when you see a situation happening to other people that makes you uncomfortable? Even if it's when you watch a cheesy scene in a movie, when someone forgets their speech in front of an audience, or when you have to sit through an awkward situation on the public transportation system where other people can see your reaction. Sometimes we just look away because we cringe. You know that secondhand embarrassment where it is so hard to watch?

One of the most powerful moves we can make is preventing ourselves from constantly blocking the awkward feelings and actually looking at each other. For example, my college had less than 3,500 undergrad students on our campus. I could never walk to class without seeing at least one person I knew. The campus was small, so I always waited until five minutes before the class to walk to class. But the problem was that we pass about thirty minutes of conversation as we rush to the classroom. There were so many times when I had just rolled out of bed and was still squinting from the sunlight, not wanting to talk to anyone before having to sit in a room for over an hour learning at 8 a.m. But I would tell myself, "I don't always need to avoid making a connection. Interacting could put me and someone else in a better mood!"

Even when I wanted to look down at the ground so badly when I saw someone I kind of knew from class but did not know if they would say hi back, I would force myself to look up and say hello, whether they reacted or not. I did this so many times that I actually looked forward to putting away my phone for my walk to class. I started to feel comfortable and not guilty when I told someone I had to get to class if they would stop to talk when I was about to be late.

These little healthy habits I formed helped me own my voice even in small situations, as well as connect with others on a daily basis. I learned not to constantly turn away from hard moments, big or small. Heck yes I still turn away at times and I cringe when I see a super cheesy love scene in a movie. But even if I turn away, I am now aware and know that I have a choice. I more often than not choose not to be quick to turn away before I try to sit with an uncomfortable feeling, to find the good in a situation. Think of how many people we can make smile, and how many people would make us smile, with a simple and genuine hello, a real acknowledgement.

Sometimes I am truly on my phone while walking sending a last-minute email or text that I should have sent when I was laying in my bed watching Netflix. Sometimes I am studying a screenshot of my notes before an exam, trying to take in every last detail of my studies. Sometimes I want to listen to music while on a stroll, or want to pump myself up before class with an upbeat song. But when I am not in the mood to talk to anyone, that's when I challenge myself to talk to others. I notice that when I'm not looking at my phone all the time. And I am getting used to it.

When We Screw Up When Attempting to Listen to Others (Because It's Inevitable)

Yup, jealousy and comparison can try to get in the way of listening to someone.

Assumptions can get in the way of listening to someone.

Trying to fix each other can get in the way of listening to someone.

And so can simply talking over people, not giving each other the patience and chance to speak.

I've come a long way embracing my vulnerable side. But I still suck at it sometimes.

And I finally figured out the big secret: that's totally normal. Shocker!

As I write a book on vulnerability, I openly endorse the practices that I tend to misplace in my mind from time to time.

Lights! Camera! Cue the authentic example:

Let's set the scene. One night, as my boyfriend and I were sitting in the car heading to see Christmas lights, you'd have thought the car ride would be magical and filled with excitement as we sung holiday tunes and held hands, but I was being a little pain in the you-know-what.

"Let's talk!" I said excitedly, hopping around, jamming to music. Michael, being a lot calmer than I am, had a slight smile on his face listening to the music and focusing on the road. "We are talking!" he said, his famous line every time I ask to engage in more conversation.

"Why aren't you peppy like me right now?" I said as my face moved to a pout.

After a second, we started to briefly talk about something, and I asked him another question.

He stopped for a moment, and my focus was all over the place, as I was still excited from all the Christmas festivities. He did not answer, and I pouted more, saying, "Hey!!! I asked you a question!"

He looked at me and smiled, saying, "Julia, I am thinking! Take a page out of your own book and wait!"

Michael and I are very honest with each other, and when we have something to say, we try to say it in the most respectful way that we can. I definitely need to improve my patience in all areas of my life. Although I would usually feel irritated with these side comments (hey, it's normal to feel annoyed when we are called out on our BS), when Michael reminds me to take a step back and really let people think and take in the moment the way they want to, it opens the possibility for true connection and comfortable interaction for both parties. Michael and I joke that when one of us is upset, if we do not say the perfect thing to cheer one another up that "we are not following the script." We joke because we have expectations for each other at times, but there is no specific script that is set in stone when a relationship starts. You have to talk things out *and* listen to one another to fully understand why someone feels uneasy or upset. No matter how similar a situation can be, the results can pan out differently from another, so let's put those assumptions behind our attention.

I am writing a dang book on vulnerability and appreciating reflective silence without force and connection, all the while having so much trouble putting my own practices to use every second of every day.

I continually learn about vulnerability and have improved at embracing myself in my own life in many ways, but I am not anywhere near perfect at opening myself up to discomfort and always staying patient.

When people are honest with me about the way they are feeling, we can also figure out if we identify with the comments given to us. When someone criticizes us or harms us through emotional means, we have the ability to think about it in our own minds, take the time to process the words, ask ourselves if we identify with what was said. When Michael asks me to wait, instead of becoming defensive right away, I think, *You know, I actually identify with that. I do need to calm the heck down!* I would have never realized that myself because I was so emotionally in the moment, only thinking about myself.

Some people may criticize you just to hurt you, and others may honestly approach you to state their opinion. Don't let someone else's opinion define you, but don't shut down something that you can learn from.

If we don't understand vulnerability ourselves, how can we help others understand it?

Being able to admit that we mess up sometimes is powerful in itself. Michael has respectfully shared his vulnerability with me, asking me to stay patient with him because he is more calm, collected, and reflective at times, and I still try to force connection in my own way. Although we are all the same, we have different experiences and practices that make us comfortable.

We can take this minimal example and apply it to conflict situations in which we force answers, interaction, and are impatient.

Let's take a page out of this book and listen to one another. Let's work past our temptations to always speak or to always be right or to always have to prove ourselves. Let's learn to listen. Heck, I may even literally take the page out of this book and hang it on my wall as a reminder! Just kidding—but seriously.

Communicating and Listening Through Times of Conflict

One of the most important lessons I learned is the power of patience: actually taking the time to listen to someone, not always trying to think of the next comment I am going to make.

Read that sentence again and again. It may sound cliche, especially the more you read it, but we need to highlight and keep reminding ourselves of these little nuggets of wisdom. It's hard, but do we actually sit in silence when the other person is talking, truly letting another person speak?

Ask yourself this. Do you truly listen to what others are saying, or rather just listen to some of the conversation and assume what you want to hear to prove your own point?

Why do we shut down vulnerability? We may think to ourselves, *People can talk to me; I'll listen! I am excited to connect with others!* This is my go-to line. I always want people to feel that I am here for them and that if they need to talk to me they shouldn't hesitate to ask. But I am not perfect. I have situations in which I think I am right even before I talk to the other person or people involved. And when conflict arises, usually the other parties think they are right before the actual conversation too.

One of the most common questions I am asked when I talk about my viewpoint on conflict and vulnerability is, "What if I do everything that I can to listen to others, but they never show that they really listen to and value what I have to say?"

If someone does not listen to us, it's not always entirely their fault. Knowing myself, I grew up watching a ton of people around me handle conflict in messy ways. I learned that being defensive every moment of every day may keep you in the clear, but I also realized from experience that it is a bit annoying and quite destructive in a conversation. But it's something that every single person, especially myself, does at times. We want to defend ourselves, of course! I wanna have my own back!

The difference is once we learn that when we communicate truthfully but respectfully, the best we can do is lead by example. We will create these patterns that others will notice, by hearing them out and sharing what's on our mind, being kind but sticking to our word. It can be frustrating, but I am talking to you from experience.

When my mom and I bicker, we both love to bring up past events that hurt us to prove our point. Over the years of doing this, we both never move forward; we keep moving backward into a time when we made mistakes that we cannot go back and change. As much as we want to, it's not effective to bring up past events to prove ourselves. We say what is on our minds now, giving them the opportunity to notice it and respond. This gives respect to the other person's feelings, while not discounting our own feelings. When in conflict, we tend to move away from interaction. We may blame others, ignore others, or completely lose our cool. We do not always welcome vulnerability, then become confused and angry when our voice isn't welcome.

One of my favorite books is *Crucial Conversations*, which reintroduced me to the importance of fight or flight—yes, those terms that circulate in almost every psychology discussion. Do we fight, shutting others down? This is when we are most vulnerable, and letting our emotions control our actions from the moment they hit without even taking the time to sit with and process how we feel. Or do we take flight and leave a situation silenced? Do we ignore conflict?

Crucial Conversations helped me learn that when we make others feel unsafe in the conversation, they will become defensive and react, which leads to either silence or violence. The authors talk about how people in conflict tended to "push others to silence, which signaled agreement."[59] We should ask ourselves in the midst of conflict, "what we want for ourselves, others, and the relationship."

---

59 Patterson, Kerry, Joseph Grenny, Ron McMillan, and Al Switzler. 2012. *Crucial Conversations : Tools for Talking When Stakes Are High.* New York : McGraw-Hill, copyright 2012.

When we feel unsafe, we may lie, feel fearful and anxious, overexaggerate a story, stay silent, gossip about others—we may not be able to feel like we can trust people. We may feel like we are angry not because our argument didn't win but because it was regarded as stupid. We may refrain from talking to others, letting fears and entitlement hold us back.

We help others feel safe when we show that their voice is welcome and being their true self is okay. If you struggle with defensiveness, that's okay. If you struggle with a short attention span, that's okay. Becoming aware of these things does not mean you'll be perfect right away, but it's the vehicle to improving listening and communication skills. People's feelings are real even if we don't agree with them. Massive change happens when we work to understand others, to show that we hear their voices.

I always remind myself: I want to be truthful *and* respectful. Remind yourself, even as cliche as it sounds!

We may think that reacting from the moment a strong emotion hits is going to solve the problems and show our power. But the real power comes out when we are able to stick to our word, but still open our ears to the people on the other side of the conflict. We show maturity, openness, and a willingness to learn. We can always learn and take something away from a situation whether we know it at the moment or not.

Pay attention to vulnerability. Pay attention to the intensity of conflict, and how constantly voicing our opinions may not be the most effective way to really welcome vulnerability full circle. Let's not move away from connection, but rather find ways that help us cope with the strong emotions, and allow ourselves and others to process how we really feel.

What are you saying to others, and are you living by the words you preach? What are others saying to you? Do you feel like you need to be "fixed" or need to "fix" someone when giving advice? It's okay to feel that way! But let's remember, just like Sophia said, that we need someone to listen to learn and understand rather than always listen to fix.

What to expect:

- Expect that really listening to one another can be very, very difficult. Writer Josie Fisher once said to me, "Anybody could think you're crazy for what you say. You might nudge a person out of their comfort zone, and you can get push-back. But there have been times when people sharing vulnerable stuff with me has cracked open my mind a little bit. What they say might really challenge the way I think about the world or how I think about myself. So, I am looking at all of these preconceived notions I have and all of these behaviors that I have that are not necessarily all beneficial to me. But If I can get my head cracked open – – even for a little while to think in a different way – – I say thank you, to whomever helps me do that." When you are learning something new, when you are working out differences with others, the process will not always be easy. Accepting each other's faults and viewpoints is surely a hard route but essential to build a connection past your differences. Leaving a situation and/or working on listening to one another both come with challenges. You accept each other, and it's the harder road, but one that builds stability over time with work. "If we cannot now end our differences, at least we can help make the world safe for diversity." —John F. Kennedy.[60]

- Sophie Hodess, from Oakland, California, once shared with me how she has been in therapy since sixth grade, recalling her experiences with depression, anxiety, and self-harm. She highlights the importance of turning away from judgment to understand that everyone is going through a hard time. "You don't have to be living on the street to have problems," she said. "I grew up in a relatively affluent life, but struggled with my mental health a majority of my life. Throughout my lifetime, I've run into barriers when trying to explain to others that I just needed someone that could listen to listen, not to respond and try to 'fix' me. I did not want someone to fix me when I felt depressed; I was looking for someone to say, 'I understand.'" Let's listen to listen, not to respond.

- Know that you are lucky. Jordan Corcoran, the creator of the mental health awareness platform Listen Lucy, shared with me her beautiful words of wisdom: "I'm

---

60 "Excerpt, Commencement Address At The American University, 10 June 1963 | JFK Library". 2019. *Jfklibrary.Org*. https://www.jfklibrary.org/asset-viewer/archives/TNC/TNC-319-EX/TNC-319-EX.

lucky enough that other people want to share with me." Someone trusting you enough to open up to you over time is extremely rewarding. Be that ear for them, and hopefully they will be one for you as well.

- Think of something you really, really wanted with all of your heart. Think of something you told yourself was the only way, and then life panned out differently. We may have the tendency to think what we wanted was ripped away from us when we had the ability all along. It's not easy to think about, heck no. But I want to keep reminding you of that: it's not easy, but if we keep focusing on the things we don't have we will surely miss the opportunities others have to change the world for the better. We do not need to do everything, and if we did, we would be pretty darn exhausted at the end of each day.

- Behind the stereotype, behind the thoughts, is someone just like us. A human. A human with blood flowing through their veins who is taking a breath as we speak. A human who is just trying to get to experience the next day.

- Just a reminder: in my last college leadership class, a student quoted the Greek Stoic philosopher, Epictetus, "We have two ears and one mouth so that we can listen twice as much as we speak."[61]

---

61 "A Quote By Epictetus". 2019. *Goodreads.Com*. https://www.goodreads.com/quotes/738640-we-have-two-ears-and-one-mouth-so-that-we.

What you can do:

- Ask meaningful questions. Paraphrase and repeat what they say back to them. Say you are not trying to judge or waste their time; you just want to understand how your unique perspective is interpreting the information given to you.

- Keep a notebook with you. It can be super small, but when I am bored in class or a meeting and cannot seem to focus, I will pick out side comments and quotes that inspire me and that I can apply to my life and jot them down. It helps me recall the conversation in a creative way when I lose focus.

- Senior year of college, my friend Sean offered this advice to underclassman: "Actually take the time to ask someone, 'How are you?' and mean it." Engaging with and seeing the beauty and worth in others can be as simple as participating in authentic conversation. My friend Vinnie agreed with this comment, adding:
"You can't always just tell people, 'If you need anything let me know; I'm here for you.' You have to show them through your actions and connections with others and your behavior in everyday scenarios. The skills to converse and to listen lead to many other solutions in the future. It is not always about finding a solution. The service of 'being' with one another and ourselves goes far beyond the service of fixing. The service of being and sitting with someone

through their joys and pain and providing companionship, by being in solidarity with them, gives you not only the opportunity to learn about themselves, but you even learn more about yourself. It's a process. You don't always have to have the right thing or say, if you just look at them and actually take in what they are saying. Yes, ask the question of 'How are you? How is your heart?' When people brush it off and say, 'Oh, I'm good,' stop them and let them know you really want to know how they are doing. Some people are right now longing for people to ask them that question."

- On the retreat I mentioned at the beginning of the chapter, we all had a partner with small groups of eight retreatants. We were advised to stay silent as long as we could after asking questions, no matter how awkward the vibe of the room becomes. Try staying silent after you ask someone a question. If they are thinking and need some time to think, just know it takes time and is a process for others to open up. You can set an example for them, but always find time for another person to share their voice when they feel ready. Silence is hard because we tend to make assumptions about what is being thought by the others in the room, as well as assumptions about what may happen if no one speaks up. Maybe it will feel awkward at first, but know that giving someone that opportunity to think and speak is so very powerful.

- It's easier to drown things out with the presence of media. If you catch yourself distracted when someone else is talking, take the extra second to say excuse me.

CHAPTER 11

'We Can Create a Safe Space for Vulnerability'

———

I love beer. But I hate the concept of drinking.

After a couple of drinks, I start to feel the light sway of the world. I feel electricity throughout my body, giggling at everything in sight, laughing with the people feeling that same sway beside me. That doesn't sound so bad, does it?

Ever since high school, I viewed drinking alcohol as something that you had to do to *be* someone. I viewed drinking as an action that allowed me to be vulnerable.

Although I could count on my two hands the number of times I drank in my life before my senior year of college, the times when I did drink were not always because I wanted to taste and enjoy what was in front of me. Most of the time,

I held a drink in my hand to make a statement, to have an excuse to act myself.

The best way I could describe how I felt when drinking is captured by the lyrics of *With Lifted Hands* by Ryan Stevenson:

> I have tasted
> All that this world has to offer
> The here and gone that leaves you wanting more
> But can't satisfy.[62]

Although this song is not about drinking, when I first heard these lyrics, I personally thought about my false perception toward alcohol: how I thought when I had a drink that I would make more authentic connections and be more accepted by the majority. I was not satisfied. I was confused about who I needed to be to connect with others when I did not have a drink in my hand. And I thought I wanted—no, *needed*—more, to experience connection with others.

Many of us do not need to have a drink to have a blast, but it can be very hard for people to understand that. When I turned 21, there were tons of people who acted surprised and proud of me when I had even one sip of a drink, followed by applause and a loud, "Finally! She's doing it!"

One night, I was laying down talking with some friends when they started to touch upon how open and honest they

62 "Ryan Stevenson – With Lifted Hands (Official Lyric Video)". 2019. *Youtube*. https://www.youtube.com/watch?v=hBEyUsB7olI.

are when they drink alcohol. "I cannot have the time of my life at a concert unless I've had a couple of drinks," one said.

"Agreed. I'd rather dance drunk then embarrass myself sober," said another.

Alcohol = time for vulnerability.

Alcohol can loosen people up, creating a chill and upbeat atmosphere in many situations. Many say it's the perfect literal ingredient to welcome in vulnerability. Alcohol gives you the power to be vulnerable, to connect with one another.

People love when others come out of their shell, but many feel like they do not have permission to be themselves without the presence or effects of alcohol.

So, I guess that's the big secret then. Have a drink to be invincible (no, not exactly).

Have you ever felt like you needed a drink in your hand to be more accepted by a group? Or a drink in your hand to dance as wildly as you please?

I would always think I needed a drink in my hand to be someone, making me feel like I could act authentic. It was an excuse to act like myself. It was an excuse to get people off of my back who wanted me to drink, thinking I would not have fun otherwise.

I started carrying a drink to connect with others. I started carrying a drink to look approachable.

Why do we need something or someone else to allow us to express our true selves? When we dance like crazy at a concert or party, why is it frowned upon by some when we are coming out of our shell, letting our emotions flow?

We may even think people will forget everything that happened when a group is under the influence, so we can act as crazy as we want, and we can go about the regular norms the next day.

Have you ever heard, "Sorry if I said anything crazy yesterday or danced like a maniac! Soooo embarrassing"? Alcohol can be a built-in excuse for honesty.

Why is it so hard to say our feelings sober? What's changed in today's society?

We want an excuse to be vulnerable and connect with one another. We do not want to be judged, even though judgment is inevitable.

How can we create a safe space for vulnerability when it seems that there are so many requirements or barriers before we can actually connect with one another? Where can we look for inspiration in today's world?

Yes, I like my beer and sometimes do feel a bit more loose after having a drink or two. Yes, sometimes people do seem to open up more, and yes, some people do prefer having a drink when they are out. This does not make you a bad influence or inauthentic. I just had a beer last night... I'm not anti-alcohol y'all! But some people do not need a drink to have fun and loosen up. When I have a drink, I now keep in the back of my mind that this is not the only time we can create a space for vulnerability for both ourselves and others. And I challenge myself to act like myself without always holding a drink in my hand.

A Safe Space Within Myself

I once saw alcohol as an authentic way of being. But when I really looked within myself and thought hard about what continues to strengthen my own connection with myself and others, I looked toward my faith.

What really does a "safe space of vulnerability" mean? I look at a safe space as an opportunity for a person to not be afraid of acting as their truest self. A space where they can yell and scream if needed, and a space where they can genuinely laugh until their head hurts (Oh, and that includes a place where they can pee their pants or puke on me and I'd still love them).

As always, whatever religion you identify with, wherever you are on your journey pertaining to faith, this message goes deeper than what you—and only you—believe to be true. What I am about to share is a continuation of how through my experience, I found love in my life through the faith and hope I possess.

As mentioned earlier, spirituality and faith have always been very important to me: a complete safe space of vulnerability. I remember my spiritual director in college saying to me, "When you are feeling at your worst, imagine God looking at you with a smile on his face, proud of his creation, loving you exactly where you are right now." It is so difficult to wrap my mind around the concept of someone loving me despite all of my mistakes and imperfections, but the God I believe in does. And that is beyond my understanding but creates this safe space of vulnerability within us.

Even though faith has been present in my life for as long as I can remember, I definitely stopped prioritizing my commitment to my spirituality practice in college and lost sight at times of what made me feel true connection to myself and others. I can best describe my mental state at the time as falling out of love with myself and with my faith. Although I would still talk to God every night and try to pray throughout the day, I became distracted and put other tasks and my stress in front of my commitment to my faith. I became convinced that I was too late in receiving love in my life, and thought it was impossible to fall back in love with myself.

I look toward my belief of Jesus as a mentor for my thoughts. My senior year of college, I started learning more about Ignatian spirituality with all of the resources available at the Jesuit university that I attended. Ignatian spirituality is a form of Catholic spirituality following the teachings of Saint Ignatius of Loyola of how to live alongside God's presence in our daily lives. To learn more, I first read *Ignatian Spirituality: A to Z* by Jim Manney. This book defines the various concepts present within the Jesuit faith in a simplified, understandable manner.

As I was reading Manney's explanation of who Jesus is and what he represents, I stopped in my tracks when

I read that Jesus "identifies with the poor and vulnerable."[63] Instead of identifying with status, wealth, and material goods, Jesus stood alongside of each and every human when they were experiencing both pain and happiness. The reason I look to Jesus as a mentor in my life is through the way he lived out the true example of love for others no matter where they were in their life. I always felt insecure growing up that once something difficult was happening in my life, others would not want to hear me complain. I thought that people would not want to stand alongside of me if I made a mistake, and I did not even want to stand alongside of myself at times.

Manney goes on to explain that the concept of love is not just an emotion, but rather "love is always a verb. ... Love isn't one-sided, it's mutual." Pay attention to how he defines the definition of love: It's a verb. It's mutual between two or more persons (or with yourself), and always a work in progress. This does not mean that if one person is feeling off or feeling less motivated that love is not possible. This does not mean if you do not agree with someone or something, if there are hardships, that love is not possible to rekindle. This does not mean that love is a perfect, constant state of being. It's a commitment—an active commitment to understand others and love the negative traits just as much as the good. Just because I fell away from my faith, just because I lost sight

---

63 Manney, Jim. 2017. Ignatian Spirituality A to Z.

of the love I had for myself, did not mean it was impossible to fall in love all over again.

I've found that love is the action I challenge myself to commit to in times of uncertainty. We tend to focus so much on what we cannot control, rather than the things we can control. Just as my friend Robin Sacks, motivational speaker and author, explained, there are typically more things about ourselves that we can control than things we can't, but we tend to focus on what is out of our control.

To expand upon this point, one of my favorite passages in the book is when Manney defines the word "uncertainty" in the terms of Ignatian spirituality. He first quotes Saint Francis: "If a person said that he met God with total certainty and is not touched by a margin of uncertainty, then this is not good." Manney then writes, "It seems like uncertainty is built into the nature of things. ... There will always be surprises." He touches on how the way of life is not guaranteed, and even if we are good it does not mean everything will go our way all the time. Discovery is a continuous process. We think once we reach a high and become clear on life that the rest of life is clear. It's okay to be sad, to disagree, to experience loss. It's okay to trail off the path for a second. He continues to say, "But we can have confidence that the decision we make now in these circumstances is the right one."

To summarize, uncertainty is inevitable when developing a strong foundation. Love is uncertain. Love is an action. Love is all around us. Love is able to be strengthened. And when we stand with the vulnerable, and live as our own truest self with and for others, we are showing love in its truest form.

My daily mantra, which represents God's love in my life, comes from a quote Manney provides from a character in Rob Hansen's novel *Mariette in Ecstasy*:

> We try to be formed and held and kept by him, but instead he offers us freedom. And now when I try to know his will, his kindness floods me, his great love overwhelms me, and I hear him whisper, 'Surprise me.'[64]

Just as I see God looking at me with a smile every day, I challenge myself to stop expecting so much out of others when, at the end of the day, we are all human and all imperfect. I challenge myself to stop trying to mold and shape other people into someone who I want them to be, and rather accept them for who they are. I challenge myself to be that example of a safe space for vulnerability. Let others surprise you. A surprise comes when you least expect it.

I challenge myself to stop trying to control what is out of my control, and make a decision even amid uncertainty. And when we model that behavior for others, no matter what level of faith we possess, we allow others to simply be.

---

64 Hansen, Ron. 1991. Mariette in ecstasy. New York, NY: E. Burlingame Books.

Growing in Love

It's hard to understand that life is out of our control. We plan and plan and plan, and still plans can change. Especially with the presence of media, the opinions, the comparisons, the criticisms, the research, we have to realize that we are all living our own experiences. We want others to realize that we are just humans with our own unique set of thoughts and feelings that are not confined to a page on Google. But just like we want others to realize that we are growing every day, we have to remember that of them as well.

When we think about a safe space for vulnerability, we may come to the realization that we all have our own emotions, feelings, opinions, and experiences that may try and get in the way of connections we have with others. When we are struggling, we may try to push people away, including ourselves.

One of my favorite songs highlights an example of the concept of loving one another through the twists and turns of life: *Grow As We Go* by Ben Platt. The lyrics go:

I don't think you have to leave
If to change is what you need
You can change right next to me
When you're high, I'll take the lows
You can ebb and I can flow
And we'll take it slow
And grow as we go
Grow as we go

You won't be the only one
I am unfinished, I've got so much left to learn
I don't know how this river runs
But I'd like the company through every twist and turn.

These words represent how we are all growing and changing and that everything good in our lives can prove to be difficult at times. Whether a family member growing old is in need of extra care, or a relationship is long distance and you cannot feel the warmth of another's skin in the exact moments you may want to.

The lyrics continue:

I don't know who we'll become
I can't promise it's not written in the stars
But I believe that when it's done
We're gonna see that it was better
That we grew up together.[65]

As much as it may look like someone has it together, we are constantly growing and experiencing new life; we cannot escape the inevitability of pain. As negative as that may sound upon first glance, to me that now sounds empowering. Love is uncertain, it's a commitment where we do not know what is going to happen in our lives. Feelings will arise and emotions will run high and low, but they always do. We are creating a safe space of vulnerability by accepting that life

---

65 "Ben Platt – Grow As We Go [Official Video]". 2019. *Youtube*. https://www.youtube.com/watch?v=aDeNQNtW1f8.

is not perfect. Just as Kiyomi said, every day we have the opportunity to "fall in love over and over again."

Leading by Example

Just as Jesus serves as a role model for me in my life, there are countless examples of people who represent what it means to lead with love.

A friend of mine who inspires that absolute crap out of me and always reminds me how we are all a work in progress is John Tucci. When I felt unsafe being myself, John was there to say, "I appreciate your vulnerability."

In college, John created the campuswide movement Work in Progress, bringing awareness to students' mental health. To be completely honest, even with my experience with mental health and knowing that everyone has their own story and experiences, as far as I knew, it seemed like John had it all together.

When the Work in Progress campaign released, students were asked to share a snippet of their mental health story and mention some of the ways they implement self-care in their own lives. Students shared statements that were hung up on posters all around campus and posted on social media. When I saw John's poster, I could relate to the words written on the page. "I am John Tucci," the sign read. "I have depression and anxiety. I handle this challenge by attending counseling sessions as well as talking to and spending time with my friends. I am a work in progress."

Wait, he struggles with depression and anxiety? I didn't know that! I said to myself.

When I asked him about his poster and his "why" behind creating the movement, he described that "it's putting a face to the name. I hope to create a welcoming environment for all of us students. Sometimes, it's challenging to truly say, 'This is me.' I hope to help others embrace who they are." John set the tone by speaking out himself, embracing who he is and how he is a work in progress.

He explained that "Vulnerability is human connection; it does not matter if you're black, white, purple, green, or blue. We are all people. We all have things going on. We are all on the same team." John's mission is to help at least one person live a better life. He wants to foster a culture where "it's okay to not feel okay." He wants people to know that when we are working through tough times, we are making progress. He says, "Vulnerability is needed in our world, and we need people to be okay with it. Vulnerability allows me to become a better friend, son, and community leader. Others don't give me that permission; rather, understanding vulnerability does."

John stresses the importance of realizing that loving one another can be super hard. "I have to love the good, the bad, and the ugly about myself and others," he said. "For example, one of my best friends cries *all* of the time. It feels annoying sometimes, but I love it."

John helps us understand that life is not perfect and we all have quirks, but loving one another is seeing past the little inconveniences that may come up in our lives. John helps us realize that no matter what feelings, assumptions, and thoughts try to get in the way of human connection, understanding one another goes farther than just looking.

Freudian Slip: Did I Really Just Say That?

Speaking of John, his acceptance and vulnerability reminds me of a time he made me feel comfortable after making a mistake.

Have you ever slipped up and said something you did not mean? Do you have a fear of saying the wrong thing at the wrong time? We may think that we are offending someone when we say how we really feel. But talking about it is the first way to change and understand each other.

Think about a time something slipped that you did not mean to say. How did people react? Were you anxious that you offended someone? Did someone blow up with anger in your face? Did you accidentally reveal your mom's birthday gift a week in advance?

I remember sitting in my first psychology class in high school when my teacher first described the Freudian slip.

"Okay," he started as he stood at the front of the classroom. "Say I was teaching and had a really busy day. I was also in the mood for a cold beer, wanting to hang out with my friends and kick back. Instead of asking for a piece of chalk to write on the board, maybe I'd accidentally ask for someone to 'pass me the beer' when I actually wanted to say, 'pass me the chalk.'"

This is an example of a Freudian slip. The psychologist Sigmund Freud described that a Freudian slip is something we unintentionally say based on actual feelings we have stored in our subconscious.[66]

But what if I accidentally say something that someone interprets wrong or pronounce a word the wrong way or, or, or…

One day, when I was sitting with John, we were talking about who knows what, and I said, "Okay, so imagine you own a huge retail store," I started. "Let's think of Forever 21." My mind panicked after the words "Forever 21" left my mouth.

He's a guy! He probably does not care much about Forever 21. Think, Julia—what is something a guy would care about? I thought.

"Wait, let's change the store to Dick's Sporting Goods," I said quickly. I wanted to frame the question with something he loved, and I knew he played football.

"Oh, because I am a guy you changed it to Dick's Sporting Goods?" he joked back.

The joke was lighthearted, but I flinched and immediately my face was flushed as I moved into a defensive state. "I didn't mean to say that. I just thought because you played football, uh…" I paused.

---

66 "Definition Of Freudian Slip". 2019. Merriam-Webster.Com. https://www.merriam-webster.com/dictionary/Freudian%20slip.

As little as this example may seem, I was mortified, thinking I offended him by assuming what he liked and preferred.

Although my face was as red as a tomato, he created a safe space of vulnerability for me, knowing that I make mistakes and sometimes word something in a way that might not be in another's favor. He gave me a chance to understand another perspective and was still able to make a connection with me.

Are we afraid to say anything anymore because we fear people will not engage with us? Or do we feel like we can say everything and not listen to one another, expecting to get shut down without giving other people a chance?

Connection and Authenticity in the Media

More often than not, we feel like we are not in the safest space to make a connection. Whether online or in person, there are always fears, stimuli, and judgments present that can influence our decision to form an authentic connection with another. There are many mediums through which people spread the power of vulnerability, especially television and social media platforms.

When I think about authenticity in the media, Ellen Degeneres first comes to mind. Ellen is constantly using her platform and voice to spread happiness, laughter, and open people up to sharing their true emotions. She will shed a tear with you, or scream in fright with you as she successfully pranks A-list celebrities.

Through her content, she shows the world that we can both speak and listen to one another. She sparks imagination not only for kids, but for people of all ages and genders. She shows us that even when we are expected to present ourselves formally, we can have fun.

She brings attention to the authentic side of human beings and offers a helping hand to those in need. Her presence is an escape from the pressures of everyday life, a whirlwind of love and support. But most of all, she opens up to us as well. Although she does not usually place the spotlight only on herself, she shares with us moments of real emotions by crying onscreen along with guests or offering her hand for comfort. In turn, she helps others feel comfortable enough to open up, lightening the mood.

She reminds us that we do not need to overshare to gain attention from others to have worth. In an interview with *The Today Show* host Savannah Guthrie, Ellen shared her words of wisdom regarding people in the media thinking fame will give them worth: "Some people start out in this business trying to get love or approval, it doesn't fill a void. … You have to know you're good enough without someone else's approval."

She further stated in regards to her show, "I hope it's an escape for people from what's going on in the world."[67] But

67 "Ellen Degeneres Opens Up To Savannah Guthrie About Sexual Abuse | TODAY". 2019. *Youtube*. https://www.youtube.com/watch?v=EyfzJaZXb18&t=232s.

personally, to me and many others, it's not only an escape, but rather an authentic space of emotion and connection that encourages vulnerability and caring for one another.

Another amazing influence in media's history is none other than Mr. Fred Rogers, also known as Mr. Rogers. His show, *Mister Rogers' Neighborhood*, was filmed two minutes away from my high school, making it that much more exciting to wake up and attend hours of classes knowing I was close in proximity to where my childhood magic happened. One of my favorite quotes, which inspired the message behind this book, is when Fred explained: "I give an expression of care every day to each child, to help him realize that he is unique. I end the program by saying, 'You've made this day a special day, by just your being you. There's no person in the whole world like you, and I like you just the way you are.'"[68] Mr. Rogers truly explains that we do not need to be considered someone special to have worth. You do not need to be considered someone special to have a voice in this world.

**

..As for authenticity on social media, Larissa May helps us understand the ways we can start a conversation about vulnerability in a cluttered society by simply pointing out these three words: "Half the story." Larissa created her platform, #HalfTheStory which is now a nonprofit, to normalize

---

68 "'I Give An Expression Of Care Every Day To Each Child'". 1969. *Current.* https://current.org/1969/05/i-give-an-expression-of-care-every-day-to-each-child/.

the imperfect. She launched her company on Instagram where anyone and everyone can submit a struggle, experience, photo, anything that resonates with them to share with the world. #HalfTheStory started when Larissa was navigating the stress and anxiety as a student in college, creating the platform to bring awareness to mental health and human connection. Larissa is another example of someone who allows others to be vulnerable on a public platform by embracing the imperfect. She says, "Who I am offline is more than who I am online." Seeing the words: #HalfTheStory, reminds us that we are always hearing and seeing half the story. Vulnerability is present within each and every person, and there is more to the story that anyone ever knows. I would encourage you to share your story by submitting to the platform, @halfthestory on Instagram.

The Beauty of Coming Together

We've discussed a lot of information thus far. Let's check in.

Do you follow the crowd, acting different around certain friends or family members just to please them or earn some kind of approval you may think will change the course of your life?

We can't make a change by yelling and screaming at one another. We can't make a change by trying to please everyone.

We all may have passed gas in a formal setting one or more times in our lives. We may have ripped our pants in public and accidentally slipped and said something wrong in a conversation. But are we completely annihilating ourselves and others for making a mistake? A darn mistake?

I'm not sure how much simpler it can get: if we notice that we are just humans and the people next to us are too, we can create change. But every human has to realize it. That's how we can sustain the VulnerABLE movement.

No matter what you've done in your life, what mistakes you've made, what reputation you have—you're worthy of change. And if no one else in the world is giving you that chance, just know that I believe you can work toward the goal you want. We are not defined by our sickness, by our reputation, by our success or failure. We really are not. Other people will try to define us, but the opinion changes from one person to the next. Whose opinion will we let define us? Why?

My friend Katie and I were talking about her time studying abroad and meeting new friends from around the world. She looked at me and said, "When I was making these friends, we just had each other. We had nothing to gossip about, just continuing to learn about each other and the things that lights them up." Think of your best friend—maybe not the person you define as your best friend publicly, but the person you may not even know fully but feel that if something went wrong, you could be yourself around them.

Sometimes vulnerability comes out of nowhere. Someone may start a story by saying to us, "I have no clue why I am telling you this, but…" and their vulnerability was taken off guard. That typically could mean that they feel safe, and accepted to open up the conversation.

Yeah, we deserve better in the world. But we have to do better. Like motivational speaker and entrepreneur Tiffani Peterson said, "Let go of that grudge. Someone didn't show up for you when you needed it. I get it. But you wanna know what matters more than anything? You love yourself and have to show it for *you*. We love ourselves enough that we are going to let it go."[69]

She then said, "We are waiting for permission for validation. ... We are waiting for someone else. Waiting like someone else holds the keys to our kingdom or queendom."

When we realize that we are all human, we can create a safe space for vulnerability. Who would you want to sit with at night if we did not have to post our approval for others? If we did not have social media and just sat with ourselves at the end of the day, why would we be disappointed in ourselves?

Are we encouraging others to keep going and keep trying? Just like Thumper and his rabbit siblings encouraged Bambi when he was trying to walk for the first time, are we advocating for people to get up and try again?[70] Or are we shutting each other's true, authentic voice down once and keeping them at the bottom of our feet, hoping never to

69 "Tiffany Peterson – Tiffany Peterson Business & Life Coach". 2019. *Tiffany Peterson Business & Life Coach*. https://tiffanyspeaks.com/.

70 Walt Disney Productions, Felix Salten, and Felix Salten. 1941. Walt Disney's Bambi. New York: Simon and Schuster.

stoop to their level? Are we actually dedicating ourselves to be leaders not only for ourselves, but others?

It gives us an honest and genuine way for people to understand one another.

Think about a crowd cheering. Think about an audience holding hands and raising them up at an event. Think of a choir singing together. Think of a sports team celebrating after a big win. Think of the power in these moments. Think of the power of giving each other encouragement. What power is greater?

Step Into That Space

What do lettuce, laundry, and love represent to you? What experiences shape your life? How can you look back to those, encouraging others to create a safe space for vulnerability?

What to expect:

- Creating a safe space may be hard. Remember that you cannot control other people's behavior and reactions. But you can set an example for others just as Ellen, Mr. Rogers, Larissa, John, and many more do.
- Remember, we are a safe space for vulnerability. Ask yourself at the end of the day: who are we waiting for approval from and who are we letting change our mind and why?
- You'll encounter people trying to tear you down, people who just want to talk about themselves, but you'll also encounter people who really want to talk with you and

discuss. Sometimes even you may just want to talk about yourself and tear others down. But remember: vulnerability does not have an agenda.

What you can do:

- Senior year of college, a professor taught me one of the most important lessons of my life as a side comment when he was describing different persuasion theories and techniques. I never knew how the norm of shaking hands started, but this gesture goes all the way back to 5 B.C. in Greece. Shaking someone's hand represented peace, showing each other that you both had no weapons.[71] Offer a smile and your hand to another, someone will always appreciate that connection.
- Stay curious about others. Ask people what truly motivates them to move forward every day. What is that incentive they aspire to reach?
- Approach everyone like it's the last time you'll be with them. Make the most out of your time together with others.

---

71 Greece, Ancient. 2018. "From The Handshake To The High-Five: A Brief History Of Gestures". *History Extra.* https://www.historyextra.com/period/ancient-greece/a-brief-history-of-gestures-from-the-handshake-to-the-high-five/.

CHAPTER 12

How We Move Forward From Vulnerable to VulnerABLE

———

Imagine this: you're standing in a circle with everyone on the planet—the circle of vulnerability. There is someone to your left, and another to your right. One voice decides to speak first, and it creates a domino effect. The voices in the circle travel around clockwise and when it comes close to your turn, the person to the right turns and admits their biggest regret and fear.

You have the privilege to judge as a listener what the people in the circle say when they speak. You will have thoughts that pop into your mind. You'll have to really listen to understand what people say. You may not know how to respond at first. You just have to remember, when it's your turn and you decide what you want to use your voice for, that everyone else listening to you has the same privilege to judge as a listener.

How do you react when someone tells you, in confidence, their biggest regret or fear? Their biggest secret?

If you are going to judge others, people are likely going to judge you. And it's not a crime to have thoughts of judgment that pop up from time to time. The important part is working to understand different perspectives and not assume with demeaning actions and words.

How can we make an environment of inevitable judgment constructive?

Everyone's own personal experiences shape their thoughts, judgment, and communication.

Remember how we talked earlier in the book about how recovery is not a straight line?

Neither is connection. Connection comes full circle so that everyone in the world can link arms and rise together as one unified whole, not a ton of separate circles. There is room, and time, for everyone to speak.

Our experiences will change and shape us throughout our lifetime, so why be quick to judge someone when we do not want others to do the same to us and shut down our voices? Let's remember that we are not immune to new experiences and perspectives.

If we shut down other voices and others shut down our voices because of opinions and judgment, we are doing each other a great disservice. Something that you say or that someone else says can really help another in the circle. People can relate to so many different messages, even if others in the circle think it's stupid.

And something in your life has the ability to impact others. Heck, the moment I chose to highlight in the beginning of this book was me sitting in a restaurant, a part of my life that was no more than forty-five minutes at lunchtime. Never forget that there is a moment, small or large, that someone else may be able to relate to in your life. I just wanted to eat my dang lettuce, and it was so hard for me to admit how I was truly feeling.

And "lettuce" not forget that the voice next to us matters too.

Okay, puns aside, let me say that again to really highlight the power of these words:

Let us not forget that the voice next to us matters too. Invite the person next to you, across from you, 100,000+ miles away from you to tell you their very own "lettuce" story. What moment, small or large, impacted them enough to share their voice in this big, intimidating, unpredictable world? Let us refuse to silence others.

Let us refuse to silence our own voices. Do not allow others to silence your or someone else's authenticity. What story do you have that you feel compelled to share with the world?

Let's use silence to truly listen to others.

Let's use silence for reflection to learn to accept ourselves and others, to appreciate the connection of vulnerability.

So when that circle of vulnerability comes to you, what comes to mind in your life? What voice or voices in the circle, in your life, impacted you? What messages are you truly hearing from others?

As we continue learning how to express our vulnerability, we realize that we are all in this together.

We are all in this together, holding each other up, and everyone's voice comes full circle.

I stood right next to you in the circle. I stood up not so you don't have to, but so you can too. And so that we can together.

You are ABLE.

Right now, the spotlight is on you. Feel this moment. Accept what you're feeling.

It's your turn to speak.

What are you going to do with your voice?

A Note from the Author (Hey hey, that's me)!

———

To be honest, I've always wondered if an author actually wrote the title, "A Note from the Author" themselves, or if it was their publicist or whatever fancy word I would come up with in my head. I decided on my own to write the title for what you're about to read, so technically this is just a note from me. I just thought it'd be cool to check writing the words, "the author" off of my bucket list.

On a serious NOTE (pun intended)...

I've had a little bit of time to reflect on everything written in these pages, and I wanted to share with you what I've learned throughout the book writing process.

I used to be so afraid of the content in this book. Truly, for years I could not talk about my childhood. For over a year,

I was afraid to confront my fears about my relationship. For months I tried to hide how I was feeling about my dad's diagnosis. A majority of my life I felt ashamed to talk about depression. I used to wake up every single morning with a stomach ache for more than eight years, terrified of every surface I would touch and terrified that I would vomit at any time.

I experienced so many triggers. When someone nearby would talk about feeling sick, I would immediately obsess. When struggling with obsessive thoughts about Michael not loving me or me not loving Michael, even hearing the words "relationship," "break," "friend," "fate," even the word "boy" would send me into a spiral of making up stories in my head. I could not read books, I could not watch TV, and I could not interact with others without coming face to face with my triggers.

Writing about the topics in this book was extremely difficult for me. It may not seem like much to others, but writing this book was life-changing because every. single. story. in this book I was too afraid to share to even my closest friends and family members. I never wanted anyone to see my depression. I never wanted to admit that I was jealous of another. I never wanted to admit that I was in the wrong. I never wanted to admit that my life wasn't perfect. But now I have this in my hand today to finally say, "I embrace who I am *and* who I was."

I am now a pro in knowing that my fears will come back at points in my life. But they are not nearly as debilitating as they once were, and oh my goodness do I feel strong. It's been months since I've had daily stomach aches (and if you know me well, you're probably thanking God as well that you don't have to hear my repeated, 'I think I have the stomach flu' every two minutes). Even if this is a short progression, I want to honor how I feel right now. I want to honor how painful it was to write this book, and I did it anyways. And right now, I feel... great. I used to obsess that feeling good meant all of my fears would come to life. I used to think feeling good was not safe. We will always try to find a safe story to put in place of the story we actually want.

When you put down this book, I encourage you to share your story and listen to someone else's story. I also challenge you to ask yourself, "What miracle is going to happen today?" Appreciate even the smallest of wins. Three minutes where shame does not take over your whole entire body? LET'S CELEBRATE! Confront your shame! Rub your happiness in shame's face! Just like I mentioned before, even if you are at a low point in your life, you will more than likely one day look back and call the moment you're in right now "one of the good ol' days." Appreciate appreciate appreciate. It feels amazing to know you are taking another breath as you read these words.

I just returned from a Zumba class and noticed myself falling back into a habit of refusing to embrace my vulnerability. If someone would even glance my way when I was dancing, I immediately tried to hide. But then I whispered to myself, "able." When I allow myself to dance unapologetically, I am being vulnerable. I am working past the shameful feelings that I have toward myself. It's damn difficult, even in the small moments, but it works. There is not much else to say rather than show your vulnerability to others. This book has helped me snap back into awareness when I am too afraid to let loose. I hope, with all of my heart, that the words in this book can pop up in your mind when you need that reminder.

I remind myself daily that I am no better or no worse than another. As much as I want to say I am *always* humble *all* of the time, I remind myself that I am imperfect and that humbling myself is a challenge (and a commitment). And as much as I want to say I am truly confident in myself *all* of the time, I remind myself that finding confidence also proves to be a challenge in my life. I vow to remember that I am committed to learning and growing every single day by allowing others to be vulnerABLE, as well as myself.

When I remind myself that I am not any better, any more perfect of a human being than the person sitting next to me, it's relieving and refreshing to know that I don't have to bend over backwards to become someone I am not just to hold this fake image of perfection in front of others.

Please, don't give up embracing your vulnerability. If you are currently figuring out how tomorrow will pan out, not knowing how much further you can reach, the only solution is to wake back up.

Thank you for hearing me out, it means more to me than you will ever know. I'm excited to hear your voice next. You and me, we're not alone.

We are ABLE.

Forever with you on the rocky but beautiful path of love,

—Julia

Book Suggestion List

———

The books that guide me through my journey of vulnerability

There are so many amazing books out there related to channeling the power of vulnerability. I personally wanted to share with you the books that recently touched my heart and inspired me to continue writing this book.

Braving the Wilderness: This is one of my favorite Brené Brown books. There are moments in life when we have to step outside our comfort zones and stand alone to create a world we want to live in. Brené, despite her own opinions and beliefs, shows the importance of everyone's preferences, and how we can work to understand each other and develop the confidence to "brave the wilderness."

Crucial Conversations: Al Switzler, Joseph Grenny, and Ron McMillan help us learn how to navigate conflict and other common crucial conversations. When we are vulnerable with others or others are vulnerable with us, conflict has an opportunity to arise. By learning effective methods of communication, we can practice productive interaction and acceptance of someone's true feelings.

Daring Greatly: How the Courage to Be Vulnerable Transforms the Way We Live, Love, Parent, and Lead: I highly encourage you to read this book. Through years of research on shame and vulnerability, Brené covers the whole scope of how we can find courage in our lives.

Girl, Wash Your Face: Unapologetically herself, Rachel Hollis takes her readers on the journey of self-discovery and the power we all have within us. It truly feels like you are sitting one-on-one with Rachel talking about your deepest, darkest secrets and largest goals.

Permission to Screw Up: Kristen Hadeed opens up about many of her mistakes when starting her first company in college. She admits her faults and takes us through how she learns from them.

Rejection Proof: Jia Jiang describes why rejection is a common fear among most people. I love referring to some of the research and stories that Jiang provides when talking about vulnerability. When we are in a vulnerable state, it is easy and common to feel afraid of rejection.

The Miracle Morning: Ever want an idea of a morning routine to get your blood pumping and still have that "me" time to relax? This is an awesome quick read with ideas on how to maximize your lifestyle practices.

Acknowledgements

———

When I first met Doan Winkel at John Carroll University, he suggested for me to read the book *Rejection Proof* by Jia Jiang, as well as a couple of other amazing books. After hiding in my room reading book after book in a span of 3 weeks at the beginning of 2018, I felt more and more empowered to live out my childhood dream of writing a book. Who knew that months later, I would be introduced to Eric Koester and New Degree Press. Eric and Doan, thank you both for inspiring me to develop confidence in my voice and supporting me throughout every part of this process. Thank you for empowering me to keep pushing when responding to my frantic messages when I had doubts and anxieties about my own voice.

Special thanks to Katie O'Connell for connecting me with New Degree Press. Katie, you're going to change the world. I cannot stop saying that. I am so thankful that you were on this journey with me writing your very own book, *Live LIVE! A New Music Experience.* Publishing alongside you is an honor, and I cannot wait to see all of the lives you will continue to change.

Where would I be without the amazing team at New Degree Press including Barbara Hightower, Brian Bies, Catriona Kendall, Dania Z, Eric Koester, Leila Summers, Mateusz Cichosz, and NeKisha Wilkins for helping me bring my book to life. And to all of my friends who embarked on their own writing journey with New Degree Press, including the amazing Samantha Leonard who is changing the world with her voice.

Thank you to my advanced readers: Addie Macioce, Aunt Gina, Aunt Lucia, Doan Winkel, Hannah Nichwitz, Hannah Shultz, Josephine Fisher, Michael Navarro, Nick Ferchak, and Samuel Newcamp.

Huge thanks to all of those who took time out of their day to talk with me about being VulnerABLE, including: Addie Macioce, Brianne Conley, Cardin McKinney, Larissa May, Leslie Bullano, Mary Hyatt, Mike Veny, Dr. Jiani Wu, Jordan Corcoran, Josephine Fisher, Katie Dombroski, Kiyomi LaFleur, Owen Wolf, Sophie Hodess, Stephanie Martin, Taylor Malie, and Tesa Drew.

Thank you to all of my friends, teachers, mentors, and family members for lifting me up throughout some of the hardest points of this process. Addie Macioce, Aunt Gina,

Aunt Lucia, Michael Navarro, and Nick Ferchak, I would not be sane without you. Thank you for your countless hours talking with me about the book and helping me with edits at any time of the day (even if it is at 2 am).

To my Grandma Catherine and Grandpa Julius, for always watching over and guiding me as I journeyed through life's many ups and downs; for them, a very special thank you.

Thank you to Brené Brown, Kristen Hadeed, and Rachel Hollis (whom I don't yet know but hope to meet very soon) for inspiring the message behind *VulnerABLE*.

This book would not be possible without:

Alexandra Shackleton

Audrey and George Swartele

Barb and Rick Faccenda

Beth Bailie

Bonnie Solman

Christina Senchak

Cira Mancuso

Debbie Zahren Edwards

Deborah Lattner

Denise Angelo

Dorothy Nguyen

Eric Koester

Gemma and Mickey Ruggiero

Gianna Baker

Hannah Nischwitz

Hannah Schultz

Jalena Colozza

James Lyons

Janet Hordubay

Jen Marr

Jessica Bucci

Jessica Cook

Jonathan Lynch

Joseph Sapienza

Josephine Fisher

Julianne Rosa

Linda Hern

Lois Waskiewicz

Lori Whited

Luc Piskurich

Mary Libacher

Mary Lucidi

Matt Grazia

Maura Sheedy

Maxine Mulvey

Noreen Haggerty

Norene Ruggiero

Kaleigh Golamb

Karen Weltz

Karen Woods

Kathleen and Paul Ruggiero

Kathleen McMinn

Kathleen Wilcox

Katie Jansen

Karen Schramm

Kayla White

Kristina Lustri

Nick Hupka

Pamala and Sarah Grubb

Paul LaRue

Rachael Ray

Sheelagh Jackson

Shyla McMurtry

Stephanie Ruggiero

Taylor Malie

Tiffani Solman

Tim Jesteadt

Tina Costanzo

Tony Chiappetta

With special thanks to:

Doan Winkel

Gina Sapienza

James Lyons

Jennifer and Michael Navarro

Jim and Karen Suski

John McMurtry

John Tucci

Leslie Bullano

Lucia and Nick Ferchak

Michael Ruggiero

Nancy and Thomas Allen

Stephen and Theresa Ruggiero

And a huge thanks to everyone who shared my book on media as well as their friends and family. This is how we keep the movement going. For you all, I am thankful.

Thank you again to everyone who supported me along this journey, as well as each and every person reading this book. Thank you all for giving me the opportunity to be ABLE.

References

___

Introduction

1. "Definition Of FEAR". 2019. *Merriam-Webster.Com*. https://www.merriam-webster.com/dictionary/fear.
2. Brown, Brené. 2013. Daring greatly: how the courage to be vulnerable transforms the way we live, love, parent and lead.
3. *Walt Disney Animation Studios ; directed by Chris Buck, Jennifer Lee ; produced by Peter Del Vecho ; screenplay by Jennifer Lee ; story by Chris Buck, Jennifer Lee, Shane Morris. Frozen. Burbank, Calif. :Walt Disney Pictures, 2013.*
4. Brown, Brené. 2013. Daring greatly: how the courage to be vulnerable transforms the way we live, love, parent and lead.

5. "The Power Of Vulnerability | Brené Brown. " 2019. *Youtube.* https://www.youtube.com/watch?v=iCvmsMzlF7o.

6. "Definition Of VULNERABLE". 2019. *Merriam-Webster. Com.* https://www.merriam-webster.com/dictionary/vulnerable.

Part 1

7. Brown, Brené. 2013. Daring greatly: how the courage to be vulnerable transforms the way we live, love, parent and lead.

Chapter 1

8. Barrington, Jo. "Self-Loathing: Where Self-Loathing Comes From And How To Stop It". 2017. *Psychalive.* https://www.psychalive.org/self-loathing/.

9. Wier, Kristen. "Oh No You Didn't!". 2019. *Https://Www. Apa.Org.* https://www.apa.org/monitor/2012/11/embarrassment.

10. Brown, Brené. 2019. "Listening To Shame". *Ted.Com.* https://www.ted.com/talks/brene_brown_listening_to_shame.

11. Burgo, Joseph. "The Difference Between Guilt And Shame". 2019. *Psychology Today.* https://www.psychologytoday.com/us/blog/shame/201305/the-difference-between-guilt-and-shame.

12. "Tidying Up With Marie Kondo." 2019. *Netflix.*

13. 14.Bernstein, Elizabeth. 2019. "Speaking Up Is Hard To Do: Researchers Explain Why ". *WSJ*. https://www.wsj.com/articles/SB1000142405297020413640457720702052 5853492.

Chapter 2

14. Chuck, Elizabeth. "Spate Of Suicides Puts Spotlight On Survivor's Guilt". 2019. *NBC News*. https://www.nbcnews.com/news/us-news/parkland-newtown-apparent-suicides-put-spotlight-survivor-s-guilt-n987011.
15. Linklater, Richard, Jason London, Rory Cochrane, and Milla Jovovich. 1998. Dazed and confused. [U.S.A.]: Universal Studios.
16. Schwartz, Mel. "Why Is It So Important To Be Right? | Psychology Today". 2019. *Psychology Today*. https://www.psychologytoday.com/intl/blog/shift-mind/201103/why-is-it-so-important-be-right?amp.

Chapter 3

17. Crowe, Cameron, Julie Yorn, Rick Yorn, Aline Brosh McKenna, Matt Damon, Scarlett Johansson, Thomas Haden Church, et al. 2014. We bought a zoo. Beverly Hills, Calif: Twentieth Century Fox Home Entertainment.
18. Jiang, Jia. 2015. *Rejection Proof: How I Beat Fear and Became Invincible Through 100 Days of Rejection*. Potter/Ten Speed/Harmony/Rodale. [2015]

19. "Definition Of EXPERT". 2019. *Merriam-Webster.Com.* https://www.merriam-webster.com/dictionary/expert.

20. *Cinderella.* 1950. DVD. Walt Disney Productions: by Clyde Geronimi, Hamilton Luske and Wilfred Jackson.

21. Elrod, Hal. 2014. *The miracle morning: the not-so-obvious secret guaranteed to transform your life before 8AM.*

22. Smith, Jim Field, Jay Baruchel, Alice Eve, and Mike Vogel. 2017. She's out of my league.

23. "Jordin Sparks – One Step At A Time". 2019. *Youtube.* https://www.youtube.com/watch?v=PIE5QtkxzvM.

24. "Motivation – Tony Robbins On How To Break Your Negative Thinking". 2019. *Youtube.* https://www.youtube.com/watch?v=GyqrYmjjqVk.

25. The Five Elements Of The The 5 Second Rule". 2018. *Mel Robbins.* https://melrobbins.com/blog/five-elements-5-second-rule/.

Chapter 4

26. "Doterra Awards Kristin Van Wey With The 2018 Elevation Award". 2019. *Prnewswire.Com.* https://www.prnewswire.com/news-releases/doterra-awards-kristin-van-wey-with-the-2018-elevation-award-300729720.html.

27. "Mandisa – Bleed The Same (Official Lyric Video) Ft. Tobymac, Kirk Franklin". 2019. *Youtube.* https://www.youtube.com/watch?v=UEzCQBwQkdA.

28. "Tidying Up With Marie Kondo." 2019. *Netflix.*

Chapter 5

29. "Charlie Bit My Finger – Again !". 2019. *Youtube*. https://www.youtube.com/watch?v=_OBlgSz8sSM.

30. Atwood "finding something that you can give away each day."

31. Ciulla, Joanne B., Clancy W. Martin, and Robert C. Solomon. 2014. *Honest Work : A Business Ethics Reader*. New York : Oxford University Press, [2014].

32. Brown, Brené. 2019. "Listening To Shame". *Ted.Com*. https://www.ted.com/talks/brene_brown_listening_to_shame?language=en.

33. "SBSK – Normalizing The Diversity Of The Human Condition". 2019. *SBSK*. https://sbsk.org/.

34. "Cecilia's Life With Schizophrenia (Living With Hallucinations)". 2019. *Youtube*. https://www.youtube.com/watch?v=7csXfSRXmZo.

35. "Guided Meditation For OCD/Anxiety – Detachment From Intrusive Thoughts". 2019. *Youtube*. https://www.youtube.com/watch?v=e5sI6qujzIs&t=423s.

Chapter 7

36. Hollis, Rachel. *Girl, Wash Your Face: Stop Believing the Lies About Who You Are so You Can Become Who You Were Meant to Be*. Nashville, Tennessee: Nelson Books, an imprint of Thomas Nelson, 2018.

37. Smith, Jim Field, Jay Baruchel, Alice Eve, and Mike Vogel. 2017. She's out of my league.

38. "The 4th Space". 2019. *The 4Th Space*. https://www.the4th. space/.

39. "A Series Of Unfortunate Events | Netflix Official Site". 2019. *Netflix*. https://www.netflix.com/title/80050008.

40. "Cara Delevingne's Powerful Life Advice On Overcoming Depression And Anxiety (MUST WATCH)". 2019. *Youtube*. https://www.youtube.com/watch?v=CfvYlWG1cA0.

Chapter 8

41. *Matilda*. Directed by Danny DeVito.

42. "Honoring And Working With Male Vulnerability | David Hatfield | Tedxedmonton". 2019. *Youtube*. https://www. youtube.com/watch?v=rotwI8lSyQo&t=75s.

43. Hollis, Dave and Rachel Hollis. *Made for More*. Documentary. Directed by Jack Noble. 2018.

Chapter 9

44. Cherry, Kendra. "How We Use Selective Attention To Filter Information And Focus". 2019. *Verywell Mind*. https://www.verywellmind.com/what-is-selective-atten-tion-2795022.

45. "Marshmello Ft. Bastille – Happier (Official Lyric Video)". *Youtube*. https://www.youtube.com/watch?v=RE87r QkXdNw.

46. "Brené Brown: The Call To Courage. https://www.netflix. com/title/81010166.

47. Peters, Ange. HOL:FIT Talks

48. "Traditional Wedding Vows From Various Religions".
2019. *Theknot.Com*. https://www.theknot.com/content/
traditional-wedding-vows-from-various-religions.

49. LaFleur, Kiyomi. 2019. *You Are Not Alone: The ROCD
Journey*.

50. Heart of the Ocean: The Making of 'Titanic'. (1997).
[DVD] United States: Ed W. Marsh.

51. Brown, Brené. *Rising Strong*. First edition. New York:
Spiegel & Grau, an imprint of Random House, 2015.

52. Smith, Jim Field, Jay Baruchel, Alice Eve, and Mike Vogel.
2017. She's out of my league.

53. Smith, Jim Field, Jay Baruchel, Alice Eve, and Mike Vogel.
2017. She's out of my league.

Chapter 10

54. "Jealous Vs. Envious". 2019. *Merriam-Webster.Com*. https://
www.merriam-webster.com/words-at-play/jealous-vs-en-
vious.

55. Alwill Leyba, Cara. 2017. *Girl Code : Unlocking the Secrets
to Success, Sanity, and Happiness for the Female Entrepreneur*. Penguin Group USA 2017.

56. Alwill Leyba, Cara. 2017. *Girl Code : Unlocking the Secrets
to Success, Sanity, and Happiness for the Female Entrepreneur*. Penguin Group USA 2017.

57. Gwenn, Edmund, Natalie Wood, Maureen O'Hara, John
Payne, and George Seaton. 1947. Miracle on 34th Street.
Los Angeles, CA: FoxVideo, Inc.

58. Hollis, Rachel. *Girl, Wash Your Face: Stop Believing the Lies About Who You Are so You Can Become Who You Were Meant to Be.* Nashville, Tennessee: Nelson Books, an imprint of Thomas Nelson, 2018.

59. Patterson, Kerry, Joseph Grenny, Ron McMillan, and Al Switzler. 2012. *Crucial Conversations : Tools for Talking When Stakes Are High.* New York : McGraw-Hill, copyright 2012.

60. "Excerpt, Commencement Address At The American University, 10 June 1963 | JFK Library". 2019. *Jfklibrary.Org.* https://www.jfklibrary.org/asset-viewer/archives/TNC/TNC-319-EX/TNC-319-EX.

61. "A Quote By Epictetus". 2019. *Goodreads.Com.* https://www.goodreads.com/quotes/738640-we-have-two-ears-and-one-mouth-so-that-we.

Chapter 11

62. "Ryan Stevenson – With Lifted Hands (Official Lyric Video)". *Youtube.* https://www.youtube.com/watch?v=hBEyUs-B7olI.

63. Manney, Jim. 2017. *Ignatian Spirituality A to Z.*

64. Hansen, Ron. 1991. Mariette in ecstasy. New York, NY: E. Burlingame Books.

65. "Ben Platt – Grow As We Go [Official Video]". 2019. *Youtube.* https://www.youtube.com/watch?v=aDeNQNtW1f8.

66. "Definition Of Freudian Slip". 2019. Merriam-Webster. Com. https://www.merriam-webster.com/dictionary/ Freudian%20slip..

67. "Ellen Degeneres Opens Up To Savannah Guthrie About Sexual Abuse | TODAY". 2019. *Youtube.* https://www.youtube.com/watch?v=EyfzJaZXb18&t=232s.

68. "'I Give An Expression Of Care Every Day To Each Child'". 1969. *Current.* https://current.org/1969/05/i-give-an-expression-of-care-every-day-to-each-child/.

69. "Tiffany Peterson – Tiffany Peterson Business & Life Coach". 2019. *Tiffany Peterson Business & Life Coach.* https://tiffanyspeaks.com/.

70. Walt Disney Productions, Felix Salten, and Felix Salten. 1941. Walt Disney's Bambi. New York: Simon and Schuster.

71. Greece, Ancient. 2018. "From The Handshake To The High-Five: A Brief History Of Gestures". *History Extra.* https://www.historyextra.com/period/ancient-greece/a-brief-history-of-gestures-from-the-handshake-to-the-high-five/.

Made in the USA
Middletown, DE
01 October 2021